Computers in Small Bytes

NLN PRESS SERIES

NLN
PRESS

Computers in Small Bytes
A Workbook for Healthcare Professionals

THIRD EDITION

Irene Joos, PhD, MN, MSIS, RN

Nancy I. Whitman, PhD, RN

Marjorie J. Smith, PhD, RN, CNM

Ramona Nelson, PhD, MN, MSIS, RNC

JONES AND BARTLETT PUBLISHERS
Sudbury, Massachusetts
BOSTON   TORONTO   LONDON   SINGAPORE

World Headquarters
Jones and Bartlett Publishers
40 Tall Pine Drive
Sudbury, MA 01776
978-443-5000
info@jbpub.com
www.jbpub.com

Jones and Bartlett Publishers Canada
2100 Bloor Street West
Suite 6-272
Toronto, ON M6S 5A5
CANADA

Jones and Bartlett Publishers International
Barb House, Barb Mews
London W6 7PA
UK

PRODUCTION CREDITS
SENIOR ACQUISITIONS EDITOR   Greg Vis
PRODUCTION EDITOR   Linda S. DeBruyn
MANUFACTURING BUYER   Kristen Guevara
TEXT DESIGN   Argosy
EDITORIAL PRODUCTION SERVICE   Argosy
TYPESETTING   Argosy
COVER DESIGN   Stephanie Torta
PRINTING AND BINDING   Malloy Lithographing

Library of Congress Cataloging-in-Publication Data
Computers in small bytes / Irene Joos ... [et al.]. — 3rd ed.
       p. cm.
    Includes bibliographical references.
    ISBN 0-7637-1041-5
    1. Medicine—Data processing.   2. Medical informatics.
3. Computers.   I. Joos. Irene Makar.
   R859.C65   1999
   610'.285—dc21   99-37277
                                                           CIP

Printed in the United States of America
02 01 00 99   10 9 8 7 6 5 4 3 2

Contents

Preface

This third edition of *Computers in Small Bytes* is designed to keep you up-to-date with the ever changing computer world and the "real" world in which we work. All chapters have been updated and revised. Lessons continue to emphasize basic concepts and terms related to using computers. They provide a foundation for understanding the computer world and reflect the changes essential to being literate in computers and information use. Chapter 2 Computer Systems—Hardware and Software, presents basic concepts and terms necessary to understand the current technology. Chapter 3 The Computer and Its Operating System Environment, now includes Desktop and Windows management concepts and exercises in addition to basic material on managing files and folders. The next chapter, Software Applications—Common Tasks, provides information and activities that span Windows software programs. It describes how to create, open, save, delete, and copy files as well as how to use Online help. The software chapters use the MS Office suite (for either Windows or Macintosh OS) to demonstrate the concepts; the exercises and assignments have been updated to include features of the software. A new chapter, Using the World Wide Web, is added to provide you with an understanding of the Internet, including addressing, connecting, using browsers, creating and evaluating Web pages, and managing your Internet files. Chapter 10, Computer-Assisted Communication, is enhanced to include more information about e-mail, Internet conferencing, chat, and online learning. Following the theme of enhancing the Internet components in this book, Chapter 11 Information—Access, Evaluation, and Use, includes concepts and exercises about finding, evaluating, and using information found on the Internet. The next chapter, Legal and Ethics Issues Related to Electronic Data, provides current information about privacy and confidentiality concerns related to patient data and now includes more issues regarding Internet concerns. The book concludes with the chapter, Health Care Informatics and Information Systems. This chapter provides the learner with an introduction to information system concepts and theories as they apply to information systems in heath care.

The goal of this book is to assist the novice and experienced computer user to develop a set of computer skills useful for both school and work, and to develop a basic understanding of health care informatics. The lessons for each chapter contain basic terminology and concepts necessary for understanding that chapter. The chapter exercises help you to develop greater skills in working with the concepts. Assignments assess your understanding and skill. Where appropriate you are referred to other related chapters in the book. Each chapter stands alone, so you can choose which skill to develop or build upon. This book can also be used with learners who design their own learning goals and complete assignments according to their skill level.

Our sincere hope is that this book will serve as a springboard to help you, a health care professional, develop basic computer skills. With basic skills and knowledge, you will be surprised at how quickly you will go on to develop intermediate and advanced skills.

Biographical Sketches

IRENE JOOS

Irene Joos is president of J3 Consultants, a computer and document management firm, adjunct professor, administration and management division, at LaRoche College, and an instructor with Catapult, Inc. Dr. Joos received her baccalaureate degree in nursing from Pennsylvania State University. She holds a master's degree in both medical-surgical nursing and information science as well as a doctorate in education from the University of Pittsburgh. She is a member of Sigma Theta Tau and Beta Phi Mu.

Dr. Joos has taught medical-surgical nursing, foundations, basic nursing concepts and theories, professional nursing role, and nursing informatics courses at diploma, baccalaureate, and master's programs. With a FULD grant, she was instrumental in the installation of interactive video units in the skills laboratory and also managed both the microcomputer and skills laboratory at the University of Pittsburgh School of Nursing, Learning Resources Center. Currently, she teaches office automation, information systems, cyberspace, and distributive data processing courses.

Dr. Joos's area of interest is the use of technology to help end users work in an efficient and effective manner. This includes using technology in whatever arena the work may be—education, research, and practice. This has been the focus of her publications and presentations.

NANCY I. WHITMAN

Nancy I. Whitman is dean of health sciences and professor at Lynchburg College, Lynchburg, Virginia. Dr. Whitman received her baccalaureate degree in nursing from Alfred University, her master's degree in pediatric nursing from University of Virginia, and a doctorate in nursing from University of Texas, Austin. She is a member of Sigma Theta Tau, Omicron Delta Kappa, and Phi Kappa Phi.

Dr. Whitman has taught pediatric nursing, patient education, nursing research, introduction to nursing, and professional issues courses. She developed and taught an elective in Computers in Nursing for both master's and undergraduate students. She has been active in a variety of nursing assessment and college program assessment activities.

Dr. Whitman has made presentations to nursing faculty, practicing nurses, and other health care educators on a variety of topics including those related to computers and computer-assisted instruction. She has developed an interactive video program that teaches concepts and correlated basic nursing skills for infection control and is now designing Web-based course materials. Dr. Whitman received the new investigator award from the NLN Society for Research in Nursing

Education Forum (1989). She has co-authored three editions of the book *Health Teaching in Nursing Practice: A Professional Model,* currently published by Appleton & Lange. She is a member of the National League for Nursing, American Nurses' Association, Virginia Nurses Association, and Association for the Care of Children's Health.

MARJORIE J. SMITH

Marjorie J. Smith is an emeritus professor of nursing at Winona State University, Winona and Rochester, Minnesota, where she was formerly the director of the master's program in nursing. Dr. Smith received her baccalaureate degree in nursing from the University of Wisconsin, Madison. Her master's degree in childbearing family nursing and doctorate in adult education are from the University of Minnesota. She is a Certified Nurse Midwife And a member of Sigma Theta Tau and the American College of Nurse Midwives.

Dr. Smith has taught medical-surgical nursing, pediatric nursing, and obstetrical nursing at the undergraduate level in diploma, associate's degree, and baccalaureate programs. She taught advanced courses at the master's level in nursing theory, research, women's health care, instruction and evaluation, nursing informatics, and health care technology and computers. She was chief editor of the textbook *Child and Family: Concepts of Nursing Practice,* published in 1982 and 1987 by McGraw-Hill. She has also written a computer-assisted learning program, The Client Using the Birth Control Pill, published in 1991 by Medi-Sim. She was instrumental in implementing laptop computers into the graduate program in 1998–1999. Dr. Smith received the 1998 Outstanding Educator Award from the Mayo School of Health Related Sciences and the 1999 Excellence in Education Award from Kappa Mu Chapter of Sigma Theta Tau. In retirement Dr. Smith will continue her work related to Centering Pregnancy, an alternate model of prenatal care; computers; and enjoy an active travel and family life.

RAMONA NELSON

Ramona Nelson is a professor at Slippery Rock State University and holds an adjunct appointment at the University of Pittsburgh School of Nursing. In addition she is the assessment specialist for the State System of Higher Education Center for Distance Education and co-director of the health care informatics program at Slippery Rock University.

Dr. Nelson holds a baccalaureate degree in nursing from Duquesne University, and a master's degree in both nursing and information science, as well as a PhD in education from the University of Pittsburgh. She is member of and actively involved in the informatics work of the American Medical Informatics Association, National League for Nursing, and Tri-State Nursing Computer Network. Dr. Nelson is a Sigma Theta Tau Distinguished Lecturer.

Dr. Nelson has taught foundations, medical-surgical nursing, leadership, and nursing informatics courses. She currently teaches health care informatics, managed care, and community health nursing.

Dr. Nelson's area of interest is the use of technology in health care and health care education. This includes using technology to deliver education as well as identification of health care informatics content for students and continuing education programs. These topics have been the focus of her publications and presentations from a local to an international level.

Chapter 1

On Your Way to Computer and Information Literacy

INTRODUCTION

Health care professionals rely increasingly on information systems to assist them in providing quality care. They realize that a large percentage of their practice is the management of information. Computers help them to perform functions such as sorting and addressing patient materials; documenting care; organizing, calculating, and managing patient financial data; providing remote patient care through tele-medicine facilities; and organizing and accessing health care literature. To take advantage of evolving computer technologies, health care professionals must be computer and information literate.

This book is designed to help you develop computer and information literacy. Its focus is the introduction of basic concepts that cross specific application programs and the development of practical computer skills. The exercises provide practice in applying the concepts and skills, with examples from the health care arena.

LITERACY

Health care providers learn to use a stethoscope as a tool to assess patients. This involves understanding the function and purpose of the stethoscope as well as developing skill in using it. Just as health care providers must learn to use the stethoscope, they also must learn the function and purpose of computers in health care and develop skill in its use. In other words, health care providers must become "computer and information literate."

Literacy   Literacy means the ability to use printed and written information to function in society. This includes both your personal and professional lives.

Computer literacy   Add computer to the term *literacy* and it refers to the ability to use the computer to do work. There are a variety of different beliefs about what actual skill computer literacy entails, but there is agreement that it involves the skill of using computer applications to accomplish work in your discipline.

| Information literacy | This is a term used to describe a set of skills that enables a person to locate, evaluate, and use information effectively. It also includes the ability to recognize when information is needed. Information literacy is becoming more important with the growth of the Internet and the quick access to a multitude of information resources. |

People who are computer and information literate:

- Use the computer and associated software as tools to complete their work in a more effective and efficient manner.
- Recognize the need for accurate and complete information as the basis for intelligent decision making.
- Access appropriate sources of information using successful search strategies.
- Evaluate and manage information to facilitate their work.
- Integrate the technology and information strategies into their daily professional lives.

ORGANIZATION OF THE BOOK

This book consists of 13 chapters and an index featuring highlighted computer terms. With the exception of this chapter, each chapter is organized in the same way, beginning with a lesson that introduces the content, describes key concepts and terms, and, in application chapters, provides descriptions of common application functions and keystrokes. Each chapter also includes one or more exercises for use in the classroom or computer lab to practice application of lesson concepts, and one or more assignments intended for users to demonstrate knowledge and skill with the chapter topic.

The first chapter provides material useful to understanding and using this book. Chapters 2, 3, and 4 contain content about hardware, software, and operating systems. Computer hardware and software terms are introduced in Chapter 2. Chapter 3 focuses on managing your computer environment, while Chapter 4 covers tasks that are common to most application programs. This means that many applications in a graphical environment have common looks and functions.

The next four chapters include lessons and practice exercises for word processing, presentation graphics, spreadsheets, and databases. We use Microsoft Office 97 to illustrate the basic concepts of each of these chapters.

Basic Internet concepts for connecting and browsing, and related software such as Netscape and Internet Explorer, are then introduced. Chapters 10 and 11 discuss use of the Internet for communicating and accessing informational resources. While we made every attempt to select Internet sites that we felt would be around for awhile and that demonstrate the concepts presented, please note that Internet sites do change. The remaining two chapters outline the ethical and legal use of computers in health care and introduce the concept of informatics in health care.

WEB SITE ENHANCEMENTS

With the fast and continued growth of the Internet, this book includes many Web enhancements. Three of the chapters were rewritten to emphasize and introduce you to the Internet and related functions such as surfing, communicating, searching, and evaluating information obtained from the Internet. Where appropriate, each chapter incorporates Web sites to visit that expand the content of the chapter, and exercises and assignments that build your Web skills.

BEFORE YOU START: SOME HELPFUL INFORMATION

Every computer system and every computer lab have subtle differences that can cause problems for the beginner; therefore, you must learn something about the computer environment in which you will be computing. Your teacher or computer lab personnel can assist you in answering the following questions.

Accounts	Do you need an account to use the computer lab? If so, how and where do you get an account? Note that many places have at least a 24-hour wait time before you can use the labs. On the other hand, some schools automatically create your account when you register or provide facilities and directions for you to create your own instant account.
Computer labs	Where are the computer labs located and who has access to them? Do you need to present an ID card to use the equipment and software? Are some labs reserved for specific student populations, that is, health professional students or engineering students, or are all the labs general-purpose labs available to all students, staff, and faculty?
Cost	Is there a user charge for accessing and using the computer equipment and software? Do the rates vary (less at night or off-peak times)? Do you pay a computer fee with your tuition charges? What does the fee cover?
Documentation	Does your computer lab have user documentation? Where is the documentation? Are there handouts available in the computer lab or are the documents online for you to read and/or print? What documentation do you need to start? Most computer labs have user documentation that can help you to start and to learn specific software programs. For example, your lab might have a document called "Getting Started with Eudora" or "Accessing the Computers with a Modem."
Equipment	What type of hardware will you be using? What type of diskettes do you need and where do you get them? What do you need to do to turn on the equipment and what do you see?
Lab hours	What are the lab hours? Do they change during the term? Are they open over the weekend? Some labs expand their hours of operation toward the end of the term when many papers and projects are due. Does a lab assistant need to be present for the lab to be open or is the lab left unattended?
Lease or buy	Does your university have a program whereby you can lease or buy a laptop computer for use at home, in the dorm, or in class? If so, how does the university support you in terms of repair, software, etc.?
Logging in	Is there a log-in procedure (a series of steps to access the computer software)? If so, how do you go about logging into the system? Is there a help sheet to guide you?
Policies	What are the policies that govern use of the computer lab? Policies can include anything from how often you must change your password, to how many pages you can print each term, to respecting the rights of others. What are the penalties for not adhering to the policies? Penalties can be anything

from a warning for a minor offense to dismissal for a major offense. Most computer labs and organizations or businesses give you the policies when you obtain an account or give you directions for viewing them online after you obtain your account. If this is not a student account but an employee account, you may have to sign a statement about confidentiality of data, confirmation that you read the policies, and protection of your password.

Printing	What printing capabilities do you have in the lab? Do you have access to color printing? Is there a charge for printing? Some schools use a prepaid print card or keep an electronic record of your printing and then bill you. Other schools permit unlimited printing.
Rules	What are the rules that govern use of the lab? Many labs prohibit eating and drinking. Some labs also check all diskettes that are brought into the lab for viruses.
Support	What support is available if you need help? Many labs provide user consultants to assist patrons who have questions or are having problems. Others provide online help services and quick reference guides for their users. Are there orientation classes for the labs and/or training classes on specific software?

GETTING STARTED WITH THE WORKBOOK

You should review the material in this section before you begin work on the computer.

Enter	Used throughout this workbook, enter refers to the enter or return key. When you see **Enter**, do not type it. Press the Enter or Return key; it is sometimes marked with a left pointed arrow.
Bold	Text in bold tells you what to click on, what keys to press, or what to type. Computers are very exacting. A misspelled word or failure to place a blank where you need a blank results in error messages. Make sure what you type is exactly what is **Bolded**.
Ctrl+X	When you see a Ctrl, Alt, or Shift followed by a plus sign (+) and function key number or letter, press the first key, then while holding it down, press the correct function or letter key. Release both keys together.
Version	Specific sequence and location of commands vary with different versions of software. We use MS Office 97 for the word processing, presentation graphics, spreadsheet, and database content; and Internet Explorer and Netscape Navigator 4.0 for the two browsers. If you use another version, some of the specific commands will be different. You may need to use the manual or other reference materials to guide you in completing the exercise.
Macintosh/ Windows	While the exercises written for Word, Excel, Access, PowerPoint, Internet Explorer, and Netscape Navigator were done using a Windows operating system, you can use Macintosh-based programs just as easily for these exercises. Most of the keystrokes are exactly the same. A few menu items and a few keys on the keyboard are different.

Some additional tips are described here that you might find helpful as you develop your computer and information literacy through use of this book.

1. Don't try to complete all the book exercises at once. Sometimes it is helpful to come back later, especially when the exercises aren't going well or you are tired.
2. Pay attention to messages on the screen. This is the computer's way of trying to help you.
3. Use the software sequences found at the end of each lesson on an application program to complete your exercises or assignments for that software program. You don't need to memorize the commands, mouse clicks, or sequences of events. Use the screen clues, prompts, and online help to guide you through the sequence.
4. Try additional functions by referring to other reference sources like the online help, manual, or reference books. The functions given in this book were chosen to permit you to complete the exercises and learn some basics of how the programs work. There are many more functions you can do with each of the software programs presented.
5. Always make a backup of your files. This is especially important for the beginner so you don't lose hours of work.
6. Practice doing assignments from all courses using the computer. It takes practice to develop computer literacy. You will find things become easier and take less time when using the computer as a tool to help do your work.
7. Be patient with yourself. You will be learning a new vocabulary and developing new skills; these efforts take time and energy.

FOR THE PROFESSOR

Using the Workbook

- You may use the entire book or parts of it within a computer course. You may reorganize the lessons to fit the course outline. We have found, however, that the general information about computers and operating systems is important before learning about specific software applications. We also have found that the chapter on word processing is best introduced before the other lessons about specific software programs. Our experience indicates that word processing is one of the most readily useful applications for students, thus one of great interest. Learning to use the keyboard and mouse for word processing provides the basis upon which to build other computer skills. In addition, the student can convey knowledge of other computer concepts using word processing, thus providing further opportunity to practice and expand word-processing skills as they progress through the book.
- You may use selected chapters of the workbook within individual courses to prepare students to use the computer as a tool in health care settings. For example, you could introduce the database and information literacy chapters in an introductory nursing course to guide students on the use of computerized literature databases and to help students begin to organize nursing care plans. You might use the spreadsheet chapter in an administration or leadership course, and the presentation graphics chapter in courses about patient teaching.
- You can use the book as a stand-alone for students lacking the required computer and information literacy competencies. The student then could demonstrate the required competencies by completion of selected assignments.
- If the book is used in an informatics course, it is helpful for students to contract for projects and a final grade. This allows students to set their own objectives dependent upon their experience, skill level, and learning needs.

Organization of Chapters

Lessons You may use the lessons as a foundation for classroom presentations. The lessons were developed to introduce concepts related to the topic as well as to provide direction for some of the exercises that follow. You can use readings in current textbooks, journals, and the Internet to expand the content and provide examples of applications for health care settings. We introduce appropriate concepts and terms in each chapter lesson. Sometimes the concept or term may be repeated in other chapters as necessary to understand the new material.

Exercises We designed the exercises for each lesson for use in the classroom or computer lab setting. You can use all or part of them. The step-by-step exercises designed to introduce a computer skill were developed to require minimal assistance. However, because novice users can find the most imaginative problems, it is helpful if the teacher or a lab consultant is available to help students handle problems and decrease initial frustration. We designed some of the exercises for use as a foundation for class discussions. They have been successfully used for entire class discussions and for small groups within the class.

Assignments You can use the assignments, included with each lesson, for independent evaluation of individual students or small groups. You can use all or part of them. We have found that requiring assignments within one or two weeks after the class presentation encourages students to practice the concepts immediately, and helps them identify misconceptions or problems in applying the material. Grading criteria for assignments requiring use of software programs can include competence, accuracy, and pleasing visual presentation. Teachers may attribute grade points to these assignments in any way they wish.

Orienting Students

Throughout the workbook, wherever possible, we made an effort to use content that is generic to any computer. Thus, you may need to supplement the workbook with some specific information that students need to be successful with the computer exercises and assignments. Since computer labs are set up in a variety of ways, students need an orientation to the computers they will be using. Even starting the computer can be a challenging and fear-provoking experience for the novice computer user. Step-by-step instructions on starting the computer and accessing each software program are essential.

Information about where the computer stores data is also important. Some computer programs are configured to automatically save data on a floppy disk (diskette); others have space set aside on subdirectories of the hard drive or file server. Even on the same computer, various programs may be configured differently. We have found that students have difficulty initially understanding data storage concepts, and often think files are lost when they are saved on the hard drive or file server data space. Explanations and written guidelines about the data storage configurations for each program the students will be using can save the student many hours of frustration.

SUMMARY

This chapter provides you with an orientation to the terms *computer literacy* and *information literacy*. It describes how this book is organized and the conventions used to denote user actions. Some helpful information about getting started using the school or lab facilities is also presented.

Chapter 2

Computer Systems—
Hardware and Software

OBJECTIVES

1. Define information systems.
2. Describe the major components of computer systems and their related functions.
3. Define basic terminology related to hardware and software.
4. Describe the main classes of computer software.
5. Appreciate the language of information systems.

INTRODUCTION TO INFORMATION SYSTEMS

We live in an information age and use information systems to help us deal with the wealth of information available to us. A system is a set of interrelated parts; an information system is a system that has as its purpose the production of information using the input/process/output cycle. The basic information system consists of four elements—people, procedures, communication, and data, while a computer information system adds computers and software as elements of the structure of the system. Types of information systems include transaction systems like payroll and order/entry systems; management information systems that facilitate the running of organizations; decisions support systems that facilitate decision making; and expert systems that provide advice or make recommendations regarding diagnosis or treatments.

The purpose of the information system is to provide information to the users that will facilitate the work of the organization. Chapters 11 and 13 provide more information about health care systems. People are the most important part of the system; they, and ultimately the organization, benefit from the information provided by these systems. There are two basic types of users of systems—end-users and professionals. End-users are the people who use the computer, but don't have a lot of technical knowledge about it. Professionals are the information technology users who develop, maintain, and evaluate the systems.

Procedures are the step-by-step directions for how the system works and how things are done to accomplish the end results. Most systems have manuals or documentation that include the directions and/or instructions, rules or policies, and special guidelines for using the system. Many of these procedures are now online.

Communication refers to the electronic transfer of data from one place to another. This is an area of rapid developments that change how we do our work. Chapters 9, 10, and 11 review some of the basic concepts regarding communication.

Data and information are described in detail in Chapter 13.

Hardware and an introduction to software are the focus of this chapter. Later chapters address more information about specific software programs.

INTRODUCTION TO COMPUTER SYSTEMS— HARDWARE

The hardware for a computer system consists of input devices, system unit (processing unit, memory, boards, power supply), output devices, and secondary storage devices. The following definitions are important to understanding the upcoming sections on hardware. Refer to these definitions as you encounter them throughout this chapter.

Common Computer Hardware Terms

Bit
A bit is the smallest unit of data, the lowest level. Bit is an abbreviation for binary digit. A bit represents one of two states for the computer, 0 or 1, off or on like a light switch. Everything the computer understands uses combinations of 0s and 1s.

Byte
A string of bits used to represent a character, digit, or symbol is a byte. It usually contains 8 bits.

Cursor
A cursor, more commonly referred to as a pointer, is a "visible indicator" on the screen that marks your location and the point at which you begin your work. The cursor can appear as a pointer (generally an arrow), a vertical or horizontal line, rectangle, or an I-beam (looks like a capital letter I). The cursor also changes to reflect processes and functions. For example, in Windows it changes to an hourglass when the program is processing your command. In Netscape, an Internet browser, it changes to a hand when you are over linked text or objects (text or objects that take you someplace else).

Diskettes
A magnetic storage medium for your data is a diskette. The common size for Windows computers is $3\frac{1}{2}$" (720K, 1.44MB, and 2.88MB). The common size for the Macintosh is $3\frac{1}{2}$" (440K, 800K, and 1.4MB). Some computers also contain zip drives that use zip diskettes. They are slightly larger than conventional diskettes, and about twice as thick. They can hold at least 100MB of data.

Icons
Icons are pictorial symbols or figures on the desktop that represent a computer function or command. For example, clicking the picture of the printer starts the print command.

Laptop	A laptop is a portable computer. Configuration of laptops is similar to microcomputers.
Mainframe	A large computer that accommodates hundreds of users simultaneously is a mainframe. It has a large data storage capacity, large memory, multiple input/output (I/O) devices, and speedy processor(s). Many universities and hospitals run their computer systems on mainframe computers.
Menu	A list of options available to you in that window is a menu.
Microcomputer	A small, one-user computer system with its own central processing unit, memory, and storage devices is a microcomputer. Micros are growing in processing power, speed, and storage.
Minicomputer	A term that describes medium-sized computers that are faster and store more data than PCs, and are cheaper than mainframes. Size wise, they are between mainframes and microcomputers.
Modem	Modem stands for **mo**dulator/**dem**odulator. It converts computer signals (digital) into an analog (wavelength) form that can be sent over the telephone lines. They come in internal (placed inside the computer) and external (sits on the tabletop) types.
PC	PC is an acronym for a microcomputer or **p**ersonal **c**omputer. In this class are desktop models, laptops, and notebooks. Notebooks are usually $8\frac{1}{2}$" $\times$ 11" and fit into a briefcase. Laptops are slightly larger than notebooks and usually have a full-size keyboard.
PDA	An acronym for **p**ersonal **d**igital **a**ssistants (also called palmtop). These are the smallest portable computers and are currently less powerful than PCs. PDAs are useful for special applications like small spreadsheets, addresses, schedules, and small databases.
Pointer	See cursor definition.
Sector	A pie-shaped segment of tracks on a disk is a sector.
Storage	A place or space for holding data and application programs is referred to as storage. The computer has both primary (memory) and secondary (floppy diskettes, hard drives, optical drives, and tape drive) storage spaces. In addition, the storage space may be either temporary (e.g., memory RAM space or floppy diskettes) or permanent (e.g., memory ROM space or most optical discs).
Toggle	Toggle means to switch from one mode of operation to another. For example, pressing the Insert key toggles you from Insert mode to Typeover mode.
Track	Tracks are concentric rings on a disk or diskette.
Upgrade	Upgrade means to buy the newest release of a software program or to enhance a piece of equipment.

Workstation In hardware terms, a workstation is a computer with capabilities beyond a normal PC. It looks like a PC, but uses a different CPU design known as RISC (reduced instruction set computing). Most of these use the Unix operating system. When used in a network context, it means a computer node on a network.

Major Input Devices

Input devices are hardware components that convert data from an external source into electronic signals understood by the computer. Two major input devices are the keyboard and mouse.

KEYBOARD

The keyboard is an input device that looks like a typewriter, but it has more keys. The most common layout includes the typical typewriter keys with the function keys at the top, cursor movement, and numeric keypad on the right. Note, however, that laptop computers have a slightly different layout due to size limitations. Most keyboards have four components: alphanumeric keys (typewriter key layout), function/special keys, cursor keys, and numeric keypad (calculator layout). Described next are some of the common special keys for many computers.

Alphanumeric keys These keys resemble the typewriter keyboard layout.

Cap Lock is a toggle key used to switch between upper and lower case letters.

Backspace deletes characters to the left of the cursor.

Delete, sometimes labeled Del and located above the arrow keys on most keyboards; use it to delete characters to the left of the cursor.

Enter or return key works like a carriage return. Press it after entering commands or at the end of paragraphs. Also use it to accept the outlined button in a Windows dialog box.

Some texts use the symbols ⏎ or <CR> to represent the enter key. This text uses **Enter** to mean press the enter key.

Insert key is above the arrow keys on most keyboards. It inserts characters located directly under the cursor. In many programs, INS serves as a toggle switch to move between Typeover and Insert mode.

Shift key functions like a typewriter shift key. It produces uppercase letters. On many keyboards, an up arrow ($\uparrow$) represents the shift key.

Tab functions like a typewriter Tab. It permits you to move along the screen at defined intervals or to the next field in a dialog box. For example, pressing the tab key moves the cursor five spaces at a time, the default tab setting for many word processing programs.

Function/special keys (Most frequently located at the top of the keyboard.)

ALT, **CTRL**, and **Shift** extend the number of functions possible with the F1–F12 keys to 48. These keys, in combination with other keys, initiate commands or complete tasks. These keys also provide keyboard short-cuts to some commands. For example, CTRL+S represents the Save command in many applications.

ESC allows you to back out of a program or menu one screen or menu at a time.

Fn is short for function. The Fn key is used in conjunction with other keys to produce special actions that vary with applications. It is most commonly found on portable computers without full-size keyboards.

Function keys are special keys used by application programs to complete tasks. Their specific function varies for each software program. They are typically labeled F1, F2, and so on usually to F12. With the advent of the windows environment, the use of these keys has diminished in favor of mouse clicks and shortcut keystrokes like CTRL+P for print and CTRL+O for open.

Print Screen is used alone or in combination with the Alt key to place the screen or active window onto the clipboard. Once on the clipboard, you can paste the image into an application program.

Cursor keys

Arrow keys are generally clustered together in a group of four with directional arrows on them. On most keyboards, they are on the lower right. Pressing the arrow keys moves the cursor around on the screen in the direction of the arrows. Some people refer to these keys as cursor keys.

Page Up/Down, Home, and **End** keys are above the arrow keys on most keyboards. These keys serve to move you quickly from one place in the document or on the screen to another and vary within applications.

Numeric keypad

Numeric keys are used to enter numbers and they function like a numeric keypad. Some keyboards require the Num Lock indicator light to be on when using the numeric keypad numbers.

Special Windows 95 and **natural keyboard** keys

Application key , located under the right shift key, displays the shortcut menu for the selected item. This is a new key introduced on the new natural keyboards.

Windows logo key displays or hides the Start menu. It is also used in combination with other keys to execute commands. For example, pressing the Windows logo key and F opens the search for a file or folder dialog window. This key was introduced with the Windows 95 and natural keyboards.

Macintosh keyboards Your Macintosh can have a variety of keyboards. Most common is the standard with the keypad at the end or an extended keyboard with all the function keys at the top. Most keyboards have many of the same keys as the Windows-based computers. For example, the arrow, control, alt (options), escape, return, shift, delete, backspace, tab, and spacebar keys function similarly. The main keyboard differences are:

Command key, the key with the apple or the cloverleaf symbol on it, works with other keys as an alternative to choosing a menu command.

Power On key is in the upper-right corner of extended keyboard. It turns on the computer.

Today, keyboards are undergoing many changes. These changes reflect the increasing knowledge of the relationship between health problems and repetitive use of the keyboard. The new designs are intended to decrease your risk of repetitive stress injuries by designing ergonomic keyboards.

MOUSE

Currently, most computers come with another input device, a mouse (trackball). This input device rolls, has a ball on it to roll, or uses the finger on a pad to direct the position of the cursor. You use the mouse to access menus or functions, open application programs, and create graphic elements without using the function or cursor keys.

Button is a place on the mouse that you press to invoke a command or activity. It clicks when you press it.

Click (Press) means to press and hold the mouse button down, as on a menu item to see the commands, or to scroll through a window until you can select the command you want.

Single click means to press and release the left mouse button once to activate a command or select an icon or menu option. Use a single click to insert the I-beam (cursor in the shape of a capital I) at the point in the document where you want to type. This is the default; use it when instructed to click.

Double click means, with the cursor on an icon or option, press and release the mouse button twice in quick succession. Use the double click to start an application program, open a file or folder, or select a word for editing.

Right click activates the shortcut menu. To right click, press and release the right mouse button once. Make sure you are right clicking the appropriate place. Different menus appear for different areas of the desktop or window. Use it when instructed to right click; otherwise, use the left mouse button.

Drag means to left click an icon, menu option, or window border; and then, without lifting your finger off the mouse, roll the mouse to move the object to another place on the screen, change its size, copy a file or document, select text, or take something to the trash.

Right drag means to hold down the right mouse button, move the mouse to a different location, and then release the mouse button. This generally results in the appearance of a shortcut menu from which you select a command.

Point means to move the mouse so the cursor is on or over the command or icon on the screen.

OTHER INPUT DEVICES

Light pen is an input device that uses a light sensitive, pen-like device with a special monitor to enter data. Hospital clinical information systems commonly use this input device. Light pens and electronic pens are not the same; electronic pens permit electronic signatures and require you to hold the pen and write on a special pad. Light pens enable you to enter data only with special screens.

Scanner is an input device that converts character or graphic patterns to digital data (discrete coded units of data). Software programs then import this converted data. Two main types of scanners are image (for text and graphics) and barcode (for database work) readers.

Touch screen is a special screen that allows the entering of commands or actions by pressing specific places on the screen with your finger. Most interactive video programs and ATMs also use touch screens as the main input device.

Tablets require a special stylus that is used to create an image on the tablet surface. These tablets then convert the marks or images to digital data the computer can use.

Voice input devices use a microphone that converts a person's speech into a data form understood by the computer. This input device has a lot of potential for use with handicapped persons and in emergency and operating rooms for recording events.

System Unit

The system unit contains the control center or "brains" of the computer; it is not visible to the eye on most computers unless you remove the cover from the computer.

Processing unit This unit consists of several semiconductor chips mounted on a single circuit board (called by many the motherboard or system board), often referred to as the CPU and memory.

Chip A chip is a tiny piece of semiconducting material, usually silicon, that packs many millions of electronic elements onto an area the size of your little fingernail. Computers contain many chips that are placed on circuit boards. A specialized chip, CPU, contains an entire processing unit while memory chips contain only memory.

CPU A special type of chip, the central processing unit (CPU), is the computer circuitry that interprets and executes program instructions. It is sometimes referred to as the processor or central processor. It has two parts, control unit and the arithmetic/logic unit (ALU). The control unit coordinates the computer activities. It receives, interprets, and implements instructions. The arithmetic unit performs math functions like add, subtract, multiply, and divide. The logic unit compares two values of data (equal to, greater than, and less than). The ALU temporarily uses registers and memory locations to hold data being processed.

Microprocessor In computers, the CPU is a single chip or microprocessor. Large computers found in hospitals have many chips plugged into circuit boards that communicate with each other. Microprocessors are of two types: CISC (Complex Instruction Set Computing, commonly found in small computers), and RISC (Reduced Instruction Set Computing), commonly found in Macs and workstations. We generally refer to them by numbers and manufacturers, such as Intel Pentium series and Motorola RISC series. This is the heart of the computer, and it controls and coordinates many functions.

Memory Memory storage (primary) is fast, but has low density (amount of data stored per square inch), and costs more per amount of data stored than secondary storage. Read only memory (ROM) is memory burned on the chip at the factory; the computer can read instructions from it, but cannot alter them. This memory is permanent. Computer startup instructions reside in ROM; these are instructions that tell the computer what to do when you turn it on.

Although not common, there are other variations of ROM, such as PROM (programmable read only memory), which permits you to program instructions once, and EPROM (erasable programmable read only memory), which permits you to program the instructions many times. Random access memory (RAM) is memory that stores data the computer needs to use temporarily. It is volatile and erased when the power is off. The common unit of measurement for RAM is byte; a byte is the amount of storage it takes to hold a character. The more RAM a computer has, the more it can do.

Ports Ports, carrying information, are the highways that lead into and out of the computer. They are the interface between the computer and devices. They are plugs or sockets located on the back of most system units. Ports allow the computer to communicate with peripheral devices. For example, many computers have built-in game, mouse, keyboard, and monitor ports. This allows the computer to talk with these devices. The ports described here are also considered external data buses (a bus is a series of connections or pathway over which data travels). Most computers have at least one serial and one parallel port.

- A **serial port**, called by most people a "com" port, arranges data in serial form, one bit at a time. This allows data to move from the internal, parallel form in the computer to external devices. Since it allows two-way communication, the reverse data flow occurs from external devices back to the computer. Most modems connect to serial ports.
- A **parallel port** is a unidirectional port set up to send parallel data. Parallel data are data moving abreast, in groups of 8 bits or a byte of information. Parallel ports commonly connect the computer to a printer (one way communication). A version of this port is the enhanced parallel port (EPP) that permits bi-directional communication.
- **Small computer systems interface** (SCSI), or "scuzzy," is a parallel port that supports faster data transfers than traditional parallel ports. These ports are standard on many Apple and Unix computers, but generally require an adapter board for PCs. Scuzzy ports permit attachment of up to seven peripheral devices in a daisy, or linked, chain fashion. This interface also contains a set of command protocols or instructions for data transfer. There are many varieties of SCSI ports from SCSI-2 to Fast SCSI to SCSI-3; they vary in terms of the pin connectors and data transfer rates.
- **Universal serial bus** (USB) is a new external bus or port standard that supports faster data transfer rates (12 million bits per second). Some manufacturers now include this port along with the serial and parallel ports. USB supports up to 127 peripheral devices and plug and play technologies.

Note that serial, parallel, and SCSI often refer to the configuration of pins and the size of the physical connection.

Expansion slots Expansion slots are places on the system board where you can add cards, adapters, or other computer boards. Cards or adapters provide the option to run additional devices or provide for such options as internal modems, sound cards (containing synthesizers for playing sound files), and hard drives (secondary storage devices). On laptops these PMCIA (Personal Computer Memory Card International Association) slots permit adding devices like modems, memory, sound cards, and hard drives via credit card-like expansion modules. There are three types of these slots—Types I, II, and III; each is differentiated by its thickness. Type I cards are usually used for memory chips; Type II are more commonly used for fax and modem cards; and Type III are more commonly used for portable disk drives (storage).

Power supply box The power supply box provides the conversion from the power available at the wall socket (120 volt 60MHz, AC current) to the power necessary to run the computer (+5 and +12 volt, DC current). The power supply must ensure a good, steady supply of both 5 and 12 volt, DC power for the computer to operate effectively.

In addition to the processor of the computer, other factors in the system unit affect how fast the computer works. These are the registers, RAM, clock speed, internal data bus, and cache.

Registers The size of the registers (temporary storage spaces used by the CPU when processing data) affects processing speed. The larger the register, the faster the computer processes data. For example, a 16-bit register is slower than a 32-bit register.

RAM The amount of RAM increases the speed of processing. A program runs faster when more of it fits into RAM simultaneously. Keeping the program in RAM means the computer doesn't have to access files it needs from the hard drive thereby speeding things up.

Clock speed The faster the internal clock (used to time process operations) runs, the faster the computer works. Measurement of clock speed is megahertz (MHz) or one million cycles per second. Theoretically, the higher the number the faster the computer works.

Internal data bus Data moves around in the computer on an internal data bus, which is a collection of wires. A data bus is a path between computer parts such as the CPU, memory, and other devices. The wider the bus (number of wires or pins), the faster it can move data. All buses consist of two parts—an address bus (where the data is going) and a data bus (the actual data). What is critical about this bus is the width (16, 32, and 64 bits) and speed. The width determines how much data it can move at a time and the speed determines how fast it moves the data. Some terms used to describe the internal data bus are ISA (Industry Standard Architecture), EISA (Extended Industry Standard Architecture), VLB (Video Electronics Standard Association Local Bus), and PCI (peripheral component interconnect). The older ISA and EISA buses are being replaced with the faster PCI bus. Because of the intensive demand for graphics, new to the scene is the accelerated graphics port (AGP), which is an internal bus between the graphics controller and main memory. It is dedicated and designed specifically for the video system. While this might not mean much to you at this point, when reading about computer configurations you will see these terms used to describe the system architecture.

Cache The amount of cache a computer has also affects how fast the computer works. A cache is a memory space similar to RAM but extremely fast. It is time consuming to move data back and forth between the CPU registers and memory. Data stored in a cache is accessible faster than other data.

Output Devices

Output devices take the processed data, called information, and present it to the user in display, print, or sound form.

Monitor Display screens, CRT (cathode ray tube), VDT (video display terminal), or LCD (liquid crystal display) are terms used to describe the monitor. The term *monitor,* however, generally refers to the entire box, while the term *display screen* refers to just the screen. Monitors are of two basic types—CRTs used with desktop systems or flat panels used with laptop and some desktop computers. Monitors vary in their size, color, resolution, refresh rate, and dot pitch.

- **Size** refers to the diagonal measurement from corner to corner of the monitor. Active viewing area is another name for size. The size needed depends on what is being done. Common sizes are 15 to 17 inches; larger sizes are used for desktop and Web publishing.
- **Color** refers to whether the monitor is monochrome (one color, green or amber, on a black background) or color. The number of colors displayed varies from 256 and upward. Most monitors sold today for general purpose use are colored. You may see monochrome monitors in such places as retail sales or hospital information systems.
- **Resolution** is how densely packed the pixels are. The monitors display images via pixels (tiny dots) and vary in number of pixels per screen (resolution). The more pixels on the screen, the sharper the image. A common resolution is 1024×768 pixels, but some monitors are capable of 1600×1280 pixels. The capabilities of the video card influence the quality of the images a monitor displays more than the monitor itself. The video card or controller is a device between the CPU and monitor. It contains memory and other circuitry necessary to display information on the screen. **Multi-synchronous** monitors can display images in multiple resolutions.
- **Refresh rate** is the number of times a monitor scans the screen vertically each second. Hertz (Hz) is the measurement unit used for refresh rates. The higher the refresh rate, the less flickering you notice on the monitor. To avoid flickering the refresh rate should be at least 72Hz. Another important concept related to refresh rate is **noninterlaced**. Noninterlaced monitors scan every line with each refresh; interlaced monitors scan every other line with each refresh.
- **Dot pitch** is the measure of the distance between the red, green, and blue phosphors that make up the colors of the monitor. The closer together they are, the sharper and denser are the screen colors. Here, the smaller the number, the better the colors. Dot pitch measurement is in millimeters (mm).

Another term, used to describe monitors on laptop computers, is *backlit*. LCD panels don't emit enough light for contrast between images to make them legible under all conditions. The backlit screens increase the display of the images. The trade-off for legibility under all conditions is an additional power requirement.

The last point about monitors relates to their conformance to standards. There are three standards you should look for with your monitor. First, it needs to be energy efficient and conform to the Energy Star guidelines. This requires a monitor to idle down to 30 watts or less when not in use. The second guideline relates to emissions. This refers to the amount of electromagnetic emissions produced by your monitor. You monitor should comply with the MPR-II or the more rigorous TCO-92 or TCO95 standards. The last guideline is the ISO 9241-32 standard for front of screen ergonomics. This means the monitor must be easy on your eyes.

Printers Printers produce either black and white or color output. Use black and white printers for papers, correspondence, handouts, and reports. Use color printers for overheads, poster presentations, and documents where color enhances the message.

- A **nonimpact** printer is one whose mechanisms do not touch the surface of the paper. Some examples are laser, thermal, and ink jet printers. Laser printers are the most expensive of the printers. They produce high-quality print, are fast, and produce little noise. Ink jet printers are less expensive than laser printers. They produce a better quality output than dot matrix and serve as an excellent middle ground between laser and dot matrix printers. Many ink jet color printers are very reasonably priced.
- An **impact** printer is one whose mechanisms touch the surface when printing. Some common examples are dot matrix, daisy wheel, and plotters. Dot matrix printers are the least expensive, but are noisy and produce lower quality print. Use dot matrix printers for carbon forms such as invoices and statements. Plotters are used for graphic design work such as design plans.

Sound cards Sound cards are boards that attach to the motherboard. They have synthesizers for playing MIDI (musical instrument digital interface) files. This file standard permits you to connect musical instruments to the computer and to store musical instrument data. They are able to record and play WAV (Waveform Audio) files, which enable you to record sounds, music, or narration. Multiple-media computers come with a sound card and stereo speakers.

Secondary Storage

Secondary storage is media that holds the application programs and user data when not in use. Attributes of secondary storage are slower access to data, higher density or amount of data per square inch, and lower cost than primary storage. Two main types in use today are magnetic and optical. Floppy disks, hard disks, and tapes are examples of magnetic media. CD-ROM, laser discs, and WORM (Write Once, Read Many) drive discs are examples of optical medium. Data storage uses the same concept as that which holds data in memory—bytes. Kilobytes, megabytes, gigabytes, and terrabytes are size terms that describe the amount of data a medium holds. A kilobyte is 1024 bytes or characters. A megabyte (MB) is 1 million+, a gigabyte (GB) is 1 billion+, and a terrabyte is 1 trillion+ bytes or characters.

Floppy drives A floppy drive reads floppy diskettes. Floppy diskettes store programs or data files. Early floppy drives were one-sided, meaning they could write to and read only one side of the diskette. Today's are double-sided (DS) meaning they can write to and read both sides. Most disk drives are high-density and read high-density (HD) and double density (DD) diskettes. Common floppy diskettes hold data from 720,000 to 2,880,000 characters and come in $3\frac{1}{2}$" size. Common terms to describe these diskettes are double sided, double density (DS/DD) and double sided, high density (DS/HD or just HD). The trend for data storage is smaller physical sizes and larger amounts of data.

Zip drives While considered floppy disk drives, the diskettes read by these drives are slightly larger in size and about twice as thick. They hold at least 100MB of data and are commonly used for storage of graphic files, larger program files, and to back up hard drives.

Hard drives The hard drive is a data storage device fixed in a sealed case that reads data stored on platters in the drive. It stores more data (in the gigabyte range) and permits faster retrieval than floppy drives. Hard drives are either external to the system unit or contained within the system unit. They are also available as hard cards inserted in an expansion slot, or as portable drives inserted in a bay designed for them. Some interface standards for moving the data between this storage device and processor are IDE (integrated device electronics), EIDE (enhanced IDE), and SCSI. When you buy a computer or hard drive, you will see these terms used to describe the hard drive.

Tape drives A tape drive is a secondary storage device that allows backup or duplication of data stored on a hard disk. It stores data sequentially (one right after the other) in magnetic form much like an audiotape.

Optical drives Optical storage drives are the main alternative to magnetic storage. They hold large amounts of data, usually written (pressed) once and accessed many times. Some examples are CD-ROMs (compact disc—read-only memory) and laser discs. Some optical drives permit erasing and rewriting data many times. Two of these are CD-Rs and CD-RWs. This storage device can store digital audio, full motion video, graphics, and animation in addition to text data. The latest addition to the CD-ROM storage technology is the DVD (digital versatile or video disc). These discs hold a minimum of 4.7GB and up to 17GB of data and are enough for full-length movies.

Care of Floppy Diskettes

To prevent a disaster with your data files, the following are some helpful hints for care of your floppy diskettes.

- When transporting or storing diskettes, place them in a special carrying case designed for that purpose. *You may damage diskettes if you carry them around unprotected.*
- Keep diskettes dry and away from heat and cold. Extreme heat and cold can affect the data stored on the diskettes.
- Handle diskettes by touching the top or labeled part. For $3\frac{1}{2}$" diskettes, do not touch the area under the silver shutter. Do not try to remove the silver shutter. For a CD-ROM, do not touch the surface of the disc. Hold it on the outside rim with the finger in the center circle.
- Slide diskettes into disk drives gently with the label side up and toward you. This means to hold the diskette by the label with the label up. For CD-ROMs, place them in the drive door right side up. Use the Close and Open button to close and open the disk drive door or select the commands from the desktop icons.
- Insert or remove diskettes from the disk drive when the disk drive light is off on PCs. Removing them when the drive light is on may damage the disk surface and destroy data beneath it.
- Keep diskettes away from other devices or magnetic fields. This includes electrical appliances, monitors, magnets, and phones. If they are taken into a library environment, do not place on circulation counter! Many library security systems use some form of magnetic tapes and magnets to secure materials.
- Label your diskettes using felt tip pens. Ballpoint pens can cause permanent indentations on the diskette surface. Pencils can also cause damage if you press them too hard.
- Write-protect your diskettes to avoid accidental deletion of important files. This is especially important when making backups of original work. To write-protect your diskette, slide the write protect shutter open so you can see through the hole.

- Check with the computer lab assistants for the correct type of diskette to purchase for your lab. There are many types of diskettes and all are not interchangeable with every computer. This is especially true for zip disks.
- Initialize or format (prepare to receive data) diskettes before creation of your data files. You can store data only on formatted diskettes. Many diskettes today come preformatted, but do not assume all do.

Labeling Disk Drives

Disk drives are referred to with letters. Letters and icons with letters help the user direct the computer to the drive from which they want to access stored information or assign as the default drive. The letters C and D usually refer to the hard disk. CD-ROM and zip drives usually use the letters D, E, F, or G. The computer reserves the letters A and/or B for floppy drives. In the Windows environment, you will see words next to the letters describing the nature of that storage device. For example, $3\frac{1}{2}$" floppy appears next to the letter A. Since there are many variations for drive labeling, consult your lab assistant or teacher for the conventions used in your lab.

INTRODUCTION TO COMPUTER SYSTEMS— SOFTWARE

Computers are multipurpose machines. They are, however, unable to complete any task without directions from software programs. Software programs consist of step-by-step instructions that direct the computer hardware to perform specific tasks such as multiply, divide, fetch, or deliver this data. They provide instructions for the computer. All computers require software to function. When the computer is using a specific program, users say they are running or executing the program.

Common Software Terms/Concepts

Boot Boot is a term that means to start the computer so it can execute the necessary startup routines.

Default Default is the setting the computer uses unless told otherwise. It is the setting the program uses to retrieve and save files, unless told otherwise. This is an important term because you will have difficulty retrieving or finding your files if you don't know where the computer is storing them. Most college labs require you to store your data on your diskettes or your folder on the file server. Most do not want students storing their data in the MS Office My Documents folder.

Software Categories

The following are three major categories of software.

Operating systems (OS) The OS is the most important program that runs on a computer. The operating system tells the computer how to use its own components or hardware. No general-purpose computer can work without an operating system.

Operating systems perform some functions necessary to all users of the computer system. Some of the basic tasks they perform include keeping track of files and folders; communicating to peripheral devices like printers; receiving and interpreting input from the mouse or keyboard;

displaying output on a screen; and managing how data moves around inside the computer. In other words, operating systems coordinate the computer hardware components and supervise all basic operations.

The most common operating system for PCs is the Windows family (Windows 95, 98, 2000, and NT), and for the Apple, the Macintosh operating system. Some computers also use OS/2 or variations of Unix called Linux and Xenix. Portable computers may use Windows CE. For larger computer systems and workstations, you may work with VMS and Unix, or a Unix variation like Solaris. The important point to remember here is that all computers need an operating system to work and that operating systems will change to reflect changes in technology and user needs. Chapters 3 and 4 go into more detail about working in the Windows environment.

Languages Language software presents a simplified means, called a language, to execute a series of instructions. It consists of a vocabulary and an accompanying set of rules that tell the computer how to work. Languages permit the user to develop programs that do specific tasks. Some common languages are Pascal, C, C++, COBOL (Common Business Oriented Language), JAVA, and Basic. You do not need to be a programmer to use the computer; however, programming skills are helpful when you want to do more advanced things on the computer.

There are four levels of programming languages. Machine-level languages are the lowest level and consist of numbers only. Assembly languages are the next level giving the programmer the ability to use names instead of numbers. High-level languages are what we normally think of when we say programming language. They include the above-mentioned languages such as Basic, C, and Pascal. They consist of a set of keywords or commands and related syntax for organizing the program. The last level of programming languages is called fourth-generation languages or 4GL. This level of programming language is the closest to human language. They are usually used in artificial intelligence type programs. LISP (List Processor) is one example.

While many people include HTML (HyperText Markup Language) and SGML (Standard Generalized Markup Language) as programming languages, in reality they are not. They are considered organizing and tagging languages designed to manage the layout and formatting of documents over different computer systems.

Applications Application programs meet specific task needs of the user and are considered the core of any computer system. Applications use language software to write the application program. Major types of applications or programs are:

- General purpose software such as word processors, spreadsheets, database managers, presentation graphics, and communications programs
- Educational programs
- Utility programs such as virus scanners, hard disk managers, and menu systems
- Personal programs like calculators, calendars, and money managers
- Entertainment programs like games and simulations

This book covers some common general purpose application software.

- General Purpose Software

    Communications software permits one computer to "talk" to another by using standard communication protocols (rules and procedures that govern the communication).

Database software helps organize, store, retrieve, and manipulate data for the purpose of later retrieval and report generation.

Desktop publishing software permits the user to create high-quality specialty publications like newspapers, bulletins, and brochures. It handles page layouts better than word processors and permits importing of a variety of text and graphic files from other application programs.

Graphics software facilitates the creation of a variety of graphics. Three types of graphics programs exist. **Presentation** graphics permit the user to create or alter symbols, present a variety of chart styles, make transparencies and slides, and produce slide shows. **Paint programs** permit users to create symbols or images from scratch. **Computer-aided drafting (CAD)** programs meet the schematic drawing needs of architects and engineers.

Integrated software includes in one program some capabilities of word processing, database, spreadsheet, graphics, and communication programs.

Spreadsheet software permits the manipulation of numbers in a format of rows and columns. Spreadsheet programs contain special functions for group additions, division, and statistical and financial formulas. Use them for financial functions and number crunching.

Statistics software permits statistical analysis of numeric data.

Suites are value packages that include a word processor, spreadsheet, database, presentation graphics, and sometimes a personal information manager. The main advantage of these suites is the cost (lower than each program individually) and the ability to share data easily between each program.

Word processing software are programs that permit creating, editing, formatting, storing, and printing text. Most have spell and grammar checkers built into them.

■ Education

Computer-assisted instruction (CAI) software are programs that help users learn concepts or specific content of their discipline or area of study. In some circles they are also referred to as training software.

Interactive video disc (IVD) is a form of CAI software that integrates the capabilities of the computer with sound and motion of video. CD-ROMs and DVDs also hold programs that perform these integrated sound and motion programs.

■ **Utilities:** A group of software programs that help with the management or maintenance of the computer. Some examples are hard disk managers, virus detectors, compression/decompression programs, and viewers.

■ **Personal:** Personal software programs help us manage our personal lives. Some examples are appointment calendars, checkbook balancing, money management, and calculators.

■ **Entertainment:** A class of software programs that provides us with fun. Many games exist to lighten up our lives including golf and football; others challenge our problem-solving abilities; still others are more video-arcade type programs.

When discussing software developments, the trend is for easier-to-use, graphical or icon driven programs that are available in suites.

SUMMARY

The focus of this chapter was to present you with sufficient terminology and concepts necessary to become an intelligent computer user. To that end, the term *information system* was defined and the major components of computers were described. Software basics were presented including the three major classes. Keep in mind, however, that while some of the specifics of the computer system will change as technology develops, the basic concepts will remain. You will always need the input-process-output cycle and some form of software.

REFERENCES[*]

Advanced System Products Incorporated (1998). *AdvanSCSI—drivers made easy.* Retrieved January 9, 1999 from the World Wide Web: http://www.advansys.com/white_paper/wpide.htm.

Kozierok, C. (1999). *Accelerated graphics port (AGP).* Retrieved April 10, 1999 from the World Wide Web: http://www.pcguide/com/ref/mbsys/buses/types/agp-c.html.

Mueller, S. & Zacker, C. (1988). *Upgrading and repairing pcs.* Tenth Edition. Carmel, IN: Que Corporation.

Pabst, T. (1999). *The CPU guide.* Retrieved April 14, 1999 from the World Wide Web: http://www.tomshardware.com/guides/cpu.

Wright, M. (1999, January 21). The disk drive: Winner and still storage champion. *EDN Magazine, 2,* 60–72.

EXERCISE 1: IDENTIFY COMPUTER COMPONENTS

Objectives

1. Identify the specific computer hardware in front of you.
2. Use the proper terminology to describe the computer.

Activity

1. What make of computer is in front of you? (Make refers to the company that manufactures it. Some examples are IBM, Gateway, Compaq, Dell, and Apple.)

   What model computer is in front of you? (Model refers to different computers manufactured by the same company.)

   How do you know?

   How do you turn this computer on?

2. Look at the monitor in front of you. Is the monitor part of the system unit or separate from the system unit?

   What type of monitor is it? (color or monochrome; resolution)

   Do you need to turn it on separately from the system unit?

   If so, how do you turn it on?

---

[*]When entering an URL, do not type the period that follows it in this list.

3. How many floppy disk drives are on this computer?

   What size are they?

   What capacity diskettes can you use in these drives?

   Draw and label your disk drive setup:

4. Do you have a CD-ROM? Zip drive?

5. Do you have a hard or fixed disk drive on this computer?

   How do you know?

6. What type of input devices can you use with this computer?

7. What type of output devices can you use with this computer?

   Describe them:

8. Does your computer share a printer with another?

   How do you know?

9. Are there places to plug in a mouse, modem, printer, or other peripheral devices?

10. Is your computer connected to another computer that serves as a file server (a file server is a computer that contains software and data shared by those using the system)? Is your computer networked?

    How do you know?

11. Turn on your equipment. Do you need an ID and password to access the system?

12. List the software available for use on this computer.

EXERCISE 2: COMPUTER CONFIGURATION

Objectives

1. Identify questions you would ask and information you would obtain when buying a computer.
2. Relate information from a newspaper computer ad to material presented about hardware.

Activity

Using the following ad information, fill in the blanks below: Dell Dimension XPS T450, 128 MB RAM, Pentium III (450MHz) processor, one 3.5 inch diskette drive (1.44MB), 9.1GB Ultra ATA hard drive, 40X Max Variable CD ROM, Yamaha G 64V Wavetable sound, Harman/Kardon HK-195 speakers, Iomega Zip 100MB built-in drive, 3Com USRobotics V.90 WinModem, Dell mouse, Dell 17" (.26dpi) M780 monitor, Microsoft Windows 98, Microsoft Office.

Microprocessor	Memory	Speed
Floppy Disks	Diskette Size	Diskette Capacity
Hard Disk	Size	
Zip Disk	Type	
Monitor Model	Size	DPI
CD-ROM	Speed	
Sound System		
Operating System		

What type of diskettes would you buy? What size? Density?

What would you use to backup your system?

What type of keyboard do you receive?

Is your monitor color? What size? Type?

Do you get any software?

What additional questions would you ask before buying the computer? List them.

EXERCISE 3: COMPUTER SPECIFICATIONS

Objectives

1. Specify minimum hardware requirements for different scenarios.
2. Identify software needs.
3. Justify your recommendations for your requirements for both hardware and software.

Activity A

You are in charge of a local health clinic. The budget requests are due to the clinic board and you are submitting a request for a microcomputer, related peripheral devices, and software. You want to use the computer to help with the clinic management duties. Itemize and justify your request.

Activity B

You are the system's analyst in the Center for Research in your institution. The director decides to purchase computers for the center. You must now specify the hardware and software to meet the computing needs for the center. The center staff consists of a director (PhD), two associate directors (PhDs), three research associates (master's degree prepared), one statistician, and three clerical staff.

Activity C

You want your parents to purchase a computer, printer, and related software as a present for you. They need some help from you to determine what type of computer and software you need and whether the cost is reasonable. Itemize what you want and justify it to them.

Use hardware and software ads from newspapers, computer magazines, and computer retailers to obtain hardware and software specifics. If you know how to use the Internet, you may also use it as a resource for collecting this information.

EXERCISE 4: ACCESSING APPLICATION SOFTWARE

Objectives

1. Start application programs using a variety of techniques.
2. Identify the software programs available on the computer.
3. Identify the operating system.
4. Shut down the computer.

Activity

1. Start an application using the double click method.

   Turn on your computer system.

   If necessary, press **Ctrl+Alt+Del** to obtain the login screen. That means to hold down the Crtl key, hold down the Alt key and then press Del. **Release** all three keys.

   If necessary, type your login (**User ID**) and **Password** and press **Enter**.

   Double click the **Internet Explorer** or **Netscape Navigator** icon on the desktop. The browser program opens.

   Click the **Close** button on the browser window to close the application.

2. Start an application using the Start button on the taskbar.

   Click **Start** button on the taskbar.

   Select **Programs, Accessories,** and **WordPad**. WordPad, a word processing program that comes with Windows, now starts.

   Click the **Close** button on the WordPad window to close the application.

3. Start an application using **My Computer**.

Double click **My Computer** 🖳 icon.
Double click **C drive** icon, **Windows** folder.

Double click **Calc** ⌨ icon. The calculator program opens. Note: you will need to scroll through the window to find the calculator icon.

Click the **Close** ☒ button on the Calculator window to close the application.

4. Start MS Office application using the MS Office Toolbar.

Click the Word 🅆 icon on the toolbar MS Office Toolbar on the desktop.

MS Word opens. Click the **Close** ☒ button to close the application.
You may start any of the MS Office applications using the MS Office Toolbar on the desktop.

5. Identify application programs on your system.

Click the **Start** 🏁 Start button on the taskbar.
Select **Programs**.
List the applications programs that are accessible to you on this computer.

6. Identify the operating system.

Click the **Start** 🏁 Start button, select **Settings, Control Panel.**

Double click the **System** 🖳 icon.
Note: If you are using Windows 98, you can also access this information by selecting **Start** button, **Programs, Accessories, System Tools,** and **System Information.**
What version of Windows are you using? _____

Click the **Close** ☒ button on the top, right of the System Properties window.

Click the **Close** ☒ button on the top, right of the Control Panel window.
Close all remaining open windows.

7. Shut down the computer.
Click **Start** button.

Select **Shut down.**

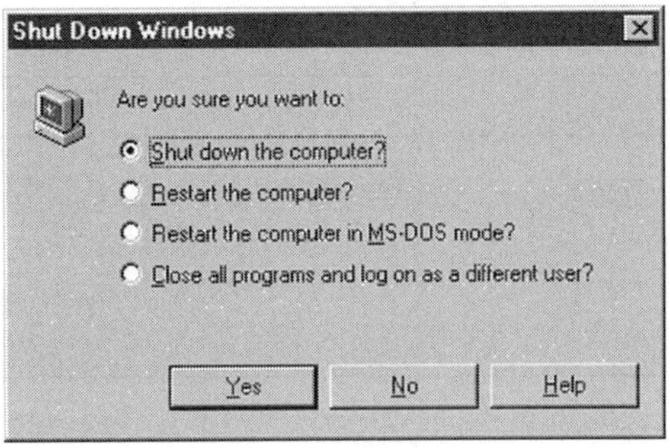

FIGURE 2–1.
Shut Down Dialog Box

Click the circle next to **Shut down** OR click the circle next to **Close all programs and log on as a different user**.

Click **OK**.

If you have been instructed to turn off the computer in the lab when finished or are using your computer at home, wait until a message appears on the screen telling you it is OK to turn off the computer. If the computer doesn't turn itself off, **turn off** the computer and monitor.

ASSIGNMENT 1: COMPARE TWO COMPUTERS

Directions

1. Obtain *two* ads for a microcomputer. Obtain them from the newspaper, computer magazines, or from a store that sells computers.
2. Compare the two computers by filling in the following form.
3. Make a recommendation for one.
4. Turn in both the form and the computer ads.

NAME:_____

Features/Specifications	Computer 1	Computer 2
System Unit:		
Make/model		
Microprocessor type		
Speed	MHz	MHz

Features/Specifications	Computer 1	Computer 2
RAM	MB	MB
# of expansion slots		

# of ports 	
  Serial
  Parallel
  SCSI
  USB		

Secondary Storage:		
Hard drive	GB	GB
Floppy drives	Yes/No	Yes/No
Zip drive/superdisk	Yes/No	Yes/No
CD-ROM If yes, speed	Yes/No	Yes/No
DVD drive	Yes/No	Yes/No
Tape drive	Yes/No	Yes/No
Input/Output Devices:		
Keyboard included	Yes/No	Yes/No
Mouse included	Yes/No	Yes/No

Monitor included
  Resolution (dpi)
  Size (inches)
	Yes/No	Yes/No

Printer included
  If yes, make
  If yes, type
	Yes/No	Yes/No

Modem—type/speed		
Additional Information:		
Sound system?	Yes/No	Yes/No
Operating system? If yes, what?	Yes/No	Yes/No
Additional software? If yes, what?	Yes/No	Yes/No
Cost:	$	$

Recommendation:

Rationale/Comments:

Chapter 3

The Computer and Its Operating System Environment

OBJECTIVES

1. Describe the Windows operating system environment.
2. Describe a graphical user interface and operating system trends.
3. Identify the process for managing your desktop and windows.
4. Identify basic concepts of file and disk management including file-naming conventions.

INTRODUCTION

This chapter describes the operating system environment in the Windows world. For a definition and description of operating systems, refer to Chapter 2. Windows is an operating system designed for PC computers with Intel microprocessors such as Dell, IBM, Gateway, and Compaq. It uses a graphical user interface (GUI) to help you work in this environment. A graphical user interface takes advantage of the computer's graphic capabilities along with the mouse to make using the commands and applications easier. The Macintosh also uses an operating system with a graphical user interface. Many of the concepts and functions described in this chapter have their equivalent concept and function in the Macintosh environment.

Critical to working in any operating system environment is the ability to manage your files and folders. Files contain your work and folders are storage places for your files. This chapter also includes information on managing your files and folders using My Computer and Windows Explorer.

OPERATING SYSTEM ENVIRONMENT

Operating systems are responsible for many of the "housekeeping" tasks needed by the computer. The operating system "wakes up" the computer through a set of commands and routines that lets the computer recognize the CPU, memory, keyboard, disk drives, and printers. The purpose of the operating system is to supervise the operation of the computer's hardware components and coordinate the flow and control of data. Without the operating system, you cannot run language or application software.

Today, most operating systems come preinstalled on the hard drive of your computer. There are several versions of Windows operating system in use such as 95, 98, and NT 4, and others about to be released such as 2000 and NT 5. The general trend in these various versions is the integration of Internet capabilities, ability to perform multiple tasks at the same time, ability to work in network environments, and increased inclusion of security and multimedia capabilities.

To become proficient in using your computer, you need to acquire a basic understanding of how the system works and how to manage your desktop environment. This means learning how to customize your desktop, manipulate the windows, switch between applications, and manage your folders and files.

The Boot Process

The boot process refers to turning on the computer and initiating a series of actions.

POST test When you turn on the computer, the CPU performs a POST, or Power On Self Test. This test analyzes the memory, drives, and ports to make sure all hardware is working properly. It locates the bootable partition on the hard drive and loads the master boot record (MBR). This test runs very quickly, and if problems are found, makes beeping sounds and then stops running.

MBR and bootstrap Once the bootable partition is found, the MBR passes control over to the boot sector in that partition on the hard drive. This boot sector contains the programs and/or directions necessary to continue the set-up and configuration of the computer before you can use it.

The above information is not critical to using a computer. It does, however, increase your ability to problem solve when something goes wrong during the boot process. For example, when you see a message "nonsystem disk error," this means you have a nonbootable disk in the A drive. You left your data disk in the drive and your data disk does not have the necessary system files for the computer to proceed. If your remove the data disk and press any key, the computer will proceed with configuring the computer for your use.

Booting the computer Computer users also use two other terms when talking about starting the computer.

Cold boot   This means to turn on the computer with the on switch. It also includes using the restart button if the computer has one.

Warm boot   A warm boot is pressing, in sequence, the **CTRL+ALT+DEL** keys together.

GRAPHICAL USER INTERFACE

Both Windows and Macintosh OS use graphical user interfaces for the user to interact with the operating system. Figure 3–1 shows you a typical Windows desktop with its graphical interface. Some features common to both are listed here.

Mouse   A device used to select objects and issue commands. The idea is to make issuing commands faster especially for the nontypist. GUIs depend on the mouse or other pointing devices to select objects or commands from menus or toolbars. Note that most of the commands accessed with the mouse also have their equivalent keyboard stroke. Refer to Chapter 2 for a description of the mouse actions.

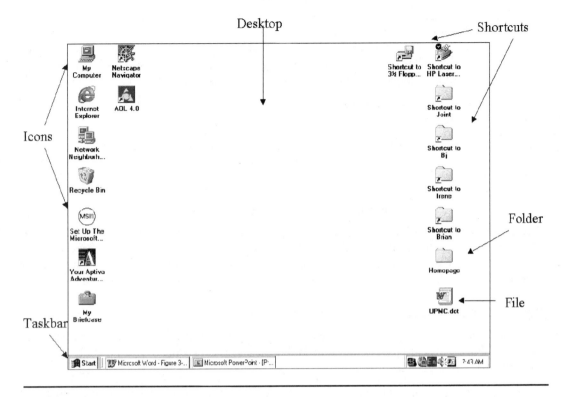

FIGURE 3–1.
Typical Windows Desktop

Pointer	A pointer is the symbol used to represent the insertion point. Many application programs change the look of the pointer to reflect the process the system is expecting. For example, the pointer changes to a double headed arrow (↔) to represent sizing the window. The pointer enables you to select commands from menus and toolbars. We will point out the different pointer shapes as they occur in our discussions.
Objects	Small pictures or graphical representation of icons, files, folders, and shortcuts located on the desktop are referred to as objects. Placing the pointer on an object and clicking selects it. Double clicking the object opens it. Right clicking an object brings up a short cut menu sometimes called a content sensitive menu.
Desktop	The area on the screen where the icons and taskbar are displayed. It is the primary work space in the Windows environment that fills the screen. This is what you first see when you turn on the computer and if necessary, log in. The desktop may be customized to suit the user. That means you can change colors, location of objects, add images to the background of your desktop, and install screen savers.

Windows   The place on the desktop where the contents of icons are displayed. Each program or file has its own window. Each window contains a title bar, menu bar, one or more toolbars, and a status bar. If all the contents of the window can't be displayed because of the window size, the window will also contain scroll bars. Additional window controls include close, maximize, minimize, and restore.

Menus   Menus are lists of commands available by selecting a command category from the menu bar.

The GUI provides you with a consistent look and easy-to-use commands. The common features and look enable the user to quickly adjust to other applications and to move between the applications easily.

MANAGING YOUR DESKTOP

This section discusses the layout of your desktop and how to manage your desktop. Most of us enjoy arranging our desks in a specific order that makes us more comfortable and productive in our work environment. We add specific personal items to provide a little personal touch to our workday. You can simulate that same touch to your computer desktop environment.

Objects on the Desktop

The desktop displays several objects by default. Default means unless you tell the computer otherwise, it will use that setting or configuration. Figure 3–1 shows some of these default objects—icons, folders, shortcuts, files, and taskbar.

Icons Icons represent applications, such as Internet Explorer, and special windows, such as My Computer, Network Neighborhood, and Recycle Bin. The list below describes some of the common icons found on your desktop in a Windows environment. You may not have all of them; you may have more of them. Icons are generally generated when you install a new program on the computer.

My Computer

Use this icon for viewing and accessing all storage drives and devices connected to the computer. In addition, the control panel and printer folder icons are stored in this window.

Network Neighborhood

Use this icon for viewing and accessing resources available to you through your network connection.

Internet Explorer

Use this icon for launching the Internet Explorer browser to access the World Wide Web (WWW or Web).

Recycle Bin

The recycle bin stores deleted files until you empty it. Note that files from external storage devices ($3\frac{1}{2}$" floppy drive) are not temporarily stored here. They are deleted immediately.

E-mail Inbox

This icon provides quick access to your e-mail inbox by launching Outlook or Exchange.

My Briefcase

Use this icon to synchronize files from your desktop (PC) and laptop. You may or may not see this icon; some places remove it from the desktop if you don't use laptops.

Folders Folders are holding places for files and may also be located on the desktop. Pictorially yellow file folders represent them. Folders are a way to organize your system by storing like programs or suites and files in them. You may also embed folders within folders to create a hierarchical structure to your system. How to create folders is discussed later in this chapter.

Files Files contain your data and are what you create through applications like Word, Excel, PowerPoint, and so forth. Files are where you do your work. Pictorially, they take the look associated with the application. For example, a Word file is represented by a W symbol on the icon representing the file. Files are created when you save your work in an application or use the create new file command from the shortcut menu.

Shortcuts These are pointers to an actual application, folder, or file. They contain the path to the executable file for the application, to the folder, or to the file. Deleting them only deletes the shortcut, not the application, folder, or file. Pictorially, shortcuts are represented by a right curved arrow on the bottom left of the icon. In Figure 3–1 there are shortcuts to the printer, floppy drive, and several folders. Use shortcuts to provide quick access to commonly used applications, folders, or files. How to create them is presented later in this chapter.

Taskbar The taskbar, by default, is located at the bottom of the screen and may be moved to any screen edge. The taskbar is actually three separate components, although it looks like one object. At the far left is the **Start Button**. This opens the **Start Menu** and provides you with access to programs, documents, find, settings, help, and shutdown. To the far right is the **System Tray** This contains the clock and often icons for programs that usually run in the background and need only occasional user input. Examples of these types of programs are Norton Anti-Virus AutoProtect and Volume. The remainder is the body of the taskbar itself. Most programs place a button on the taskbar when they are opened. Clicking one of these buttons allows the user to bring that application's window to the foreground and make it active. The taskbar helps you switch from one application to another.

Pointer Shapes

Before we start working in this environment and moving things around, it is important to discuss the varying pointer or cursor shapes. During different actions in the Windows world, the pointer changes shape. When the pointer changes shape, the computer expects to complete certain operations and responds accordingly.

Use the left slanted arrow to select objects, double click objects, right click objects, drag objects, or choose menu or icon commands.

Use the I-beam to insert text. It means you are over a text field and are expected to insert text. Note that the text is inserted at the location of the vertical bar or insertion point, not the I-beam location.

 Use the double-headed arrow to resize windows. It appears when you are on a window border. There are three versions of it—left-right, up-down, and slanted. Left-right arrows widen the window, up-down arrows lengthen the windows, and slanted arrows go in both directions.

Wait, do not type or click the mouse button when you see the hourglass. The hourglass means the computer is processing and can't process any further commands until it finishes.

 Use the hand to obtain additional information. The hand means you are over a linked object or text. Clicking the text or object will bring more information from this or another site.

No, the action you want to do is not available.

Additional pointer shapes will be discussed as they appear in specific applications.

Changing the Colors of the Desktop

The default color of the desktop is Windows Standard. This is the teal and related colors Windows uses unless you change it. Many users never change the default color scheme as they find it soothing to the eyes; others like change and stimulation in the workday world. Windows provides for both types of users by letting you choose your desktop color scheme. If you change the default color scheme, the scheme you select or develop remains until you change it again.

To change the color scheme:

Right click a blank area of the desktop.

From the short cut menu, select **Properties**.

Click the **Appearance** tab.

Select a color scheme from the scheme drop-down menu.

To see the color scheme before exiting the dialog box, click **Apply**.

If you are not satisfied with that scheme, **Change it**.

When you have a scheme with which you are satisfied, click **OK**.

You may also change the color scheme from the **Display icon** in the control panel window. To access the control panel, select **Start Button** on the taskbar, **Settings**, **Control Panel,** or double click the **My Computer** icon, double click **Control Panel** folder.

Moving Objects on the Desktop

You can move any object on the desktop and place it wherever you want it. If you don't like the location of the icons or want them to appear in a specific place on the screen, Windows gives you the option to change the location of the objects. The taskbar can be located on any of the four edges of the screen. The default is to place the taskbar on the bottom of the screen.

To change the location of the taskbar:

Place the mouse pointer on a **Blank** area of the taskbar.

Drag the taskbar to the **left**, **right, bottom,** or **top** of the screen.

Release the mouse button.

Note that when dragging the taskbar it initially appears not to move. Keep dragging the mouse towards the edge of the screen and eventually the taskbar will move.

To change the location of an icon, folder, shortcut, or file:

Select the object, **Drag** it to the new location.

Right click a **Blank area** of the desktop.

From the short cut menu, select **Line up Icons**.

The objects (icons) will now be in the general area where you moved them but will be in a straight column and row. There is an invisible checkerboard on the screen and when you choose the command **line up icons**, they are snapped into the closest square to produce straight rows and columns. If your objects (icons) snap back into place when you try to move them, right click a **Blank area** of the desktop, select **Arrange Icons**, and click **Automatic**. This removes the check mark next to automatic. The check mark causes the icons to snap back into place.

From the shortcut menu, you may also select **arrange icons**. You have four choices for arrangement—by name, type, size, and date. The icons will then be arranged on the left side of the desktop in the order you selected. The disadvantage to this option is that every time you add new objects and select arrange them, they will be in different spots on the desktop. Most people like their objects in a consistent place on the desktop so they don't spend time looking for them.

Choosing a Screen Saver

Screen savers are moving or static pictures displayed on the desktop when no activity takes place for a specified period of time. They were initially designed to protect your monitor from having images burnt onto it. Today, they are primarily used for decoration. Many screensavers come with the operating system and others may be obtained free from the Internet or purchased at computer software stores.

To set up a screen saver:

Right click a **Blank area** of the desktop.

Choose **Properties** from the shortcut menu.

Click the **Screen Saver** tab.

Click the screen saver **Down Arrow**, click a **Screen Saver Image.**

Make any appropriate adjustments with the **Settings** button.

Click **OK.**

Shutting Down the System

When you finish working with the computer, it is important to shut down the system before you turn off the computer. Shutting down the computer saves the current settings and prevents corruption of files.

To shut down the system:

Click the **Start** button on the taskbar.

Select **Shut Down.**

Select the appropriate option and click **OK.**

Most of the time the appropriate option will be either shut down or close all programs and log on as another user. The computer will proceed with shutting down. When selecting shut down, a message appears on the screen telling you it is OK to turn off the computer. Note that some computers will turn off their CPU automatically but you will still need to turn off the monitor. When choosing close all programs and log on as another user, the computer saves the appropriate data and then logs you off the system. The computer remains turned on and a dialog window appears. The message in the window is press **CTRL, ALT, DEL** to log on as a new user. Now the next person in the lab can use the computer by logging in.

MANAGING YOUR WINDOWS

This section describes the layout of the windows and the process of controlling your windows and the window's display. All applications, files, and folders display in a window. Each window shares similar attributes. To be able to efficiently work in the Windows world, you need to be able to manage your windows. Figure 3–2 displays a common Windows layout.

Common Windows Layout

Title bar This is the horizontal bar at the top of all windows. With the default color scheme, this bar is blue for the active window and gray for all other open windows. The title bar displays a graphic button to access a menu, the name of the window and/or open file, and on the far right the window control buttons of minimize, maximize, and close. These buttons will be discussed later in this chapter. Use the title bar to move (drag) the window to another location on the desktop.

Title Bar
Menu Bar

Toolbars

Scroll Bars

Status Bar

FIGURE 3–2.
Typical Windows Layout

Menu bar The next bar on the window contains names of available menus. Use the menu or horizontal bar with words on it to obtain additional drop-down options. For example, clicking **File** brings you such choices as new, open, move, copy, delete, properties, run, and exit Windows. Any command not available to you appears gray. Clicking a bold command initiates that command with a few exceptions listed below.

If an option has three periods or an ellipsis after it, a dialog box appears. A dialog box is a window that requests additional information from you before the command can be implemented. In Figure 3–3 commands new, open, save as, save as HTML, versions, page setup, and print will all bring up a dialog box. You complete the information as appropriate in the dialog box and click OK for the command to be executed.

If an option has a right arrow, another menu appears. In Figure 3–3, the Send to command will bring up another menu. This other menu is sometimes called a nested menu.

Toolbars Most windows display one or more toolbars. The standard toolbar provides access to commonly used commands such as create a new file, open a file, save a file, print a file, and cut/copy/paste data or images. These commands will be discussed in detail in Chapter 4. Additional or different commands may appear in some applications because of the nature of the program. For example, the Web browsers (discussed in Chapter 9, Using the World Wide Web) require a different set of commands. The standard toolbar in this type of application contains access to commands such as back, forward, stop, refresh or reload, home, and search.

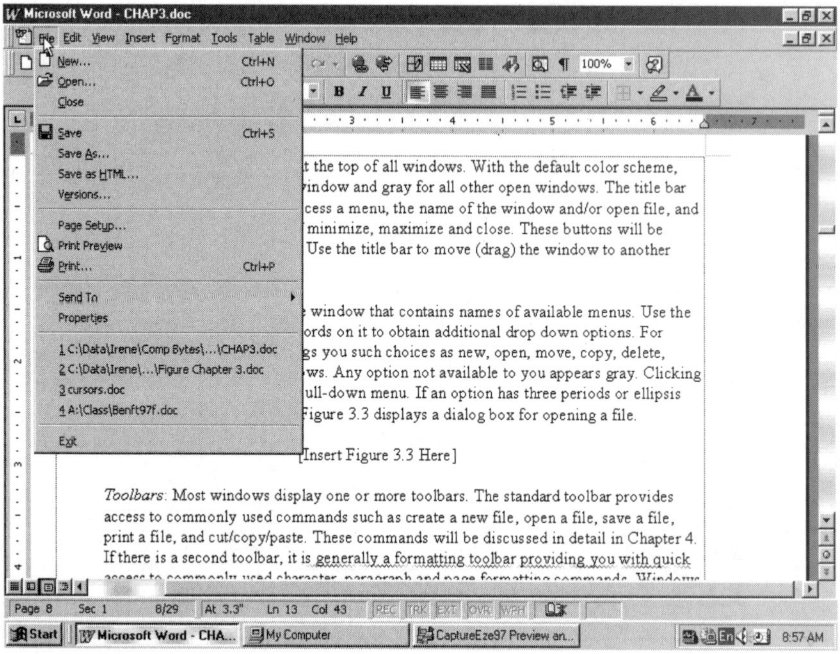

FIGURE 3–3.
Typical Menu

If there is a second toolbar, it is generally a formatting toolbar. This toolbar provides you with quick access to commonly used character, paragraph, and page formatting commands. The second toolbar under the top toolbar in Figure 3–4 is a formatting toolbar. Windows gives you the ability to display additional toolbars or hide these toolbars through the **View, Toolbars** command. Additional toolbars, such as the ruler bar, will be discussed in the appropriate application chapters.

Typical Standard Toolbars for Word Processing

Typical Toolbar for Web Browser

FIGURE 3–4.
Typical Toolbars

Status bar The horizontal bar at the bottom of the window displays such things as the number of objects in the window, description of menu commands, number of pages in a document, location of cursor, and special toggle switches like overwrite, num lock, and cap lock. Contents of the status bar depend on the application and what is important in the application. For example, in Excel it displays whether the num lock and cap lock keys are on or off and the current mode of operation.

Scroll bars Located along the right and bottom of the window are the scroll bars. They appear when there is more data than can be displayed in the window because of the amount of data. Figure 3–5 displays a horizontal scroll bar. Use it to move through your document or to view your data when the whole document is not visible. There are arrows at the top/bottom of the right or vertical scroll bar and at the left/right for the bottom or horizontal scroll bar with a box somewhere between them. Clicking the arrow buttons moves slowly through the window. The box or elevator in the scroll shaft indicates where you are relative to the total document. Dragging the elevator in the scroll bar gives you more control over viewing the contents of the window. You may also click in the elevator shaft to go to that approximate location in the document.

FIGURE 3–5.
Horizontal Scroll Bar

Opening a Window

There are several ways to open a window or program. Here are a few of them.

Double click the **Icon** representing the window you want to open.

Right click the **Icon** representing the window you want to open, and select **Open** from the menu.

Select **Start** from the taskbar, select the **Window** you want to open. For example, to open a recently used file, select **Start**, **Documents**, and the **Name of the file**. To open the control panel folder, select **Start**, **Settings**, and **Control Panel**.

Once the window is open, perform the appropriate tasks. Since you may open more than one window at a time, you will need to control your window display.

Controlling the Window

There are several controls available for working with your windows. Use these controls to move a window to another location on the desktop, change the size of a window, or close a window. Resize lets you control the actual size of the window; the maximize and minimize buttons use default standards to control the size of the window. Maximize expands the window to fill the screen. The minimize button places a button on the taskbar and removes the window from the desktop. The program remains open, but is running in the background. The restore button returns the window to the size it was before you maximized it.

You use these buttons when you run multiple programs, open multiple windows, or open several files. This permits you to view or work on each while placing the others in the background.

In addition, you may also arrange all open windows on the desktop in cascade, tile horizontally, or tile vertically. If you have many windows open, you might want to arrange them in cascade. All open windows will be cascaded from the top of the screen down showing you the title bar of each open window. Tiling horizontally and vertically is used to partition the screen into quadrants depending on the number of opened windows. Use this feature when you want to drag and drop data from one window to another.

Function	Directions
Move a window	Click a blank area of **Title Bar** of window to move.
	Drag window to new location and release mouse button.
Resize a window	Select Window to resize by clicking **Title Bar**.
	Point to a Window **Border** or **Corner**.
	Cursor turns to double-headed arrow.
	Drag the **corner** or **border** until it is the size you want.
	Release the mouse button.
Enlarge a window	Select Window to enlarge by clicking **Title Bar**.
	Click **Maximize Button** [□] in upper right corner of Title Bar.
Reduce a window	Select Window to reduce by clicking **Title Bar**.
	Click **Minimize Button** [_] in upper right corner of Title Bar.
Restore a window	Select Window to restore by clicking **Title Bar**.
	Click **Restore Button** [⧉] in upper right corner of Title Bar.
Close a window	Select Window to close by clicking **Title Bar**.
	Click **Close Button** [X] in upper right corner of Title Bar.
Arrange a window	Right click blank area of **Taskbar**.
	Select **Cascade** or **Tile windows horizontally** or **vertically**.

MANAGING FILES AND FOLDERS

This section deals with managing files and folders. The file system you use is the core for working efficiently and effectively with your computer. Knowing how to find, access, and manage your files is important to managing your system. There are two main ways to access your files—My Computer and Windows Explorer—and several different views you can use to see those files once accessed.

Some basic file and folder management concepts are introduced here. The specifics of creating, renaming, moving, copying, and deleting files and folders then follow these concepts.

Designating Default Disk Drives

A default drive is the drive the program uses to find and save files unless you tell it otherwise. Remember from Chapter 2 the drive letter designation for the hard drive is generally C, for a $3\frac{1}{2}$" drive A, and for a CD ROM or zip drive B, D, or E. Most programs use a default folder on the C drive to store data you create. For example, Microsoft Office uses the My Documents folder on the C drive to store all Office files. All programs give you the ability to change the default storage drive and folder. To do this generally requires you to find the preferences or options command which can be in the tools or edit menus. One of the options in the dialog window is generally the ability to change the location of files.

If you are not permitted to alter settings in your computer lab, then you will need to use the file Save as command to change the location of files each time you access the program. In the file Save as dialog window, click the down arrow button in the save in textbox area and select your storage device.

Write Protecting Diskettes

Sometimes you may want to protect your diskette from accidental deletions. This is especially important when you are learning the commands. Being tired or in a hurry leads to mistakes. When making duplicate copies of a master diskette, write protect the original diskette. To write protect a $3\frac{1}{2}$" diskette, move the write protect tab on the top right of the diskette so you can see through the hole. An easy way to remember this is you can't write on air. Note that when using most application programs, you will need to remove the write protect. Many programs store temporary files on the diskette, that is, they need to write to the diskette.

Diskette Preparation Command (Format)

The **Format** command initializes a diskette by placing sectors and tracks on the diskette. This process magnetically maps the diskette. You can not use diskettes unless you format them or purchase them preformatted. Formatting allows you to recycle diskettes by erasing what was previously there.

Function	Windows 95, 98 & NT 4.0
Format	Double click **My Computer** icon.
	Right click **A drive** icon.
	Select **Format...**
	Check **Capacity** text box for accuracy of capacity (generally 1.44).
	Check **Type** for what you want—erase, full or copy system.
	Click **Start**.
	Click **Close** to finish format.

See Figure 3–6 for format dialog window. The capacity text box permits you to change the capacity (amount of data the diskette holds) of the diskette. High-density diskettes are formatted

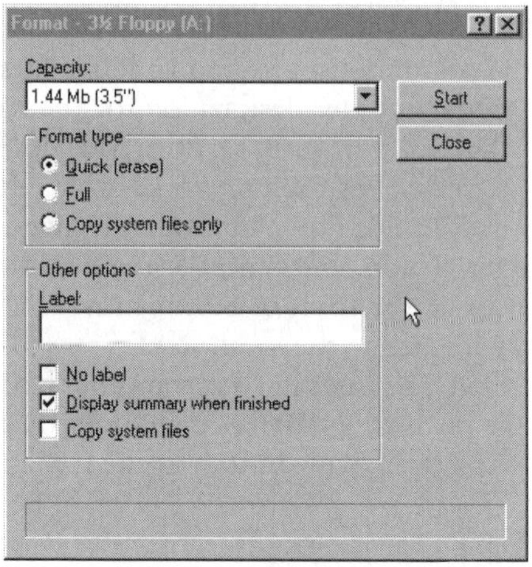

FIGURE 3–6.
Format Dialog Window

as 1.44 MB; double sided are formatted as 720K. You may also specify whether you want a full format used for new diskettes or a quick erase used for already formatted diskettes to recycle them for new use. Most of the time you will not use the last option to place system files on the diskette. That is used for creating bootable diskettes and your diskettes are primarily used for storage of data. Note that the options are circles, which means you have one choice—quick erase, full, or copy system files.

Other options you have are to place a label (name) on the diskette, display a summary when format is complete, and to copy the system files on an already formatted diskette. Note that these options are represented by squares. Squares say pick as many of these options as you want. The square acts like a toggle switch. Click once and a check or X is placed in the square; click again and the check or X is removed. All options with a check or X in the square are turned on.

It is a good idea to format a box of diskettes at one time. Doing so is more time efficient. All you need to do is respond **Yes** when prompted to format more diskettes. Format diskettes for their designed capacity. For example, if the diskette is double sided, double density, make sure you format it as such. Over time you will lose data if you format it for a different capacity.

Creating Folders

Organize and manage your files by creating folders and saving your work in them. A folder is a storage place for files and folders. How you organize them depends on the nature of what you do. For example, you might have a folder containing all files related to a specific course you are taking, another for personal items, and yet another for articles or publications. Storing files in the appropriate folders allows you to retrieve and back up your data easily. Associating files with projects or tasks allows for easier clean up when projects or tasks are completed. Saving all your files in **My Documents** or **My Files** folders make retrieving and house cleaning more difficult and time consuming. An icon represents each folder.

To create the folder:

Point to a **Blank area** of the desktop.

Click your **Right** mouse button. A shortcut menu appears.

Click the menu item marked **New**. Another shortcut menu appears.

Click the menu item labeled **Folder**.

A new folder appears on your desktop. The folder name is highlighted.

Type a **Name** for the folder and press **Enter**.

Naming Files and Folders

All files and folders have names. There are three parts to naming a file. They are filename, delimiter, and file extension. A sample filename is My Smiley Face.bmp. Folders have a name but no delimiter or extension.

Filename In the example of a filename above, the portion to the left of the period (My Smiley Face) is the filename. Filenames use letters, numbers, or some special characters up to 255 characters. Legal characters are letters of the alphabet (A–Z), digits (0–9), and all the special characters except * ? < > \ / " : and |. Use blank spaces between the characters of the filename to make the filename more readable and understandable. Filenames are not case sensitive so you may type in all lower case, a combination of upper and lower, or all upper case. Use a unique filename for each file; there can be no duplicate filenames in the same folders.

Delimiter The delimiter is the period that separates the filename from the extension. This is optional; you do not need to use the delimiter unless you use an extension to the filename or have the option selected for displaying file extensions.

Extension The portion to the right of the delimiter is the extension. Extensions help identify the nature of the file. For example, doc is the extension attached to Word documents. In most cases, the default option in the Windows environment is to hide the extensions. This means that the user does not need to type the extension. It is assigned to the file by the application used to create the file. In this environment the extension is then used to identify what application was used to create the file; and when you double click the file, the appropriate application opens and brings up the file.

Before working with files, think about some standards you might want to apply for naming files for yourself, area, or department. There are many ways to do this depending on what work you are doing, who does it, what you share, how you share it (on network or diskettes), how you access it, and who retrieves it. The important point here is for you to use some convention so in 6 to 12 months when you or someone else are looking for the file you can easily recognize and retrieve it.

To name files and folders follow the directions here.

Function	Windows 95, 98 & NT 4.0
Name File (Application)	Start **Application** like Word or Excel. **Create** the file. Select **File, Save** or click the **Diskette** 🖫. Select location from the **Save in** text box. Type **File name** in the **File name** text box. Click **OK** or press **Enter**.
Name File (On desktop)	Right click **Blank area** of the desktop or in a window. Select **New**. Select **Type** of file (Word, Excel, etc). Type **File name**. Click **OK** or press **Enter**.
Name Folder	Right click **Blank area** of the desktop or in a window. Select **New** folder. Type **Folder name**. Click **OK** or press **Enter**.

Viewing Files and Folders

Once you have your files and folders created and named, you will want to view them. You have two choices here—use My Computer or Windows Explorer.

My Computer By default, My Computer opens a new window each time you double click an object. The contents of that window are displayed on top of the previous window. You continue doing this until you locate the file or folder.

Windows Explorer Windows Explorer provides a different view of your files and folders. The left of the screen shows the organizational structure while the right side shows the contents of the selected device or folder. In Figure 3–7, the top of the structure is the Desktop. All the icons on the desktop are displayed on the left side (My Computer, Internet Explorer, Recycle Bin, etc.). Under My Computer are the storage devices (A, C, and G) and selected folders like control panel and printers. The right side of the screen shows the contents of the top of the C drive.

A plus sign next to an icon on the left side means there are more objects below it that are not displayed. A minus sign means that level of the structure is fully expanded and visible to you. You can change the look by collapsing and expanding each level of the structure on the left side. When you click an object on the left side, the contents of that object are displayed on the right.

You have four options for how the icons in the My Computer window and Windows Explorer display—large icons, small icons, list, and details. The default display is large icons. Small icons display across in a row filling the first row, then the second and so on. List places small icons in a column filling the first column, then the second, and so on. Details lists them in a column giving you more information about each icon, such as type of object, size, and date created. As you work in this environment, you will develop a preference for how these icons display.

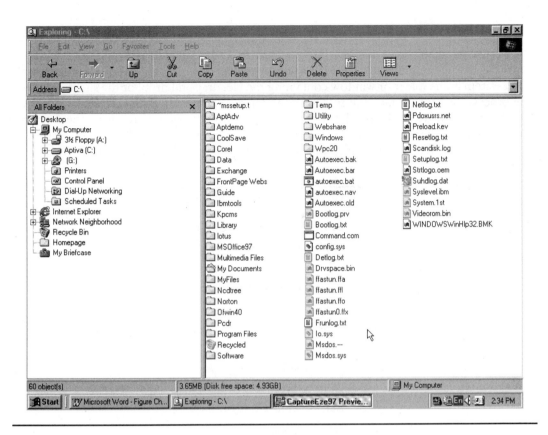

FIGURE 3–7.
Windows Explorer

Function	Windows 95, 98 & NT 4.0
View—My Computer	Double click **My Computer** icon.
	Double click the **Storage device** where file is located.
	Continue double clicking until file or folder is displayed.
View—Windows Explorer	Click **Start, Programs, Windows Explorer.**
Change View—Menu	Select **View** from menu bar.
	Click **Small, List,** or **Detail.**
Change View—Toolbar	If needed, click **View** on toolbar.
	Click **Small, List,** or **Detail** icons or commands.

Copying Files and Folders

The Copy command copies one, several, or all files from one place to another. That means you now have two of the same files. You have several options for this command. You may use the menu system in the folder or window containing the file, drag and drop, or the short-cut menu. The process for copying files and folders is the same. When using drag and drop from the A drive to another drive like C, the default is copy. When using drag and drop from the A drive to another folder in the A drive, the default is move. You can override the default option by right dragging the file. When you drop it in its new location, select copy or move from the pop-up menu.

Function	Windows 95, 98 & NT 4.0
Copy one file—menu	**Both** file and destination must be visible.
	Highlight the **File** to be copied.
	Select **Edit**, **Copy** from the menu bar.
	Go to **New location** and **Click.**
	Select **Edit**, **Paste**.
Copy one file—drag and drop	*Only works going from one drive to a different one.*
	Both file and destination must be visible.
	Select the **File**.
	Drag to **New location**.
	Release mouse button.
	If copying from A to A or C to C:
	Right drag the **File** to additional location.
	Release the mouse button.
	Select **Copy here**.
Copy one file—shortcut	Select **File**.
	Right click **File**.
	Select **Copy**.
	Go to **New** location.
	Right click in **New location**.
	Select **Paste**.
Copy adjacent files	Click the **First** file in the group.
	Hold down the **Shift** key.
	Click **Last** file in the group.
	Release **Shift** key.
	Follow any of the above as all files are selected.

Function	Windows 95, 98 & NT 4.0
Copy nonadjacent files	Hold down the **CTRL** key. Click **All** files you want to copy. Release **CTRL** key. Follow any of the above as all files are selected.

Note that you may drag a box around the files to select a group of files. Go to the top left of the group of files, hold down the left mouse button, drag the mouse to the opposite corner, and release the mouse button. Once they are highlighted, follow any of the above for copying them.

Moving Files and Folders

Moving files and folders is similar to copying. The move command takes a file or folder from one place and puts it in another. It does not duplicate it. You have three options here like you do with copying—use the menu, use drag and drop, or use the shortcut menu. When moving a file from one drive to another drive, the default for drag and drop is copy. When moving from one place on the same storage drive to another on the same storage drive, the default is move. If you want to override the default, use a right drag and select move from the pop-up menu.

Function	Windows 95, 98 & NT 4.0
Move one file—menu	**Both** file and destination must be visible. Highlight the **File**. Select **Edit, Cut**. Go to **New location** and **click**. Select **Edit, Paste**.
Move one file—drag and drop	*Only works when going from A to A, C to C.* **Both** file and destination must be visible. Select the **File**. Drag to **New location** on same drive. Release mouse button. *If going to different storage drive:* Right drag the **File**. Select **Move here**.
Move one file—shortcut	**Select** file. Right click **File**. Select **Cut**. Go to **New** location.

Function	Windows 95, 98 & NT 4.0
	Right click in **New location**.
	Select **Paste**.
Move Adjacent Files	Click the **First** file in the group.
	Hold down the **Shift** key.
	Click **Last** file in the group.
	Release **Shift** key.
	Follow any of the above as all files are selected.
Move nonadjacent Files	Hold down the **CTRL** key.
	Click **All** files you want to copy.
	Release **CTRL** key.
	Follow any of the above as all files are selected.

Deleting Files and Folders

The Delete command removes files from the storage device. Use this command to clean up your storage devices and discard files no longer needed. There are several versions of this command as noted below.

When deleting files from a floppy diskette, files are not placed in the recycle bin. They are immediately deleted. Only files from the hard drive are deleted to the recycle bin. If you accidentally delete files from the hard disk that you later need, you may recover them unless you emptied the recycle bin.

When folders are placed in the recycle bin, they are immediately deleted. If the folder contains files from an internal storage device, the files are placed in the recycle bin.

When executable files (program files) are placed in the recycle bin, you are prompted to confirm if you really want to delete the file. This is a safe guard to ensure that you really want to delete the program files.

Function	Windows 95, 98 & NT 4.0
Delete using drag and drop	Make both the **File** or **Folder** and **Recycle Bin** visible.
	Drag the **File** or **Folder** on top the **Recycle Bin** icon.
	When the icon turns blue, release **Left** mouse button.
	Click **Yes** to confirm deletion.
Delete using delete key	Click the **File** or **Folder** to highlight it.
	Press the **Delete** key.
	Click **Yes** to confirm deletion.

Function	Windows 95, 98 & NT 4.0
Delete using menu	Right click **File** or **Folder** to delete.
	Select **Delete** from shortcut menu.
	Click **Yes** to confirm deletion.

Once you send files to the Recycle Bin, you will periodically need to empty the Recycle Bin. How often you empty the Recycle Bin depends on how often you delete files and folders and how many you have deleted.

To empty the Recycle Bin:

Double click the **Recycle Bin** icon.

Select **File, Empty Recycle bin**, and click **Yes** to confirm emptying.

Renaming Files and Folders

The rename command gives the file or folder a new name. Use this command when you are reorganizing and need to change the names of files to be consistent with your new organization or when you need to clarify the name because of additional files or folders created.

Function	Windows 95, 98 & NT 4.0
Rename a file or folder—shortcut	Right click the **File** or **Folder** to rename.
	Click **Rename**.
	Type **New File Name** and press **Enter**.
Rename a file or folder—click	Click the **File** or **Folder** name.
	Pause, and click **again**.
	Type **New File Name** and press **Enter**.

Organizing Folders

Most of us store files on floppy diskettes, zip disks, or the hard drive. You must organize how you store these files, just like you do with your filing cabinet. You organize files on the storage media in folders and subfolders.

Root level The "root" is the top level on which you make the folders and store files the computer needs to access upon startup. A general rule is that a folder or file listing of the root level should not occupy more than one screen worth of information

Folders Folders organize your programs and data files. Before you create them, give some thought to how you work and what programs you use. Most software programs automatically make a directory for its program files when you install it. Be careful that these directories "fit" your organization. Customize them upon installation if needed.

Subfolders These folders are contained within other folders. Subfolders assist you in providing further divisions or structure to the organization of your files.

Some rules for creating and using the folder and subfolder structure are:

1. Place each application suite in its own folder with subfolders for each application program. This makes installation of new versions, deletions of old versions, and maintenance of files easier. You know what files go with what program. Some suites also create subfolders for shared suite files.
2. Place programs not belonging to application suites in the Programs Files folder in their own subfolder with an appropriate name representing the applications. For example, MS Frontpage for Microsoft Frontpage. You might also want to create a Utility Folder off the root and place each Utility program in its own folder. For example, Norton Anti-Virus, Norton Utilities, Acrobat Reader, and WinZip.
3. Create folders for storing your data files. Never store data files on the root as they then get mixed with essential computer files. For example, create a Data folder off the root. In the Data folder, create folders for each user on the system. Let them then create the appropriate subfolders in their data folder.
4. Create a Graphic Library folder off the root for storing graphic images you acquire. The Graphic Library folder could contain subfolders representing graphic file formats or categories. For example, JPG and Gif graphic files or pets, cities, and computers.
5. Use appropriate folder names. No two folders in the same level can have the same name. It is probably better not to name any folder with the same name as another folder.

SELECTED DISK MANAGEMENT COMMAND

This section covers a disk management command that makes a duplicate of your diskette. There are many disk management commands but this is the one you will use the most.

Copying a Disk

Once you have created and organized your files and folders, you will want to make a copy of the diskette. The Copy Disk command copies all the files, folders, and structure from one diskette to another simultaneously erasing all files on the second or target diskette. Use this command to make backup copies of your diskettes. Since it makes an exact duplicate of the disk, you need to use it with a like medium only. That means HD to HD or DS to DS. You cannot use this command to backup your hard drive to diskettes nor can you use it to backup a DS/DD diskette to a HD diskette.

To make sure you don't accidentally format the source diskette, write protect the original or source diskette before using this command. Since this command erases all files on the target diskette, check the diskette to make sure no files you want are on it.

Function	Windows 95, 98 & NT 4.0
Make exact copy of diskette	Double click **My Computer** icon.
	Right click **3½" disk drive** icon.
	Select **Copy disk** command.
	Insert **Original (source)** diskette.
	Click **Start** button.
	Insert **Backup (target)** diskette and click **OK**.
	Click **Close** to close the Copy dialog box.

CREATING SHORTCUTS

Shortcuts are used to save you time when working in the Windows environment. Instead of using My Computer or Windows Explorer to try and find your files, folders or programs, you create shortcuts for frequently used items on the Desktop. Files, folders, application programs, and storage devices can all have shortcuts. Remember shortcuts are pointers to these objects, they are not the actual object. Double clicking the shortcut opens the object it is "pointing to." The shortcut tells the computer where to find the object. The general rule of thumb for using shortcuts is to create them for frequently used objects. Many people create shortcuts to their data files, the printer, the floppy drive, and selected applications. Note that you do not want shortcuts to infrequently used items. You desktop would become too cluttered.

A shortcut is denoted with a small curved arrow in the lower left corner of the icon. Since it is a pointer to an actual object, deleting the shortcut only deletes the shortcut, not the actual object to which it is pointing.

To create a shortcut:

Find the **Object** for which you want to create a shortcut.

Right drag it to the **Desktop**. This means that you must size your windows to see the Desktop.

Select **Create shortcut here** from the shortcut menu.

SUMMARY

This chapter oriented you to the operating system and the Windows interface. The common objects found on the desktop where presented. You also learned how to manage your desktop by setting screensavers, changing desktop colors, moving objects, and managing windows. The chapter ended with file and folder management concepts and commands teaching you how to create, rename, move, copy, and delete files and folders. Also presented were some basic ideas about organizing your files and folders.

EXERCISE 1: MANAGING YOUR DESKTOP AND WINDOWS

Objectives

1. Identify and describe the desktop.
2. Apply a screensaver of your choice.
3. Arrange the desktop to work efficiently and effectively for you.
4. Change the colors of the desktop.
5. Open, close, minimize, maximize, size, and arrange your windows.
6. Switch between windows.

Activity

If necessary, make sure you turn on the computer and monitor and log on.

1. Identify desktop objects. Complete these statements:

   An object like this ⬚ is called a(n) _____. It is used for _____.

   An object like this ⬚ is called a(n) _____. It represents _____.

   An object like this ⬚ is called a(n) _____. Use it to _____.

   An object like this ⬚ is called a(n) _____. Place it on the desktop _____.
   The bar below is called the _____. For what is it used? _____.

   | 🏁 Start | 🗏 Microsoft Word - CHAP3.d... | 🖳 My Computer | | 📇 CaptureEze97 Previe... | | 🔊 🈁 En ◁ 🕐 | 8:03 AM |

2. Apply a screensaver.
   Right click a **Blank area** of the desktop.
   Choose **Properties** from the shortcut menu.
   Click the **Screensaver** tab.

   Click the screensaver **Down arrow** ▼, click **Scrolling Marquee** (see Figure 3–8).

   Click **Settings** ⬚ Settings... button (see Figure 3–9), position **Random**, background color **Blue.**
   Highlight **Text,** type **Out to lunch, back at 1 PM.**

   Click **Format text** ⬚ Format Text... button, select **Times New Roman, 72 points, yellow.**
   Click **OK, OK.**
   Click **Preview button,** click **Apply** and **OK.**

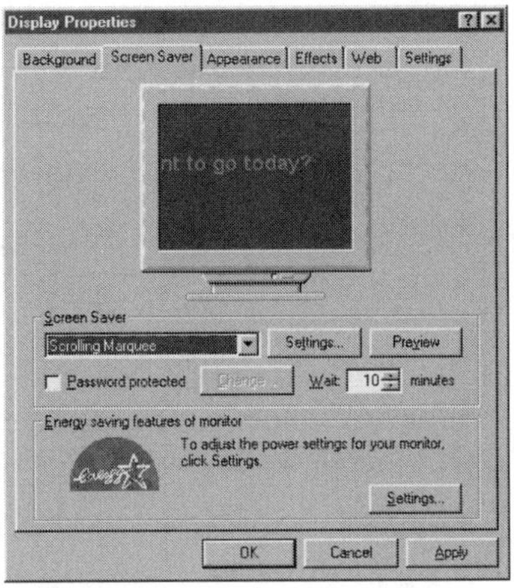

FIGURE 3–8.
Screensaver Dialog Window

FIGURE 3–9.
Screensaver Settings Dialog Window

3. Move and arrange objects on the desktop.

   Drag **My Computer**  icon to the right bottom of desktop.

   Drag **Recycle Bin**  icon to right bottom desktop.
   Right click a **Blank area** of the desktop, select **Arrange icons**, select **By name.**
   What happened to the icons? _____.

   Now, drag **My Computer**  icon to the top right of desktop.

   Drag **Recycle Bin**  icon to right top of desktop.
   Right click a **Blank area** of the desktop, select **Line-up icons.**
   What happened now? _____.
   Drag **Taskbar** to the top of the screen.

Note: If your icons snap back into place, right click a blank area of the desktop, select arrange icons, select AutoArrange. This removes the check next to the AutoArrange feature and permits you to move icons about.

4. Change desktop colors.

   Right click **Blank area** of desktop, choose **Properties.**

   Click **Appearance tab,** click **Scheme** down arrow ▼ button, select **Red, White, Blue.** Click **Apply.**

   Note to change it back to the default colors, right click blank area of desktop, choose properties, appearance tab, click scheme down arrow, select windows standard.

5. Open, browse, and manage windows.

   Double click **My Computer** 🖳 icon.

   Drag, using the title bar, the **My Computer** window to the right about 3 inches.

   Click the **Maximize** ⬜ button. What happened to the window?

   Click the **Restore** 🗗 button. Now what happened?

   Click the **Minimize** ▬ button. Now what happened?

   Click the **My Computer** 🖳 button on the task bar.

   Place your pointer on the **Right border** of the **My Computer** window.

   With the double-headed arrow, drag the **Window border** to the right two inches.

   Place you pointer on the **Bottom right corner** of the **My Computer** window.

   Drag the window border **Up and to the left** making the window about 3" square.

   What additional bars appeared?

   Why might you need to know how to open and manage windows?

   Drag to **Enlarge** the **My Computer** window making it about 6" square.

   Double click **C drive** icon. Double click the **Windows folder**.

   Notice that the default in Windows is to open a new window for every object you double click.

   Close the **Windows** and **C drive** windows by clicking the **Close** ✖ button for each window. This leaves the **My Computer** window open.

6. Switch between windows.

   Double click **Control Panel** folder in **My Computer** window.

   What happened?

   Click the **My Computer** button on the taskbar. What happened?

   Move the **My Computer** window so the **Control Panel** window is visible.

Click anywhere in the **Control Panel** window.

Now, hold down the **ALT** key and press the **Tab** key.

Press the **Tab** key again while still holding down the **ALT** key.

Release the **Tab** and **Alt** keys. What happened?

Why might you want to switch between windows?

Click the **Close** **X** buttons to close all open windows.

EXERCISE 2: MANAGING YOUR FILES AND FOLDERS WITH MY COMPUTER

Objectives

1. Format a diskette.
2. Create folders and files.
3. Move, copy, and rename folders and files.
4. Delete files and folders.
5. Empty the recycle bin.

Activity

1. Format your diskette.

   Place a **diskette** in the A drive. Double click **My Computer** icon.

   Right click the **3½" drive** icon. Select **Format** (see Figure 3–10).

   Check **Capacity** text box for accuracy of capacity (1.44 for HD diskette).

   Click **Full** in format type select area.

   Check to make sure there is a ✔ in the display summary when finished box.

   Click **Start** Button. This will take a little while to format.

   What is the total disk space? _____. Are there any bad sectors? _____.

   What is the available space? _____.

   Click **Close** to close the summary window.

   Click **Close** to close the format dialog window.

2. Create folders. We will use the diskette you just formatted for this part of the activity.

   Double click **My Computer** icon.

   Double click **3½" floppy drive** icon.

   Right click a **Blank area** of the 3½" floppy drive window.

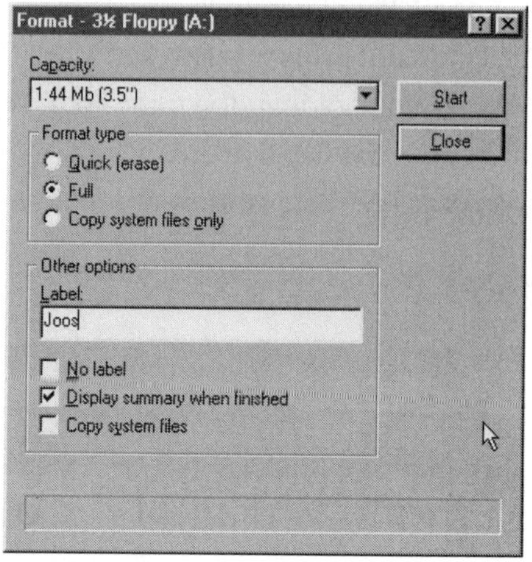

FIGURE 3–10.
Format Dialog Window

Select **New, Folder.**

Type **CIS100** and press **Enter.**

Double click **CIS100** folder.

Right click a **Blank area** of the CIS100 folder window.

Select **New, Folder.**

Type **Class Notes** and press **Enter.**

3. Create a file.

Double click **Class Notes** folder.

Right click a **Blank area** of the **Class Notes** folder, select **New, Word Document.**

Type **Hardware Notes** and press **Enter.**

Right click a **Blank area** of the **Class Notes** folder, select **New, Word Document.**

Type **Software Notes** and press **Enter.**

4. Copy, move, and rename folders and files.

Click the **Close** **X** button for the **Class Notes** and **CIS100** windows.

Double click the **C drive** ▭ icon and the **Windows** folder in the **C drive** window.

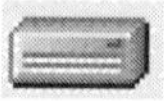

Scroll in the **Windows folder** window until the **Calc** ▦ is visible.

Arrange the **A drive** and **C:\Windows** windows next to each other as shown in Figure 3-11 below closing any other windows not needed.

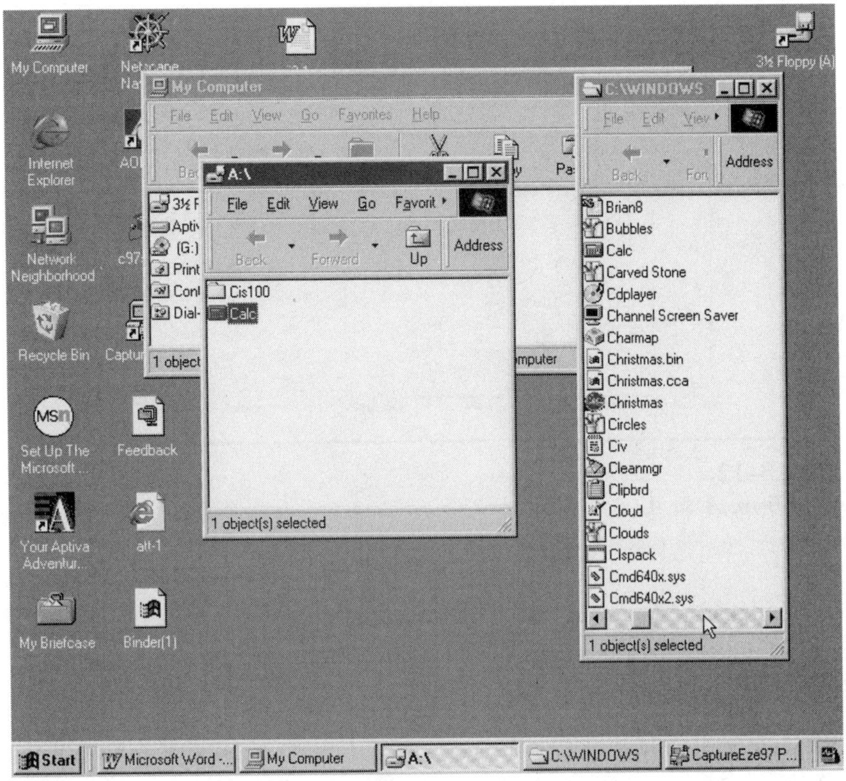

FIGURE 3–11.
Sample Screen for Copying Using Drag and Drop

Drag the **Calc** [icon] to the A drive window and drop it on a blank area of the window.

Note because you are going from the C drive to the A drive, the default for dragging and dropping is to copy. Notice that the calculator icon is now in both windows.

Click the **Close** button to close the C:\Windows window.

Double click the **CIS100** folder in the A drive window.

Arrange the **A drive** and **CIS100** windows as shown in Figure 3–12.

Right drag the **Calc** [icon] icon from the A drive window to the CIS100 window.

Drop it on a blank space in the CIS100 window.

Select **Copy here** from the shortcut menu. Notice the calculator is now in both windows. Why do you need to right drag the icon when copying from A to A?

Right click the **Calc** [icon] icon in the A drive window.

Select **Rename**.

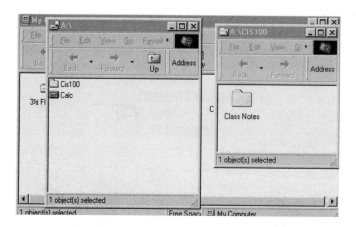

FIGURE 3–12.
Copying from A to A

Type **Calculator** and press **Enter**. The icon now has a new name.

Click over the text of the **Class Notes** folder in the CIS100 window once, then **Click again**.

The folder icon should look like this ![icon] with the text highlighted but not the icon.

Type **Lecture Notes** and press **Enter**.

Notice that there are two ways to rename files and folders and the process is the same for both files and folders.

Drag the **Lecture Notes** folder to the A Drive window. What did it do? Why?

Right drag the **Lecture Notes** folder to the CIS100 window.

Select **Copy here** from the shortcut menu. Note that you can over ride the default copy or move command by right dragging the file or folder and selecting whichever command you want.

5. Delete files and folders.

Click the **Calc** icon in the CIS100 window. Press the **Delete** key. Click **Yes**.

Close the **CIS100** window.

Move the **Icons** in the A drive window to line them up in a row or column.

If necessary, move the **A drive window** so you can see the recycle bin.

Click the **First icon** in the row or column, hold down the **Shift** key, and click **last icon**. All icons are now selected.

Drag the **Selected files** on top the recycle bin.

When the Recycle Bin turns blue, release your **Mouse button**.

Click **Yes** to confirm deletion of files and folders, and **Yes** to delete the calculator.

Close **All windows**.

6. Empty the **Recycle Bin**.

When you delete files from the A drive diskette, they are not placed in the recycle bin. They are immediately deleted. You will not need to empty the recycle bin. However, when you delete files from internal storage devices like the C drive, you will need to periodically empty the recycle bin.

Double click the **Recycle Bin** icon.

Select **File, Empty Recycle Bin**.

Click **Yes** to confirm deletion.

Close **Recycle Bin** window.

How often should you empty the recycle bin?_____

EXERCISE 3: MANAGING YOUR FILES AND FOLDERS WITH WINDOWS EXPLORER

Objectives

1. Format a diskette.
2. Create folders and files.
3. Move, copy, and rename folders and files.
4. Delete files and folders.
5. Empty the recycle bin.

Activity

1. Format your diskette.

Place a **Diskette** in the A drive.

Select **Start** button on the taskbar. Select **Programs** and **Windows Explorer**.

Right click the **3½" drive** icon. Select **Format**.

Check **Capacity** text box for accuracy of capacity (1.44 for HD diskette).

Click **Full** in format type select area.

Check to make sure there is a ✔ in the display summary when finished box.

Click **Start** Button.

What is the total disk space? _____. Are there any bad sectors? _____.

What is the available space? _____.

Click **Close** to close the summary window.

Click **Close** to close the format dialog box.

2. Create folders. We will use the diskette you just formatted for this part of the activity.

    Click the **3½" floppy drive** 📇 icon on the left side of the Explorer window.

    Right click a **Blank area** on the right side of the Explorer window.

    Select **New, Folder**.

    Type **CIS100** and press **Enter**.

    Double click **CIS100** folder.

    Right click a **Blank area** on the right side of the Explorer CIS100 window.

    Select **New, Folder**.

    Type **Class Notes** and press **Enter**.

3. Create a file.

    Double click **Class Notes** folder.

    Right click a **Blank area** on the right side of the Explorer Class Notes window.

    Select **New, Word Document**.

    Type **Hardware Notes** and press **Enter**.

    Right click a **Blank area** on the right side of the Explorer Class Notes window.

    Select **New, Word Document**.

    Type **Software Notes** and press **Enter**.

    Your screen should look similar to that screen shown in Figure 3–13.

4. Copy, move, and rename folders and files.

    Click the + sign next to the **C drive** 📇 icon on the left side of the Explorer window.

    Scroll on left side until you see the **Windows folder** in the C drive window.

    Click the Windows folder on the left side of the Explorer window.

    Scroll on the right side of the Explorer window until the **Calc** ⌨ is visible.

    Now, scroll on the left side of the Explorer window until you see the **A drive icon**.

    Drag the **Calc** ⌨ from the right side of the window and drop it on top of the **3½"**

    drive 📇 icon on the left side of the window.

    Note because you are going from the C drive to the A drive, the default for dragging and dropping is to copy. Notice that the calculator icon remains in the right side window.

    Click the **3½" drive** 📇 icon. Notice it is now also there.

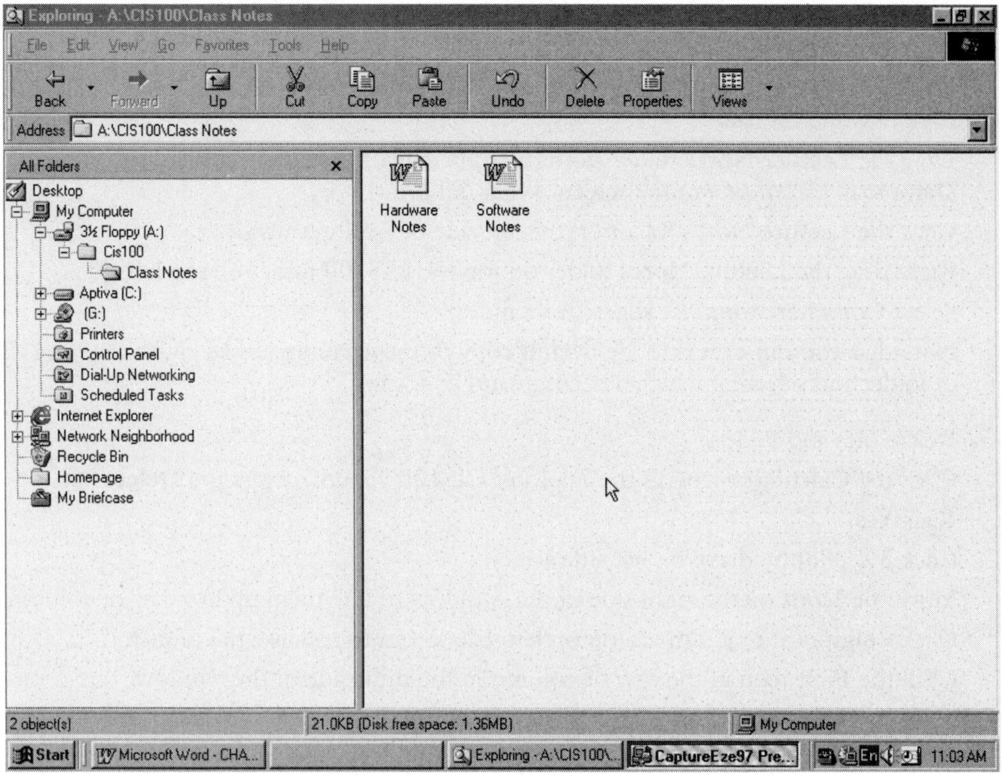

FIGURE 3–13.
Creating Files and Folders with Windows Explorer

Right drag the **Calc** ⊞ icon from right side of the Explorer window.

Drop it on top of the CIS100 folder on the left side of the Explorer window.

Select **Copy here** from the shortcut menu. Notice the calculator remains in the Explorer window.

Click the **CIS100** folder on the left side of the Explorer window. Calculator is there.

Why do you need to right drag the icon when copying from A to A?

Right click the **Calc** ⊞ icon on the right side of the Explorer CIS100 window.

Select **Rename**.

Type **Calculator** and press **Enter**. The icon now has a new name.

Click over the text of the **Class Notes** folder in the CIS100 window once, then **Click again**.

The folder icon should look like this ![icon] with the text highlighted but not the icon.

Type **Lecture Notes** and press **Enter**.

Notice that there are two ways to rename files and folders and the process is the same for both files and folders.

Drag the **Lecture Notes** folder from the right side of the Explorer window on to the $3\frac{1}{2}$" **Drive** icon on left side of the screen. What did it do? Why?

Click the **Lecture Notes** folder on the left side of Explorer window.

Right drag the **Lecture Notes** folder on top the CIS100 folder on the left side.

Select **Copy here** from the shortcut menu.

Note that you can over ride the default copy or move command by right dragging the file or folder and selecting whichever command you want.

5. Delete files and folders.

   Click the **Calculator** icon in the Explorer CIS100 window. Press the **Delete** key.

   Click **Yes**.

   Click $3\frac{1}{2}$" **floppy drive** on left side screen.

   Move the **Icons** on the right side of the window to line them up in a row or column.

   Click – **sign** next to C Drive icon on left side screen to collapse the branch.

   Click the **First icon** in the row or column in the right side of the window.

   Hold down the **Shift** key, and click **Last icon**. All icons are now selected.

   Drag the **Selected files** on top of the recycle bin on the left side of the screen.

   When the recycle bin turns blue, release your **Mouse button**.

   Click **Yes** to confirm deletion of files and folders, and **Yes** to delete the calculator.

   Close Explorer window.

6. Empty the recycle bin.

   When you delete files from the A drive diskette, they are not placed in the recycle bin. They are immediately deleted. You will not need to empty the recycle bin. However, when you delete files from internal storage devices like the C drive, you will need to periodically empty the recycle bin.

   Double click the **Recycle Bin** ![icon] icon.

   Select **File, Empty Recycle Bin**.

   Click **Yes** to confirm deletion of files.

   Close **Recycle Bin** Window.

   How often should you empty the recycle bin?_____

EXERCISE 4: SOFTWARE DECISIONS AND ORGANIZATION SKILLS

Objectives

1. Begin to select appropriate software and justify its purchase.
2. Appropriately organize a hard drive or floppy diskette with folders and subfolders.
3. Identify appropriate filenames for documents given.

Activity A

1. You are the manager on Unit 93, a 40-bed general medical-surgical unit. You received approval for a new computer for managing your information needs, but now need to specify what software you want. List the software you want and why (see Chapter 2 for brief descriptions of software categories or look in computer ads for specific software programs). Make sure you use the facility's default standards. For example, does your facility require everyone to use Word for word processing or Excel for spreadsheets? Do they let the user determine whether WordPerfect or MS Word better meets their word processing needs? Include an operating system in your request. Some examples of common categories are:

Word Processing	WP, MS Word, AmiPro
Spreadsheet	MS Excel, LOTUS, Quattro Pro
Database	Access, FoxPro, Paradox, Approach
Presentation Graphics	PowerPoint, Harvard Graphics, Freelance Graphics
Browsers	Netscape, Internet Explorer
Utilities	Norton Utilities, PC Tools, WinZip, Acrobat Reader

2. You must organize the hard drive so things are orderly and easy to maintain. Describe the organization of the hard drive. Remember each program should have its own folder and like programs and data should be in the same folders or subfolders.

3. Using a floppy diskette in the A drive, create the above folders and subfolders on that diskette.

4. It will take the Information Systems people three weeks before they can install your software. You decide to do it yourself. How will you go about installing the software?

Activity B

1. You are storing data files on the hard drive so you will not have to deal with floppy diskettes. You create the appropriate folders and subfolders as follows:

Memos:	Memos folder in the data folder C:\data\memos
Evaluations:	Jones folder in the evaluation folder in the data folder c:\data\evaluation\Jones
Teaching Materials:	Patient Teaching folder in the data folder c:\data\Patient Teaching
Budget:	Fiscal 1999 folder in the Budget folder c:\budget\Fiscal 1999

How will you name the following documents for each of the folders?

Filename:

<u>Memos</u>

Request for more staff_____

Request for communication software_____

Response to procedure change_____

Response to vacation request_____

<u>Evaluations</u>

Patient Associate Jones_____

Unit Clerk Quincy_____

Staff Nurse Walker_____

<u>Teaching Materials</u>

AIDS: What you should know_____

Orientation to our unit_____

So you are going to have surgery_____

<u>Budget</u>

Unit budget for 1999_____

Unit budget for 2000_____

Proposed budget for new furniture _____

ASSIGNMENT 1: WORKING WITH THE DESKTOP

Directions:

1. Create the following objects on the desktop. Refer to the appropriate chapter discussions if you can't remember how to create these objects.

   Shortcut to the printer and $3\frac{1}{2}$" drive icon

   A **folder** for your downloaded graphics files

   A **Word file** titled All About Viruses

2. Explain the terms icon, folder, file, and shortcut.

3. Rearrange your desktop.

   Place the **Shortcut to the printer** and $3\frac{1}{2}$" **drive** on the **Top Right** of the Desktop.

   Place the **Graphics folder** on the **Bottom Right** of the Desktop.

   Place the **All About Viruses file** on the **Top Center** of the Desktop.

   Keep the **My Computer, Recycle Bin** and similar icons on the **Left side** of the Desktop.

4. Change the color scheme of the desktop to **High Contrast White.**

   Add **Clouds** wallpaper to the desktop. Hint: The Background tab in the Display dialog window.

5. Move the **Taskbar** to the **Left side** of the desktop.

6. Press the **Print Screen** button to place the desktop image on clipboard.

   Start **WordPad** or your word processing program.

   Click the **Paste** [icon] icon on the toolbar.

   Print the **File** with the new desktop image.

7. Restore the desktop.

   Close **All windows**.

   Reset the **Defaults**—No wallpaper, color scheme Windows default.

   Place **Taskbar** at bottom edge of Desktop.

   Delete **Objects** created in 1 above.

   Turn in the **Print Screen** copy.

Assignment 2:
Working with Files and Folders

Directions

1. Create folders.

   Create a folder on your diskette titled **Test 1**.

   In the Test 1 folder, create a **Graphics** folder, a **Word** folder, an **Excel** folder, and a **Power-Point** folder.

2. Find and copy files.

   Find the file **bigfoot.bmp** on the hard drive. Click the **Start** button, select **Find, Files & Folders,** type ***.bmp,** and press **Enter**.

   Copy it to the folder **Test 1** on your diskette.

3. Create data files.

   Create a Word file titled **Word Review Guide**.

   Create an Excel file titled **My School Budget**.

   Create a PowerPoint file titled **My Presentation**.

4. Move files.

   Move the **bigfoot.bmp** file into the **Graphics** folder.

   Move the **Word Review Guide** file into the **Word** folder.

   Move the **My School Budget** file into the **Excel** folder.

   Move the **My Presentation** file into the **PowerPoint** folder.

5. Rename a file.

   Rename the **My Presentation** file **My NUR105 Presentation.**

   Place your name on your diskette and turn it in to the professor.

ASSIGNMENT 3: COMPUTER AND ITS OPERATING SYSTEM

FILE AND HARD DRIVE ORGANIZATION

Directions

1. You just bought two diskettes for use in this class. Before you can use them, you must format them unless you bought preformatted ones. Format your floppy diskettes. What is the purpose of the format command?

2. Use the find feature to search for all the .bmp files on the C drive. (Click the **Start** button, select **Find, Files or Folders**, type ***.bmp**, and press **Enter**.) Note the path and filename of one of those files here _____. Use My Computer or Windows Explorer to locate the file. Drag the file to the diskette in the A drive. What did the computer do? Copy or move it? Why?

3. As a student in college you are taking several classes this term. Think about how you want to organize your data disk so you can store and find files from your classes. On a separate sheet of paper, diagram the structure you will create to manage your files (create the organizational structure for your files). Now, create the folders and subfolders necessary to manage your files on your data disk in drive A.

4. Now, create some files on your diskette in the A drive that you might be using this term. What is the difference between folders and files?

5. Because you want to create some order to these files, you need to move them to the appropriate folders on your diskette in the A drive. How will you go about doing this? What is the default option (move or copy) when dragging from A to a folder in A?

6. After looking at these folders and files, you decide to rename them to better represent the contents. List below the old and new names, and create the new names for the appropriate folders and files on the A drive.

Old	New

7. Now, you must make a backup of your work. Use the copy disk command to make a duplicate of your diskette.

8. You no longer need some of these files. List two ways to delete files and folders you no longer need.

Turn in this sheet and your diskette. Keep the second diskette as a backup.

Chapter 4

Software Applications— Common Tasks

OBJECTIVES

1. Identify standards common to applications running in the Windows environment.
2. Describe and use the online help provided by applications.
3. Use the common toolbar and menu commands to perform the tasks of opening, creating, closing, saving, finding, and printing files.
4. Describe and use cut/copy/paste functions to move or copy data from within the same file or from one file to another in the same or different application.

INTRODUCTION

The focus of this chapter is to present some common tasks you use when working with application programs regardless of the application. In the Windows environment certain standards (CDE and Motif) exist for the development of applications. For example, in the common desktop environment, menus are used as a means of accessing commands. Menus provide the paths to the action. Commands on the menu followed by three periods (ellipsis) open a special window called a dialog box for the user to select the appropriate information before the command is executed. Commands on the menu followed by an arrow cause a submenu of commands to appear (see Chapter 3 for more details on this point). All applications use this standard or convention so you can anticipate the response you get when you select the command.

You may also have noticed that all windows display a title bar, menu bar, one or more toolbars, and a status bar. All of the title bars permit you to close, minimize, and maximize the window using the same graphical buttons regardless of the application. Using the menu and standard toolbar, you are able to open a file, create a new file, save files, print files, and obtain help. It's these common tasks and the consistency in how you access them that makes working in this environment easier. This chapter, therefore, will discuss some of these common tasks. The Microsoft Office suite is used to demonstrate these tasks.

COMMON LAYOUT

Before discussing the common tasks associated with working in the Windows environment, we present an overview of the common layout for accessing the commands used for these tasks.

As you can see from Figure 4–1, some of these tasks fall under the commands File, Edit, View, Insert, Format, and Help.

File   The file menu option permits you to create, open, close, save, and print documents. These commands are represented on the toolbar by the **New** ◻ button, **Open** ☞ button, **Save** ▣ button, and **Printer** ▤ button. The **Close document** ☒ button is on the menu bar.

Edit   Edit accesses commands such as Undo, Cut, Copy, and Paste, Find and replace, and go to. Each application may also add additional commands to this menu. For example, Word includes the commands Select all and Clear while WordPerfect includes the command Preferences and Convert case. Selected commands from this menu are represented on the standard toolbar as scissors (cut) ✂, double paper (copy) ▣, and clipboard (paste) ▣.

View   View permits you to alter the view of the screen and/or document through such commands as layouts, toolbars, and zoom. Layouts change the appearance of the document showing or hiding specific features like margins, headers, and so forth. Toolbar commands permit you to display or hide specific toolbars. Additional commands for altering the view of the screen and/or document are added as appropriate by each application. The zoom feature is generally represented on the toolbar by a number followed by a percent sign (100%) and/or a print preview ▣ button.

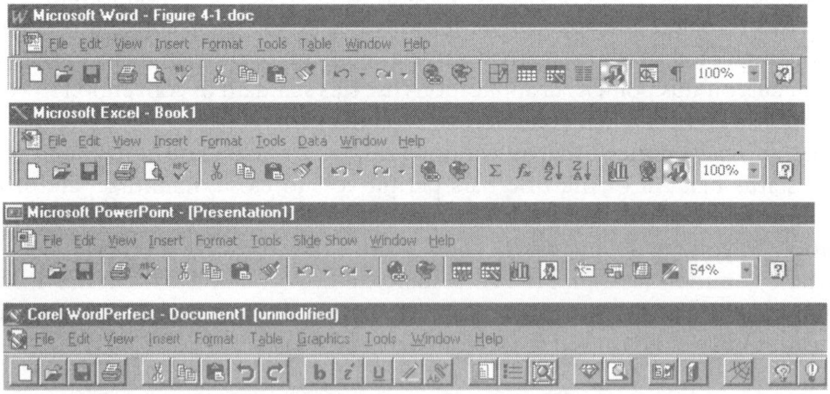

FIGURE 4–1.
Sample Menu Bars

Insert   Insert accesses commands such as dates, symbols, footnotes, files, objects, and page breaks. Basically, commands that require inserting an object, code, or special text like footnotes into the document are located here. Some applications add different commands as appropriate. For example, you might have a button for inserting clip art if that command is commonly used in that application.

Format   Most commands related to altering the appearance of the document are located in the format menu. You can alter the font, paragraphs, bullets, tabs, justification, and insert columns from this menu option. Many of these commands are discussed in detail in Chapter 5, Word Processing. Because formatting the look of the document, spreadsheet, database, or slides includes such important and frequently used commands, applications include many of these commands on their own toolbar called the formatting toolbar.

Tools   The tools option permits you to access commands related to additional features available in the application such as spell checker, thesaurus, merges, sorts, and macros. They are tools that help you use the program more efficiently by automating some of the repetitive tasks you do.

Windows   Windows accesses commands that let you switch between different documents in the same application and then display those documents by dividing the screen into different sections.

Help   Help accesses the online help system developed for that application. Note this is where you generally go to obtain the product version and/or additional registration information such as product serial number and owner. Many applications also provide you with access to the online expert through a button on the toolbar that is represented by a question mark or lightbulb.

Additional commands are added to the menu bar depending on the application. For example, in Word you also have access to Table, but in Excel you have Data, while in WordPerfect you have both Graphics and Table. What you need to remember is that there are common threads and organizational themes running through all Windows programs. Each suite tries to keep a consistent look to each application within the suite for ease of use and learning. The most commonly used commands are generally also represented on toolbars. However, there may be subtle differences in the toolbar command and menu command. Certain assumptions are made with some of the commands. For example, the diskette represents the file, save command and not the file, save as command. The printer button may print one copy of the current document to the default printer as in Word and not give you the print dialog box. WordPerfect gives you the print dialog box when you click the printer button.

COMMON TASKS

Now that you are comfortable with the common Windows layout for accessing commands, this section will cover some of the common tasks that one does in all applications.

Obtaining Online Help

All applications designed for the Windows environment provide online help to users. Very few application programs are sold with detailed user manuals. It is therefore important that you learn to use the online help.

Most applications divide the online help screen into three parts. Some applications also include a show me help option, intelligent help option, or both. Figures 4–2 and 4–3 show you the main help screen for two different word processing programs.

Notice how similar the interface is. The advantage to you is the ease of moving from one application to another and using the online help.

To access online help in an application program:

Click on the word **Help** on the menu bar.

To access Windows (operating system) help:

Click **Start**, and select **Help**.

To access content-sensitive help in a dialog window:

Click **Help** button in the window

Contents tab Use the contents tab like you do the Table of Contents for a book. Arranged in hierarchical style, this tab provides access to help screens based on commonly used functions or tasks. For example, opening, creating, and saving documents as illustrated in Figure 4–2 is one

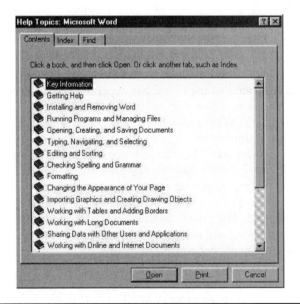

FIGURE 4–2.
Main Help Screen for Word 97

FIGURE 4–3.
Main Help Screen for WordPerfect 7

selection. This approach is most effective for new users when they are not familiar with the terminology and concepts related to this application.

To select a help topic:

Open the **Help** dialog Window. (**Help, Contents and Index,** or **Help Topics**)

Click the **Contents** Tab.

Double click on the **Book** beside the desired topic.

Repeat this process until options appear with a question mark (?) next to them.

These options, when selected, result in the display of a help screen.

You may also navigate the help topics by selecting (highlight) the **Book** and clicking the **Open** or **display** button, or pressing **Enter**. Remember that there are multiple ways of issuing almost every command.

Index Use the index tab like the index at the back of a book. Indexed words to the help screen are arranged in alphabetical order. You must know the terminology of the application in order to effectively use this tab. Typing in a word takes you to that part of the list. If you type document when you mean file, you are taken to the D part of the index.

To find help using the index:

Click the **Index** tab.

Type the **Word** or **Concept** that you have a question about.

Press **Enter**. The computer jumps to that part of the list.

Select (highlight) the **Word** on which you want help.

Click **Display** or **Open**.

You are looking for how to format characters. Figure 4–4 illustrates typing the word **format** and pressing **Enter** in Word 97. This takes you to the word format conversion. You would now either click on the word characters under formatting and then display OR double click the word characters. This takes you to a help screen on formatting characters in Word.

Find Use the find tab when you are not sure how the help screen might be indexed. This tab is designed to locate all help screens in which the word you are looking for is used. It is also case sensitive; you will locate more help screens by typing your work using lower case than upper case letters.

To use the find tab:

Click the **Find tab** in the Help window.

In Part 1 of the window, type the **Word** for which you are looking.

In Part 2 of the window, click on the **Matching word** that comes closest to what you want.

In Part 3 select the **Help screen** by double clicking it.

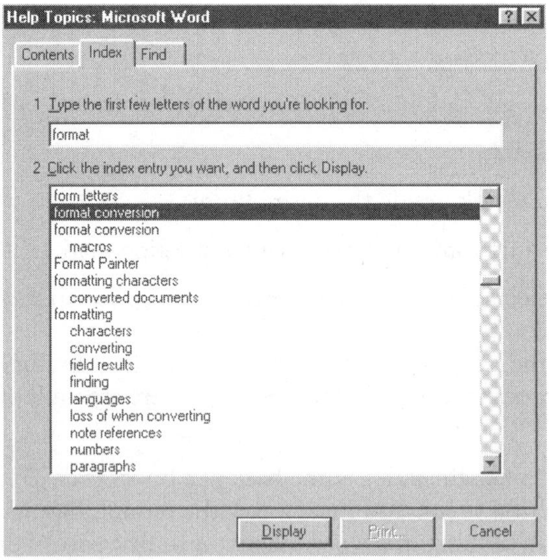

FIGURE 4–4.
Sample Help Screen Using Index Tab

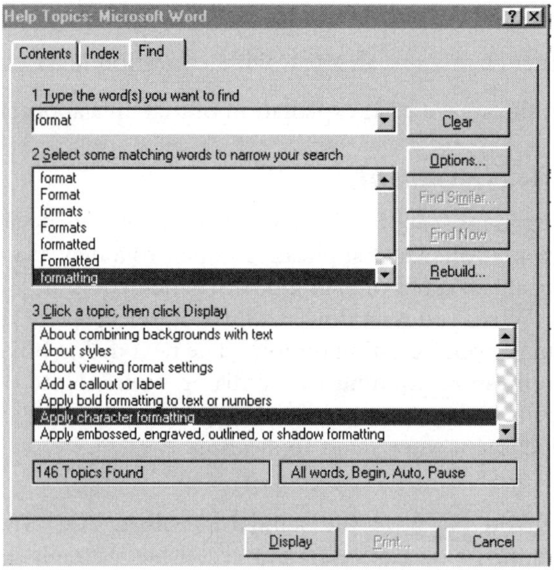

FIGURE 4–5.
Sample Help Screen Using Find Tab

Figure 4–5 shows finding help on the topic formatting characters by typing **Format**, selecting **Formatting** from the options in Part 2, and double clicking on **Apply character formatting** help screen.

Expert online help Most applications now provide you with access to intelligent help called different things in different applications. In MS Office, it is the Office Assistant, and in Corel WordPerfect, it is the Ask the PerfectExpert. This help assistant is available through the menu command or the toolbar. Sometimes it pops up while you are doing things. To use this "expert," type your question in English phrases. The "expert" then tries to match your question to a selection of help screens.

ToolTips ToolTips provides the new user with a word that describes the icon command. For example, placing your pointer over the printer icon on the standard toolbar results in a word label that says print. The new user can then learn what each icon on the toolbar represents.

What's This Help This help generally appears in dialog boxes. You access this help through a question mark on the title bar (look to the right in the title bar in Figures 4–2 and 4–3). The What's This help generally provides a brief explanation of some area in the dialog box. The idea of this type of online help is to provide you with help when you are trying to do something and do not understand the window or what is expected.

To access What's This Help:

Click the **Question mark** on the right of the title bar.

Click over the **Area of the window** where you want help.

Note that the pointer changes to an arrow with a question mark on it.

When you click on the area, a brief explanation of that area appears.

Creating a New File (Document)

In order to start working in most applications, you need to first create a new document, spreadsheet, database, or presentation. Most applications open to a new, blank document or spreadsheet OR query you through a series of dialog boxes. When you start Word, you are brought to a new blank document. When you start PowerPoint, you select a new presentation using a wizard, template, new blank, or open existing options. The next dialog box asks for the style layout, and so forth, until you finish responding to the dialog boxes. Note the word "document" is used here to represent a text document, spreadsheet, database, or presentation.

To start another document when in an application:

Click the **New button** ▢ on the standard toolbar. You now have two documents opened. All documents remain open and accessible through the Window menu command until you close them.

To use the keyboard, press **CTRL+N**. This is the same command as the new button.

A template is a predesigned style; a document that is already formatted with fonts, colors, layout, etc. A wizard is a step-by-step process for developing the document. A series of questions is asked and, based on your responses, the document is developed.

To start another document using a template or wizard: Select **File, New**.

If you are using the MS Office Suite, you may also use the MS Office toolbar found on the desktop to create new files. Figure 4–6 shows you one version of the toolbar. You can customize the toolbar so yours might not look exactly the same. At the least it should have the Word, Excel, PowerPoint, Access, open document, and new document icons. The toolbar may appear horizontally, vertically, or as a square on the desktop.

To create a new file with the MS Office toolbar:

Click the **New Document** ▤ icon on the MS Office Toolbar.

Double click the **Type of Document**. That means to select a new blank document, such as Word, Excel, or PowerPoint.

FIGURE 4–6.
MS Office Toolbar

Opening/Closing Files

Common to all applications is the function of opening and closing files. Once you create your document, you save it and open it later for additions and corrections.

Open In the Windows world, there are many ways to open a file. Since our focus here is the menu and toolbars, we will describe how to use them.

Select **File, Open** from the menu bar OR click on the **Open** button on the standard toolbar.

You will now be asked to specify the location and name of the file to open. Location is where the file is stored—the storage device (drive letter) and folder. You will use the Look In down arrow to change locations (see Figure 4-7). In this example, the file is located on the C drive, in folders Data\Irene\Comp Bytes\3rd Edition.

To change to other folders from the drop-down menu: Click the **Drive** or **Folder**.

To access contents of other folders in the list area of the dialog box: Double click. Remember, to select from menus, use a single click; to open a folder or file, double click.

Once you find the file you want to open: Double click the **File** OR select the **File** and click **Open** button.

As you now know, there are many ways to open files. Listed below are a few more ways.

- In a window or on the Desktop, double click the **File**.
- Select **Start** button on Taskbar, select **Documents**, and highlight **File**. The last 15 files that you opened are on the menu list regardless of file type.

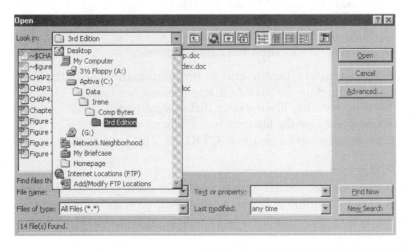

FIGURE 4–7.
Opening a File

- In an application, press **CTRL+O**.
- In an application, select **File** from the menu bar, and select **File** listed at bottom of menu for the last few files opened in this application.
- With the MS Office toolbar, click the **Open document** ▱ button on the MS Office toolbar. Select the location and file.

Close To close a file:

Select **File** from the menu bar; select **Close.**

Click on **Close** ✖ button on the document menu bar. Be careful that you close the document and not the application window whose close button is just above it. If you made changes to the file and haven't saved it, you are prompted to save the file before closing it.

To use the keyboard to close a file, press **CTRL+F4**.

Saving Files

Once you work on a file or document, you will want to save it for future reference or revisions. The first time you save a file you will need to specify a location and name (see Chapter 3 for file naming conventions). If you do not specify a location, the file is saved in the default location. In MS Office, the default location is the My Documents folder on the hard drive (C:); in Corel WordPerfect Suite, the default location is the My Files folder on the hard drive (C:); and in Lotus Smartsuite, the default location is the specific application folder in Work folder. For example, when working with Lotus your work is saved by default in the 123 folder located in the Work folder. Once the file has a name and location, the **File, Save** command updates the file saving any changes to it. You are not prompted with the **Save As** dialog window.

To access the save command:

Click the **Save** 💾 button on the toolbar OR

Select **File, Save** from the menu bar.

You are prompted for the location and name of the file.

The **File, Save As** command is used to change the location or name of the file. The **File, Save As** command always brings up the **Save As** dialog window. See Figure 4–8 for the save as dialog box. This dialog window works like the open dialog window. Select the location from the **Save In** drop-down arrow and type the filename in the **File name** text box.

To use the keyboard to save a file, press **CTRL+S**. This acts like the **File, Save** command.

Printing Files

Once the file is ready for use, you will want to print it for distribution to others or for a hard copy record. A general rule of thumb is to use the Print Preview feature most programs have before sending your document to the printer. The Print Preview feature lets you view your document as it will look when printed. By doing this, you save time and money if there is something wrong with the layout of the document. You can make changes before actually printing it.

To access the print preview command, use the **Print Preview** ▱ button in the MS Office Suite or the Zoom, Full page or File, **Print Preview** feature in some other applications.

Some applications make a distinction between the File, Print command, and the printer icon on the toolbar. For example, Word sends one copy of the current document to the default printer with the printer icon, but brings up the printer dialog box with the file, print command from the menu bar. WordPerfect makes no such distinction.

To print a file: Select **File, Print** or click the **Printer** 🖨 icon.

If you want the printer dialog box (Figure 4–9), select **File, Print** in the Office Suite. Some choices you have from the printer dialog box are changing the printer; choosing the number of copies to print; printing the total document, the current page, the selection, or selected pages; or whether to collate multiple page documents.

Pressing **CTRL+P** also brings up the printer dialog box.

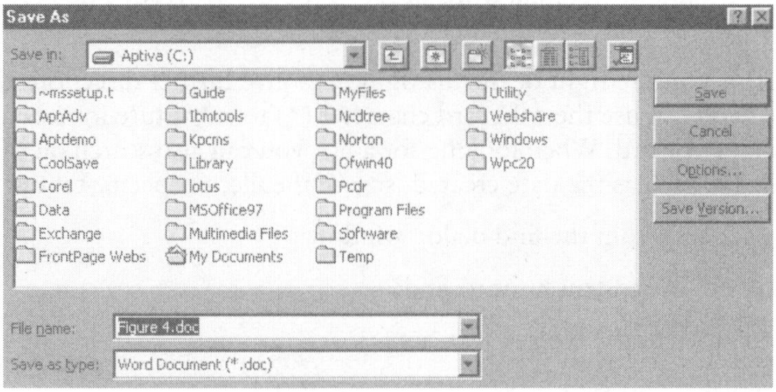

FIGURE 4–8.
Saving a File

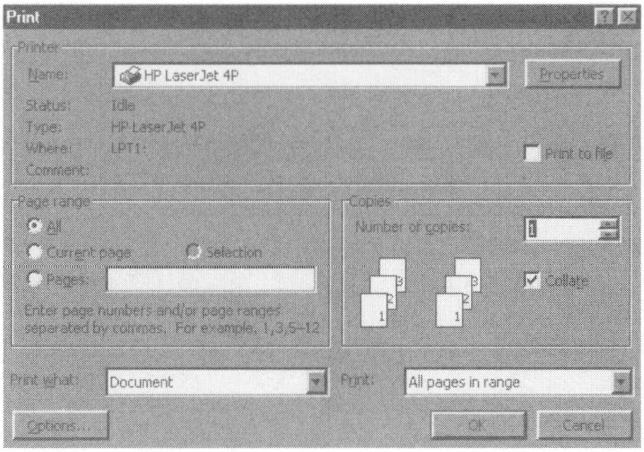

FIGURE 4–9.
Printing a File

Finding Files or Words

Another common task that computer users perform is the finding or finding and replacing of specific files or words within a folder or document. Suppose you wanted to use a document previously created and alter certain words to make it fit the current situation. Maybe you created or received a file or e-mail that you want to forward to someone else but can't find it now. Instead of manually searching for these files or replacing these words, you let the computer do it for you.

To access this feature:

> In an application, select **Edit, Find** or **Replace** OR **Edit, Find and Replace** for some applications.

> In Windows, select **Start, Find, Files or Folders**.

Once in the dialog window to find a word or file: Type the **Word** or **File** in the Find Text box and press **Enter**.

> Use the buttons on the right of the dialog box to give further directions to the computer. Note that you can use the wild card character (*) to substitute for extensions or parts of the filename or word. When looking for a file, you can also search on other information about the file such as the date created, size of the file, or specific text within the file.

To find and replace text from the find dialog window:

> Type the **Text** or **Word** you want to find.

> Press **Tab** to move to the replace text box.

> Type the **Replacement text** or **Word** and press **Enter**.

See Figure 4–10 for a sample find and replace dialog window. In this example, the word to find was school and the replacement word is college. Be careful with the replace, all button. This button results in the program automatically finding all incidents of the text "school" and replacing it with "college." This means that schoolbook will be replaced with collegebook. The find feature is not case sensitive; however, you have the option to change this default.

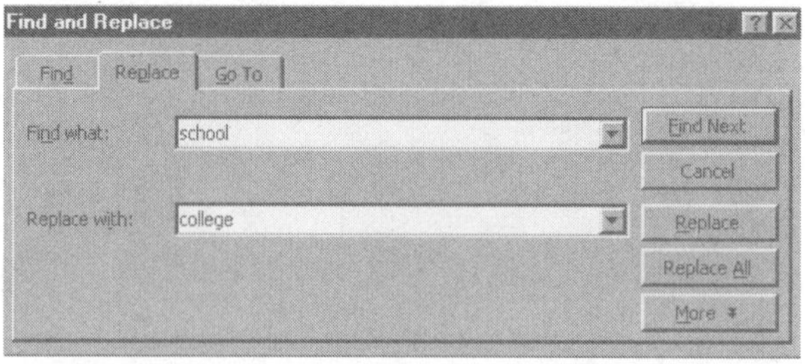

FIGURE 4–10.
Sample Find and Replace Dialog Window

Selecting Text or Object

Selecting text or object means to highlight the text or object or, for example, the cell in a spreadsheet. This is a common task when editing your documents. While it is fine to use the delete and backspace keys to complete minor editing tasks, it is not efficient for editing lines, sentences, paragraphs, columns, rows, cells, or the entire document. You also use this feature when formatting your documents (word processing, spreadsheets, and so on). Once again, you can format each item separately but that is very time consuming.

Each application has some minor variations for selecting or highlighting text and cells. Described here are some of the most common techniques for selecting them. Additional ones are presented in the applications chapters as appropriate.

What You Want to Select	Mouse Action
A word	Double click the word.
Several words	Drag the mouse over the words or select the first word, hold down the **Shift** key, and click the end of the last word.
A sentence	Hold **CTRL** and click on the sentence.
A line	Click in the quick select area (cursor is right slanted arrow).
Entire document	Triple click the quick select area.
A cell	Click the cell.
Multiple cells	Drag over the cells.

In addition to the mouse strokes, you may also use the keyboard to select text. This is especially helpful when what you want to select spans greater distances or is on the edge of the document. For example, to select text that spans several pages, place the cursor at the beginning of the text to be selected, hold down the shift key, and use the arrow keys to move down the document. As you move the cursor all the text is being highlighted. This technique also works in spreadsheets to select multiple cells.

If you want to select the whole document, press **Ctrl+A**. The whole document is now selected.

Editing Text

There are three basic editing features you will use in your applications: Insert, Delete, and Replace.

Insert means to add new text, slides, rows, columns, and so on. In word processing programs, insert is the default. When you start typing, the characters are placed at the insertion point. In applications for spreadsheets and graphics, you will need to issue a command to insert rows, columns, or new slides. These commands are covered in the appropriate applications chapters.

Delete means to remove some text, row, column, or slide from the document. Select what you want to delete and press the delete key. In some applications there are additional delete features, which are covered in the appropriate applications chapters.

Replace means to substitute one for another. In most cases you do not need to first delete the text and then type the new. By highlighting or selecting the text you are placed in replace mode. This means type the replacement and it will delete what was highlighted and insert what you type. Do not waste your time with the extra step of deleting it first.

Copying or Moving Text

The last of the common tasks presented in this chapter deals with copying or moving text from one place to another in the same document, from one document to another, or from one application to another. The most common method for doing this is using the cut/copy/paste commands; this uses the concept of a clipboard as a temporary holding place for the cut or copied material. Another method for doing this is the drag and drop method. This method relies on selecting data and using the mouse to drag it to the new spot. The general rule of thumb for selecting the method to use is based on distance to move the material. For short distances in the same document, use drag and drop. To copy or move data longer distances (to another page), to another document, or another application use the clipboard strategy.

Copy Using Clipboard To copy data using the clipboard:

Select the **Data** to be copied.

Click the **Copy** ▣ button.

Place the **Insertion point** (cursor) where you want this data to be copied.

Click the **Paste** ▣ button.

Cut Using Clipboard To move data using the clipboard:

Select the **Data** to be moved.

Click the **Cut** ✂ button.

Place the **Insertion point** where you want this data to be moved.

Click the **Paste** ▣ button.

It is important to know where the insertion point is because that's where the data will be placed when you click on paste. The mouse pointer (I-beam) does not reflect where the data will go. If moving this data to another document or application, you need to switch to it using either the **window, filename** to access the other document in this application or click on the application button on the taskbar to switch to the other application (refer to Chapter 3 if you are unsure how to do this).

Note also that data stays on the clipboard until you cut or copy something else to it or until you exit Windows; it does not disappear when closing an application. Remember the clipboard holds only one piece of data at a time.

You can also access the cut/copy/paste commands through the file menu but not as quickly or efficiently. You can also initiate these commands using the keyboard. Press **CTRL+X** for cut, **CTRL+C** for copy, and **CTRL+V** for paste. Note that the keys for these commands are in the same order on the bottom row of keys on the keyboard as the icons are on the toolbar.

Cut Using Drag and Drop To move data using the drag and drop method:

Select the **Data** to be moved.

Place the pointer on the **Selected area.**

Hold down the **Left mouse** button.

Move the mouse so the insertion point (broken vertical bar) is in the new place.

Release the mouse button.

Notice the changing look of the mouse pointer when using drag and drop. The mouse pointer turns to a left slanted arrow with a box below it and the insertion point turns to a broken vertical bar. Cut is the default option when using the drag and drop method.

Copy Using Drag and Drop To copy data using the drag and drop method:

Select the **data** to be moved.

Place the pointer on the **Selected area.**

Hold down the **CTRL key.**

Hold down the **Left mouse** button.

Move the mouse so the insertion point (broken vertical bar) is in the new place.

Release the mouse button, and then the **CTRL** key.

It is important not to release the **CTRL** key until after you release the mouse button or the data will be moved. Note that when you do this the pointer appears the same as when cutting except that there is a plus sign in the box below the pointer.

Summary

This chapter presented some standard commands used in applications in the Windows environment that make your life a little easier. It described the online help provided in applications. Common toolbar and menu commands were also presented that show how to perform such tasks as opening, creating, closing, saving, finding, and printing files. In addition, the cut/copy/paste and drag and drop functions to move or copy data from one file to another in the same or different applications were presented. These commands and tasks cross applications and provide some consistency in working in this environment.

EXERCISE 1: USING ONLINE HELP IN AN APPLICATION

Objectives

1. Use the various forms of online help available in application programs.
2. Navigate through the help screens.
3. Compare the contents, index, and find (search) tabs.

Activity

1. Find help in a word processing application.

   Start your word processing program.

   Click **Help** on the menu bar and click **Contents** or **Help topics options.**

   Click the **Contents** tab.

   Look for an option that will lead you to information about **Opening a document**. You may need to double click in several options until you find a help screen describing how you do this.

   Read the help screen on opening documents. Click the **Help topics** button in the help screen.

   Look for help on opening a document using the Index tab. Click the **Index** tab.

   Type **open document** in lower case.

   Double click the help topic for opening a document. You may have to do this another time until you find the open a document help screen.

   Look for help on opening a document using the Find tab.

   Click the **Help topics** button in the help screen. Click the **Find** tab.

   Type **open document** in lower case and press **Enter**.

   Select the lower case word **documents**.

   Look for the topic that describes how to open a document.

   Select the help screen on **Open a document**.

   Which one of these help tabs did you like best and why?

2. Find help in a spreadsheet application.

   Start your spreadsheet program.

   Click **Help** on the menu bar and click on **Contents** or **Help topics options.**

   Click the **Contents** tab.

   Look for an **Option** that will lead you to information about **Opening a file**. You may need to double click in several options until you find a help screen describing how you do this.

   Read the help screen on opening workbooks.

   Use the **Index** tab to find help.

   Click the **Help topics** button in the help screen. Click the **Index** tab.

   Type **open files** in lower case.

Double click on the help topic for opening a workbook. You may have to do this another time until you find the open a file help screen.

Use the Find tab to find help.

Click the **Help topics** button in the help screen. Click the **Find** tab.

Type **open files** in lower case and press **Enter**.

Select the lower case word **files**.

Look for the topic that describes how to open a new workbook.

Select the help screen on **Open a workbook**.

What were the similarities between this help command and the one from Activity 1?

3. Place you mouse pointer on the diskette on the standard toolbar. Do not click. What happens after a few seconds? What is this called? Why might you use this?

4. Use the Office Assistant or Online Expert in your word processing program.

   Start the Office Assistant or Online Expert (in Word, click the Office Assistant button on the standard toolbar).

   Type in lower case **how do I format a document** and press **Enter**.

   Your results are displayed. You may need to click on the see more feature to find the right help screen or about creating Web documents.

   Double click the topic for **Create or Format as a Web page**.

   What is the file type for saving your document to be published on the Web?

   What do the letters stand for? Why might you need to know this?

5. Use What's This Help

   In your word processing program, select **Edit, Replace** or **Find and Replace**.

   Click the **Question mark** on the title bar of the dialog box.

   Click the **Find Next** button in the Find and Replace dialog box.

   What is the function of this button?

EXERCISE 2: CREATE, OPEN, CLOSE, FIND, PRINT, SAVE

Objectives

1. Create a new document using the file, new command and new button on standard toolbar.
2. Use the commands from both the menu bar and toolbar to open, close, print, and save a file.
3. Use the find and replace command to replace text and the find command to locate a file.

Activity

1. Start an application.

   Click **Start, Programs, Accessories, WordPad.**

   Type **This is my first word processing document.**

   Click the **Save** 💾 button.

   Click the **Save in down arrow** ▼ button.

   Select the **3½" floppy** drive.

   Highlight the word **document** in the **File name** text box.

   Type **first document** and press **Enter.**

2. Open and save another document.

   Click **New** 🗋 button.

   Highlight **Word document** and click **OK.**

   Type **This is my second word processing document.**

   Select **File, Save.**

   If necessary, click the **Save in down arrow** ▼ button. Select the **3½" floppy** drive.

   If necessary, highlight the **document** in the file name text box.

   Type **second document** and press **Enter.**

3. Open another document, edit, and save it.

   Select **File, Open.**

   Double click **first document** file.

   Press **CTRL+End** to go to the end of the document. Press **Enter key twice.**

   Type **Isn't learning this stuff fun!**

   Click the **Save** 💾 button. Notice you didn't get the save as dialog box because the file has a name and location.

4. Print the document.

   Click the **Printer** 🖨 button. What happened?

   Select **File, Print** from the menu.

   What happened now? Click **OK**.

5. Open and edit second document.

   Click the **Open** 📂 button.

   Double click **second document** file. (If you don't see the file, make sure the Look In text box says $3\frac{1}{2}$" floppy.)

   Press **CTRL+End**, press **Spacebar**, and type **Wow, I didn't know this was so easy!**

   Select **File, Save As**.

   Type **third document** and press **Enter**.

6. Find and replace.

   Select **Edit, Replace**.

   Type the word **document** in the find what text box.

   Press the **Tab** key.

   Type the lower case word **file** in the replace with text box.

   Click **Find next** button in the dialog window.

   Click **Replace** button.

   Click **OK** and **Close** ❌ button in the dialog window.

   Notice what happened to the word document.

   Click the **Save** 💾 button to save the file.

7. Close.

   Select **File, Exit** from the menu bar.

8. Find the file through the Windows find feature.

   Select **Start, Find, Files or folders** on the taskbar.

   Change the **Look In** text box to the $3\frac{1}{2}$" **floppy drive** by using the down arrow button to the right.

   In the **Named** text box, type **second document**.

   Click the **Find now** button in the dialog window.

   Double click the **second document** in the results window.

   Close the application and find dialog windows.

EXERCISE 3: COPY AND MOVE DATA USING CUT/COPY/PASTE AND DRAG AND DROP

Objectives

1. Copy and move text from one place in the document to another using the clipboard.
2. Copy and move text from one place in the document to another using drag and drop.
3. Copy text from one document to another.

Activity

1. Start MS Word.

   Select **Start, Programs, MS Word OR double click on MS Word icon.**

2. Enter text.

   Type **This is an exercise to teach me how to copy and move text. I will create a series of lists that will be moved and copied.**

   Press the **Enter** key twice.

   Type the following text pressing the **Tab** key between items and the **Enter** key at the end of the row.

Mary Smith	Nrsg	Freshman
Ann Kay	PT	Senior
Mike Jones	Nrsg	Sophomore
Pat Roberts	OT	Junior

3. Save the document.

   Click the **Save** 🖫 icon.

   Save the document to the A drive using the filename **copy-move.**

4. Move text using drag and drop.

   Select the **Mary Smith line.** (Note the quickest way to do this is place your pointer in the quick select area. Place your pointer out at the margin across from Mary; when the pointer is a right slanted arrow, click.)

   Place your pointer on the **Highlighted** area, **Hold down the left** mouse button and **Drag** the selection to the blank line below the **P** in Pat. **Release** your mouse button. Note: If you did not press the **Enter** key after the last line, you will not be able to go to the line below Pat. Go to the right of r in Junior and place text there. Click to the left of M in Mary and press **Enter.**

   Mary Smith is now at the end of the list.

5. Move text using clipboard.

   Select the **Ann Kay line**.

   Click the **Cut** [✂] button.

   Move your pointer so the blinking **Vertical** bar is to the left of **Pat**. Do not select the whole line.

   With the insertion point to the left of P in Pat, click the **Paste** [📋] button.

   Your list should now look like this:

Mike Jones	Nrsg	Sophomore
Ann Kay	PT	Senior
Pat Roberts	OT	Junior
Mary Smith	Nrsg	Freshman

6. Copy text using drag and drop.

   Go to the **end of your document**.

   Press the **Enter key twice** to create two blank lines.

   Type the following information remembering to use the Tab key between items and the enter key to go to the next line.

Kim White	Blue Shield and Blue Cross
Joe Bloom	Keystone West
Jack Frost	UPMC Health Plan
Pat Flowers	Health America

   Click the **Save** [💾] button.

   Select the text **Kim** through **Cross**.

   Place the **Pointer over** the selected text, hold down the **CTRL** key, hold down the **Left mouse** button and **Drag** the text so the broken vertical bar is to the **left of Joe**, release the **mouse** button, then the **CTRL** key.

   The text is copied.

   Highlight **Kim** and type **Brian**.

7. Copy text using the clipboard.

   Select the text **Jack** through **plan**.

   Click the **Copy** [📄] button.

   Move the pointer to the **Left of P** in Pat Flowers and **click**. Do not highlight the text.

   Click the **Paste** [📋] button.

   Highlight **Jack** and type **Abby**.

Click the **Save** 💾 button to save the document.

8. Copy text from one document to another.
   Select all the text from **Kim** to **America**.

   Click the **Copy** 📋 button.

   Click the **New Document** 📄 button.

   Click the **Paste** 📋 button.
   The text is now inserted into a new word document.
   Save the document as **copy-two-documents**.

9. Copy text from one application to another.
   Click **Start, Programs, Excel** (or double click on the Excel icon on the desktop). Click the

   Paste 📋 button.
   The contents of the clipboard are now inserted into an Excel worksheet.

Close all files and programs. You do not need to save anything again unless requested to do so by your professor.

ASSIGNMENT 1: USING HELP

Directions

1. Use the Excel online help feature to find out how you create formulas and functions in Excel and what you need to remember in terms of order of precedence.

2. Print and place in logical sequence the appropriate help screens for future reference.

3. Using any application, select a task that you want to learn. Use the online help to learn how to complete that task in that application.

4. Submit the help prints from 2 and 3 above.

ASSIGNMENT 2:
COPY AND MOVE TEXT

Directions

1. Create a one-page document describing how to do the following tasks. Each description is to be its own paragraph.

   Save a document.

   Print a document.

   Create a new document.

   Move text in a document.

2. Print the original document.

3. Now, using the move text feature of the program, rearrange the text as follows.

   Create a new document.

   Move text in a document.

   Save a document.

   Print a document.

4. Print the revised document. Submit both documents.

Chapter 5

Introduction to Word Processing

OBJECTIVES

1. Define common terms related to word processing.
2. Create, format, edit, save, and print MS Word documents.

WORD PROCESSING

Word processing is used to create text—letters, memo, reports, proposals, newsletters, and even books! Computers act like smart typewriters when using word processing software. They make your job easier once you learn a few of the possibilities. This chapter is designed to provide the basics of word processing and to get you started with Microsoft Word.

COMMON TERMS IN WORD PROCESSING

Block   A block is a selected (highlighted) continuous section of text treated as a unit. Use it to perform formatting and editing functions. Most individual formatting functions, such as bold and underline, also work with blocks of text.

Clipboard   A clipboard is an invisible holding area or buffer for copied or cut data for later use. Users put the data onto the clipboard and then can paste it into another document, another application, or in another location within the original document.

Font   A font defines a descriptive look or shape (font face or typeface), size, style, and weight of a group of characters or symbols. For example, one font is Times Roman, 12 pt., bold, italic. Another font is Times Roman, 10 pt., italic. This term is frequently misunderstood. Several of these terms are important to understanding fonts.

      Pitch   Number of characters printed in one inch (cpi).

      Point size   Height of the font given in printing language, 72 points per inch of height.

Spacing	Proportional or fixed pitch. Proportional means allotting a variable amount of space for each character depending on the character width. Fixed- or mono-spaced means a set space for each character regardless of the character width. For example, an *I* gets the same amount of space as a *W*.
Style	Vertical slant of the character. For example, normal (upright), condensed, or italic (oblique). Many word processing programs also include bold and other effects.
Symbol set	The characters and symbols that make up the font.
Typeface	Specific design of character or symbol. Also referred to as font face. For example, Helvetica, Courier, Times Roman, Times Roman Bold, and Times Roman Italic are all different typefaces.

Footer	A footer is an information area placed consistently at the bottom of each page of a document. It can hold the name of the document, the page number, date, or anything else that is helpful.
Format	Format is the process of editing the appearance of a document by using indentations, margins, tabs, justification, and pagination; format conditions affect the document appearance. In Word, format features vary depending on whether you are formatting characters (font, size, emphasis, and/or special effects like highlight, or super- and sub-script), paragraph formatting (alignment, indentation, line spacing, and line breaks), and page formatting like margins, paper size, and orientation.
Grammar checker	A grammar checker is software that often comes with word processing programs. This software provides feedback to the user regarding errors in grammar. For example, using "there" when you want "their" or using subjects and verbs that do not agree. Within the grammar checker are several settings and styles that may be selected.
Hard return	The hard return is a code inserted in the document by pressing the enter key. This is usually done at the end of a paragraph. In Word the paragraph mark is ¶.
Header	The header is an information area placed consistently at the top of each page of a document that can hold the name of the document, page number, date, or other identifying information.
Indent	Indent refers to tab settings that place subsequent lines of text the same number of spaces from the margin until the next hard return.
Insert	Insert means to add characters in the text at the point of the cursor, thereby moving all other text to the right. It is the opposite of typeover mode and is the default in most word processing programs.

Justified	Justified is alignment of text relative to the left and right margins.

	Center	Center places the text line equidistant from both margins.
	Full	Full justification is alignment of text flush against both the left and right margins.
	Left	Left justification is alignment of text flush against the left margin and staggered on the right.
	Right	Right justification is alignment of text flush against the right margin and staggered on the left.

Move	Move is a function in word processing programs that permits the user to relocate text or graphics to another place in the document or to another document.
Outliner	Outliner is a feature of many word processing programs that enables the user to plan and rearrange large documents in an outline form.
Page break	This is the place where Word ends the text on one page before it continues text on the next page. You can insert a Page break by going to the Insert Menu and selecting Page break. The software then places the break at the point where your cursor is. It is a good idea to review your document when it is finished to determine where a page break is needed. Use it cautiously until you have completed all revisions of the document. You can also insert a Page break from the Format menu; choose Paragraph, Line and Page Breaks, and then Page break.
Pagination	Pagination is the numbers or marks used to indicate the sequence of the pages. It is a process of determining when there is sufficient text on one page, and then starting the next page. Word processing programs automatically do this if you turn this feature on. Most programs permit the variation of placement and style of the page number.
Scrolling	Scrolling is the process of moving around a document to view a specific portion of a page of text within a document. (All of the document may not fit on the screen.) Note that this does not change the location of the insertion point until you click in the document.
Soft return	Soft return is the code inserted in the document automatically when the typed line reaches the right margin.
Spell checker	Most programs come with an embedded spell checker. This program checks the words for correct spelling. A spell checker does not correct grammar or misused words.
Tab	A tab is a setting that places the following text on that line a certain number of spaces or inches in from the left margin. Tab settings by default are 5 spaces or .5 inch. The settings are changeable. There are four styles of

tabs—left, right, center, and decimal. All deal with the alignment of the text around the tab mark.

Thesaurus   A thesaurus is a built-in feature that helps the user search for alternative words.

Toggle   To toggle means to switch from one mode of operation to another mode: on or off, insert or replace/typeover.

Typeover   Typeover means to replace the character under the cursor by the character you type. It has the same meaning as overtype. It is turned on or off by double clicking on "OVR" on the bottom status bar of the Word document.

Word wrap   This feature automatically carries words over to the next line if they extend beyond the margin.

DATA EXCHANGE

Word processing software saves documents in file formats unique to that software program. Many word processing programs allow the option of saving documents under another file format by using the Save As feature. For example, you can save your MS Word 97 document in several ways such as a text file, HTML document, Word 5.1 for Macintosh, or as a Word 6.0/ 95 file. This feature permits you to exchange your file with others who are using different word processing programs, versions, or systems. It also permits you to publish the file to the Web.

SAVING WORK

Everyone has horror stories they can tell related to lost data or documents. To protect you from accidentally losing data, a few tips are in order.

1. Periodically save your work. While working on your documents, the computer holds them temporarily in RAM. Once you instruct the program to save your work on a diskette or your hard drive, the document exists in both RAM and on the diskette or hard drive. If you lose power, even temporarily, all the data in RAM is lost except for that stored on the diskette, in temporary backup files, or on your hard disk. (Remember if you are using a school computer, you will need to store your work on a diskette, not the hard drive.
2. Pay attention to warnings given by the software. These warnings are hints to remind you that doing some things will have a certain result. For example, saving a document with the same name as another one results in a message asking you if you want to replace that file. Do not respond with Yes unless you don't want the old one saved.
3. Always keep a backup or duplicate copy of your document. That backup could be a diskette or zip disk. Store the backup in another place. If something happens to the original document or your computer, you can use your backup copy.

INTRODUCTION TO MS WORD

Examples in this text use MS Word 97 for Windows. However, you should know that using MS Word 98 for the Macintosh is essentially the same. The menu and toolbars include most of the same headings and icons; and the windows are remarkably similar in all Office applications. Therefore, both Macintosh and Windows users can use the chapters in this book on word processing, spreadsheets, and graphics presentation with very few changes between operating systems. We anticipate that Office 2000 will also be very similar but with more functions that allow Word documents to be published to the Internet.

Using Keyboard Templates

Most word processing programs are menu driven with the user carrying out commands by selecting icons or choosing from a menu of options. Menu driven programs provide users with two options—select from the menus and icons with the mouse or use keystroke combinations to issue the command. Some programs are faster when the user issues commands through a series of keystroke combinations. When you click on a menu item in Word, you will see the keystroke combination on the right if there is one. For example, when you click on File, you see the keyboard command CTRL+O opposite Open. This keystroke can be used instead of File, Open to open a document. On the Macintosh operating system the Apple key (or command key), next to the space bar, acts like the CTRL key on the Windows system. Sometimes a removable template, placed around the function keys, is used as a guide to these function keys.

Starting Word

As with all Windows programs, there are many ways to start Word. A few ways are presented here.

Click **Start**, **Programs**, and scroll down to select **MS Word**.

Double click the **Word** icon in the Microsoft Office taskbar if it appears on your desktop.

Double click the **MS Word shortcut** on the desktop.

Creating a New Document

When you start Word, by default, it opens a new blank document. All you need to do is type and format the text as desired to create your new document.

Once Word is started there are several options to create another new document, described here.

To create a new document once in Word:

Click the **New** button on the standard toolbar. This opens a blank new document using the normal.dot template.

Select **File, New** from the menu bar. This opens the new document dialog window. Select the appropriate template for the new document.

Right click a **Blank area** of the desktop. Select **New, Word** document. Type the **Name** of the new document and double click the **New document** icon.

Opening a Previously-Saved Document

Once the document is created and saved and you want to make changes or additions to it, you have several options for opening the document again. Refer to Chapter 4 for additional ways to open existing documents.

To open an existing document:

Double click the **Document** icon.

Start **Word** and choose **Open** ⬜ icon, select **Location** of file and **File name**.

Start **Word** and choose **File, Open,** select **Location** of file and **File name**.

For each document, Word presents a screen with the menu bar at the top, a blank window or workplace in the center, and scroll bars on the right side and bottom right corner. A blinking vertical bar, or insertion point marker (also called the cursor), represents your position in the document. A dark horizontal line is the end mark of your document. See Figure 5–1.

The Menu and Toolbars in Word

Much of the menu bar in Word is the same as in any Office 97 program (Excel, PowerPoint, Access, etc.) for Windows or Office 98 for the Macintosh. One difference in the Windows Word menu bar is a **Table** column next to **Tools**. Each menu contains a different drop-down list of commands to help you use Word. The **Standard Toolbar** and the **Formatting Toolbar** appear below the menu bar (Figure 5–1).

You will notice that there are several icons in the standard toolbar, the row of icons (or buttons) directly under the menu bar (Figure 5–2).

You will find these same icons under the different drop-down menus when you click on a menu item. For example, the first five icons all appear under File beside the appropriate command. Clicking on the new document ⬜ button at the left in the standard toolbar opens a new document, on the open folder ⬜ button opens an existing folder or document, on the printer ⬜ button sends one copy of the current document to the printer, on the magnifying glass ⬜ button a print preview window, and so on.

The Formatting Toolbar appears directly under the Standard Toolbar (Figure 5–3). It is used mainly for font style and size and for bolding, italicizing, or underlining text. In addition the justification and outlining options appear here.

In the menu bar, when you click on each menu heading (the top row), you see a drop-down menu below the heading. (See Common layout for accessing commands in Chapter 4, also.) You will also find the keyboard commands next to the command if you don't want to use the mouse. A command in gray is unavailable to you. Clicking on a command followed by an arrow causes another menu to appear. A command followed by an ellipsis (...) causes a *dialog box* to

Menu Bar

Cursor, Endmark

Standard Toolbar

Formatting Toolbar

Ruler

MS Taskbar

Close Box

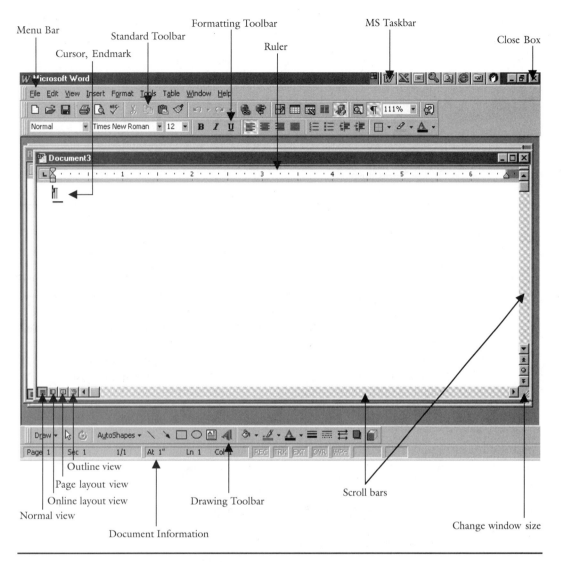

Outline view

Page layout view

Online layout view

Normal view

Document Information

Drawing Toolbar

Scroll bars

Change window size

FIGURE 5–1.
Typical New Document Screen in Word

appear. Dialog boxes communicate ways to set up your document. The more you work on a computer, the more useful the keyboard commands become. As you become more familiar with the program, you can decide which method you prefer, learn the steps, and then follow them. For this book we use the mouse since beginners usually find it the easiest. A brief description of each drop-down menu appears here.

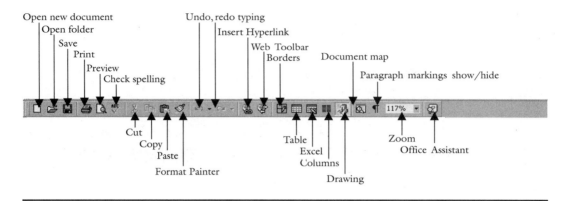

Open new document
Open folder
Save
Print
Preview
Check spelling
Undo, redo typing
Insert Hyperlink
Web Toolbar
Borders
Document map
Paragraph markings show/hide

Cut
Copy
Paste
Format Painter
Table
Excel
Columns
Drawing
Zoom
Office Assistant

FIGURE 5–2.
Standard Toolbar

File

The file commands help in document handling and printing as well as provide a list of the Word documents you worked on most recently. You select a **New Document** here or **Open** a previously prepared document that may reside on a diskette or in one of your folders. Page formatting commands appear under **Page Setup**. You can also **Close** your document or get a bird's-eye view of how your document will look when printed by selecting **Print Preview**. In the Macintosh version of Word there is a command to **Open Web Page** and instead of the **Exit** command you will see **Quit** to close the Word program.

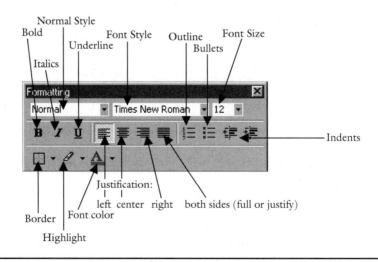

Normal Style
Bold
Underline
Font Style
Outline
Bullets
Font Size
Italics

Indents

Justification:
left center right both sides (full or justify)

Border
Font color
Highlight

FIGURE 5–3.
Formatting Toolbar

Edit	These commands allow you to copy and move text. You will also see the **Undo** and **Repeat** commands at the top of the menu. **Undo** reverses your recent delete, cut, paste, or typing change. If you hit the wrong key and something disappears that you want to keep, click the **Undo** command before you do anything else. If you have accidentally deleted a section of your document and then discover your mistake after new typing, keep clicking the **Undo** button (or icon in the toolbar) until it reappears. You can see a list of the actions that you can undo if you click the down arrow next to the **Undo** button on the **Standard Toolbar**. The **Find** and **Replace** commands have been discussed in Chapter 4. The Macintosh version also includes a **Publishing** command in this menu bar.
View	Under the **View** header, you will find commands that allow you to change your view of the document from **Normal** to **Page Layout**, **Online Layout**, or **Outline**. Icons for these commands appear in the bottom left corner of your document as well. View also contains commands that get you to the **Toolbars** or **Ruler**. You can customize your toolbars to show the Word drawing toolbar or hide toolbars you don't use frequently by clicking to select or deselect. This is also the menu that brings up the **Header** or **Footer Bars**. The Macintosh version includes a **Reveal Formatting** command.
Insert	This menu helps you insert the **Date**, a **Page Break**, or a **Footnote**. Note that a page break can be used for a column or section where you need different formatting within a document. You can also insert a **Comment**, **Text Box**, **Pictures**, **Files**, or a **Hyperlink** under this menu.
Format	These commands allow you to define the style of your document and the appearance of text or picture. Select the **Font** header and choose the size, color, and style of type. Here you add **Bullets** or **Numbers** to lists, **Borders** or **Backgrounds**, and **Change case**. This menu has justification (alignment) choices under **Paragraph** as well as tabs and line spacing choices. The Macintosh version also contains a command for **Document** and one to **Format Autoshape/Pictures**.
Tools	Under **Tools** you find **Spelling** and **Grammar**, readability level, **Word Count**, **Language** (thesaurus), **Envelope**, and **Mail Merge** commands. Word count is helpful when you need a 250-word abstract or have to write a paper of a certain length. You can also customize the layout of Word's toolbars, menus, and editing features.
Table	Under **Table** are the commands for creating and modifying tables.
Window	Here you can move between document windows, split your document into two parts if you need to see one section while working on another, and see a list of all active documents.
Help	Here you will find help with Word and learn more about it.

Moving Around the Document

There are several ways to move around a document.

Arrow keys	Move the insertion bar or cursor a line or letter at a time.
CTRL+arrow keys	Move one word or paragraph at a time.
Home key	Takes you to the beginning of the line.
End key	Takes you to the end of the line.
CTRL+Home	Takes you to the beginning of the document.
CTRL+End	Takes you to the end of the document.
Page Up and Page Down	Keys move you more quickly through the document a screen at a time.
CTRL+Page Up	Takes you to previous printed page.
CTRL+Page Down	Takes you to the next printed page.

Scroll bars are located at the right and bottom of the screen. You can place the mouse pointer in the open box in the scroll line and click or drag the box to move up or down the scroll line as quickly as you wish. The single arrow boxes in the scroll bar move you up or down a line at a time. The double arrow boxes move you up or down a page. When you click and drag the open box on the bottom scroll line you can move the document sideways on the screen.

Formatting a Document

Page formatting Described here are the options for changing page formats:

Choose **File**, **Page Setup** from the menu bar.

Select the appropriate settings.

From there the dialog box helps you choose the page size, margins, paper source, and horizontal (landscape) or vertical (portrait) orientation. Usually margins are set 1 inch at the top and bottom and 1.25 inches at the left side. If you choose **View** and highlight **Ruler,** a checkmark appears next to ruler and the ruler will appear under the heading of your Word document as shown in Figure 5–4. This is a toggle command so that if you want to remove the ruler you simply highlight Ruler again and it disappears. The ruler shows indents, or tabs, and you can make changes directly to it.

Paragraph formatting—indents Word has three indents, first, left, and right. Dragging the top indent ▽ marker to the right (first-line indent) indents the first line of a paragraph. Pressing the **Tab** key does the same thing. The bottom marker ▭ is the left-indent marker. Use it to indent all lines of the paragraph. The top and middle markers will move together with it. The middle △ marker is the hanging indent. To get a negative indent (to the right of the first line) you drag the middle marker to the right of the first-line indent marker. A hanging indent is an indentation of all of a paragraph except the first line. If you select the **Format** menu, **Para-**

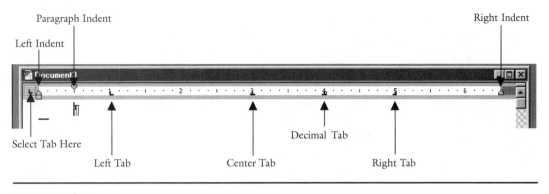

FIGURE 5–4.
Ruler and Tabs

graph, Special, it is listed as hanging indent. Word will move the indent markers together when you drag the bottom marker.

To set the indents:

Place your **Insertion** point in the paragraph you want to Indent OR highlight multiple paragraphs.

Drag the appropriate marker to the tick mark on the ruler bar.

Paragraph formatting—tabs Word has default tabs every .5 inch along the ruler. It also offers the standard four tab types shown in Figure 5–4 above from left to right: flush left tab, centered tab, decimal tab, and flush right tab. The tabs can be placed in the ruler using the mouse.

Click the **Left Corner** tab icon to change it to the one you want.

Click the **Ruler setting** where you wish the tab to be.

To remove the ruler from the screen, go to **View** and select **Ruler.**

Paragraph formatting—alignment, numbering, bullets, and borders In the Formatting Toolbar (Figure 5–3) are the icons for justification, numbering, and adding bullets or borders. The first icons involve text alignment or justification: left, centered, right, and full (both right and left respectively). Next comes a numbering tool, then one to add bullets. The next two icons move your numbered or bulleted text to the left (decrease) or right (increase). The lower icons bring up the border tool, which allows you to put a partial or complete border around selected text, the highlighter, and text color choices.

To use these features:

Highlight the **Text.**

Click the **appropriate** button.

Character formatting—font size and style When you are about to begin a document, choose a font style and size from the Formatting menu.

Click **Format, Font**.

Choose a **Font, Font Style**, and **Size** and click **OK**.

You can also use the style and font size menu bars in the beginning of the Formatting Toolbar. Business default size is 10–12 points. You can always use a size you can read easily on the screen and then highlight the document, by choosing Select All under Edit (or CTRL A) when you are finished and reduce the print size before printing by choosing another font size or print style or both. Clicking on Font under the Format Menu takes you to a dialog box where you can choose a font style and size that then can be set as the default style for all your documents. The font size and style are shown in the beginning of the Formatting Toolbar (Figure 5–3).

You will notice that there are style buttons in the Formatting Toolbar for bold, italics, and underline.

To use the Formatting Toolbar for bold, italics, and underline:

Highlight a **Word** or **Section of Text**.

Click the **Style** button.

Clicking again changes the text back to normal. You will find the same commands under the Format menu when you select Font. You can also turn on the attributes by pressing CTRL+B, I, or U to turn the feature on. Repeat the key strokes when you have finished the section you wanted in bold, and so on, and your subsequent typing returns to normal.

Headers and footers To add a header or footer to your document,

Choose **View** and select **Header and Footer**.

Type the **Text to place in the header or footer** and/or

Select **Options** such as page number, date, or filename, from the header/footer toolbar.

Click the **Close** button.

In Figure 5–5, the header is shown. The header is the default box that appears first. The title of the document could appear in the left corner, the page number in the middle, and the date on the right. If you wish to use the footer, just click in the footer box in the dialog bar. The tab key moves you from the left side to the middle and then to the right side of the box so you can choose the appropriate spot for inserting information.

If you click on the # sign a page number will appear. The calendar gives you the date, the clock the time. A running head can be placed in the header by putting the insertion point where you want the header to appear and typing it.

Preparing Your Document

There are two ways to prepare the formatting for your document. The first is to set the formatting before you begin to type the text; the other is to type the text, and then format the document. Whichever style you choose is a personal preference, but remember the idea is to create

Type in this box for header.

Change font size here by highlighting header and choosing smaller size.

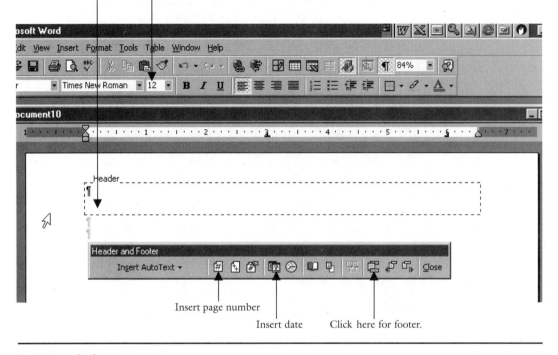

FIGURE 5–5.
Screen for Adding a Header or Footer

and format your document efficiently and effectively. Described here is the process for setting the formats before you create the document.

Although you may think that the formatting features would only be accessed from the Format menu, many of the settings can also be done under the File menu as discussed above in Page Formatting. If you plan to bind the product you are working on, you may need a 1.5-inch left-hand margin. If you are using a letterhead, you will want to measure it and make sure that the body of the letter begins below the letterhead. You may need 2.4 inches in this case. If you need to change the margins of a section of the document, go into Page Setup again, change the margins to what you need, and select "from this point forward" under "Apply to."

Next go to **Format** and choose **Font**. Select the type and size of font for your paper. Unless you change the default, the Word font and size default is Times New Roman 10 points. You may change this default by selecting the font and size in the font, dialog box, and then click Default button in the lower left of the window. Respond Yes to change the normal.dot template. This means that Word will always open to this font and size. If you want to change the settings for this document only, then change the settings and click OK.

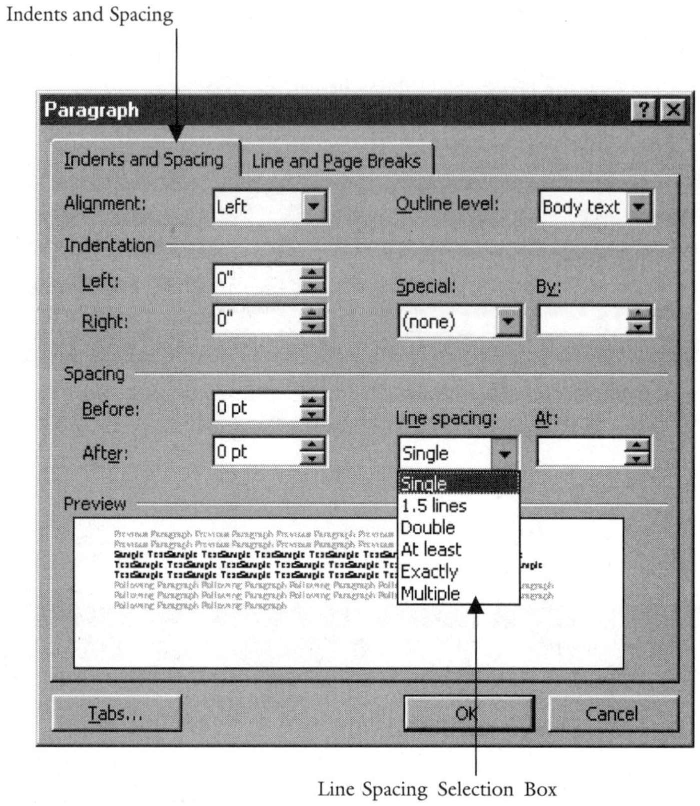

Indents and Spacing

Line Spacing Selection Box

FIGURE 5–6.
Paragraph Formatting Dialog Box with Line Spacing Choices Open

Next choose **Format** and **Paragraph**. You can select single, 1.5, or double spacing among other options under line spacing (see Figure 5–6).

You may want to work on your document using 1.5 or single spacing. Later you can change it to whatever spacing is required or that you prefer. If you highlight the document and press:

CTRL+1 you create single spacing

CTRL+5 you create $1\frac{1}{2}$ spaced lines

CTRL+2 you create double-spaced lines

In the same paragraph formatting section you will see a tab for Line and Page Breaks. Clicking the Widow/Orphan Control box adjusts page breaks so that two or more paragraph lines always begin a page or end a page. You can also use the Insert menu to set a page break. If you need to remove a Page Break simply highlight it and Backspace or press Delete.

If you click the Paragraph sign in the Standard Toolbar (Figure 5–2) you will see formatting marks for spaces, indents, and ends of paragraphs. The marks are helpful if you need to reformat a document or aren't sure why your document looks the way it does. Remember that it is always better to use tabs instead of spaces when you format a document.

Viewing Your Document

Word provides several ways to view your document on the screen. The best view for preparing your document is usually Normal.

To change a view,

> Select **View** and click the **View Option** OR

> Click the **button** on the left bottom corner of the screen that corresponds to the view you want. (See Figure 5–1.)

The first View Option is Normal. The next View is the Online Layout—a view designed to be used to read documents online. This view provides an outline view of the document on the screen's left side in a scroll box with the text on the right screen. Page Layout shows you how your document will look and can help you arrange pictures or columns, and so on. You will see spaces between each page. The Outline view displays your document in outline form using Word's Standard Headings style. This view can help you organize your thoughts when writing or reorganizing a paper.

Numbers and Bullets

Automatic bulleting and numbering can be helpful—and frustrating!

To create a numbered list:

> Put your cursor where you want to begin the list.

> Click the [▦] button in the Formatting Toolbar (Figure 5–3).

> Type the **List** pressing the **Enter** key at the end of each item.

> When finished, press the **Enter** key twice or click the numbering button to turn off the numbers.

You can also type the first number, press the Enter key and for the next item Word will add the 2. If you don't want this number, simply backspace to get rid of the number or press the Enter key twice.

To create a bullet list:

> Type the **list**.

> Highlight the **list**.

> Click the Bullet [▦] button on the Formatting Toolbar (Figure 5–3).

Spelling and Grammar Checks

Spelling and grammar checks, readability statistics, and a thesaurus are tools included in Word 97 that help with proofreading. Word automatically checks your spelling and grammar as you type. If a word is misspelled, you will see a wavy red line under the word. If it is a grammar error, the wavy line is green.

To correct the error:

Right click over the error.

Select a correction from the list, choose ignore it, or add the word to your spelling dictionary.

When adding a word to the dictionary, be sure it is correct. Note that the spelling dictionary is stored on your hard drive, so if you use other computers, it will not be available to you on those computers. Other ways to correct spelling and grammar are to choose **Spelling** and **Grammar** from under the Tools menu or click the **ABC** button on the Formatting Toolbar (Figure 5–2).

The wavy lines distract some people. Word provides an option to turn off this feature. To turn off spelling and grammar checker as you type:

Select **Tools**, **Options**, and click the **Spelling and Grammar** tab.

Click the squares **Check spelling** and **grammar** as you type and click **OK**.

Now, when you want to check your spelling and grammar:

Click the **Spelling** and **Grammar** button or select **Tools**, **Spelling** and **Grammar** from the menu bar.

Follow the directions in the dialog box and click the **Close** button when finished.

In the Spelling and Grammar dialog box, Figure 5–7, you will also see a Readability Statistics box. You can check this and learn the readability of the document you have written. The best time to do grammar, spelling, and readability checks is after you finished the document and your cursor is at the beginning of the document. Remember, however, that you must read the document over as Word will not find all the misspellings or grammar problems that might exist.

Using Word Templates

Word provides several templates for you to choose from when you select New under the File menu or click the New Document button on the MS Word toolbar. See Figure 5–8. The first screen shows the blank document icon. Note that there are several headings to choose if you want a special type of document such as a memo, report, or Web page.

In Figure 5–9, Letters and Faxes heading was selected. Here you can choose a preset style or create your own special document. You can use the Wizard to help you. The Wizard asks a series of questions and designs a document based on your responses. Note that in Figure 5–9 there are both Style (preformatted) and Wizard documents to select.

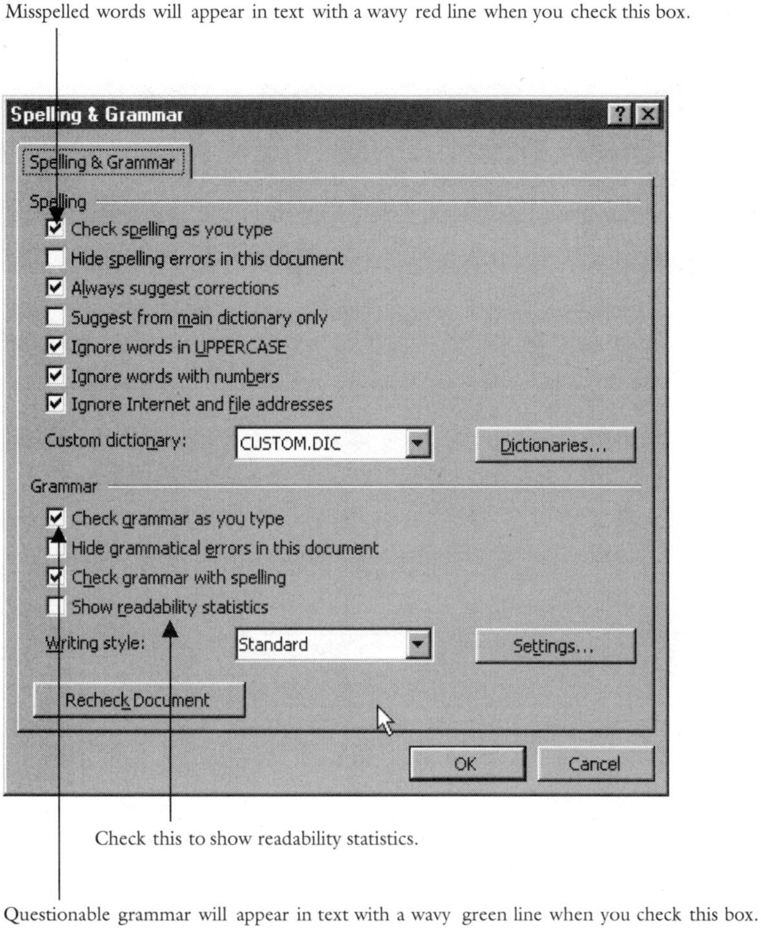

Misspelled words will appear in text with a wavy red line when you check this box.

Check this to show readability statistics.

Questionable grammar will appear in text with a wavy green line when you check this box.

FIGURE 5–7.
Spelling, Grammar, and Readability Dialog Box

If you modify a certain style and want to save it as a template, choose Save As from the File menu. In the Save as type box choose Document Type. Then name your document template. Choose the appropriate template folder in which to save it.

Creating a Table

You can use the Table feature in many ways. It helps you set columns when recording minutes, for example, or to organize any kind of information. Tables are also essential to any research reports. It is a good idea to plot out the kind of table you need in terms of number of rows and columns before you select the number of rows and columns. In the Table menu you are given

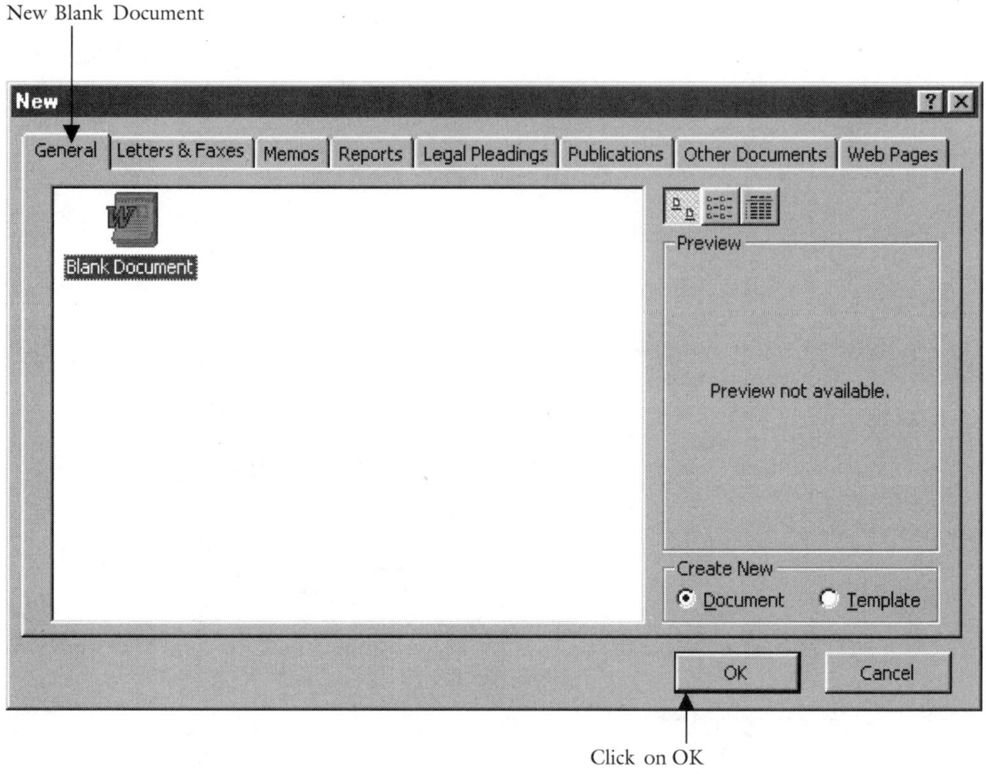

New Blank Document

FIGURE 5–8.
Open New Blank Document Screen

two choices: to **Draw** a table or **Insert** a table. Figure 5–10 shows you the dialog box when you select **Insert.** If you then choose Auto Format from the dialog box, you can customize the table with predesigned styles, as shown in Figure 5–11. Figure 5–12 shows you the box you get when you select the Table icon from the Standard Toolbar.

To create a table:

Place your **Insertion** point where you want the table in the document.

Select **Table, Insert** from the menu OR click and hold the **Table** button .

Type the **Number of Rows and Columns** and click **OK** OR if using the table button, drag over the cells for the **Number of Rows and Columns**.

Remember that you will need a row for headers. If you discover you need another row, you can insert one.

Letters & Faxes Selected

Preview of Contemporary Fax

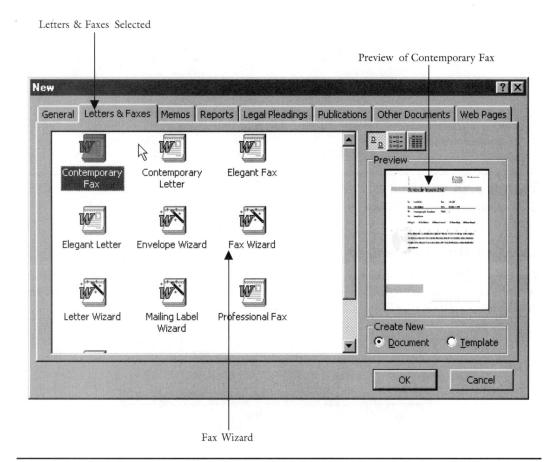

Fax Wizard

FIGURE 5–9.
Open New Document: Letters & Faxes Selection Screen

To insert a row:

Click in a **Row**.

Select **Table, Insert Rows**. You will notice that a row is added above the row where the insertion point was.

Rows are inserted above the current row, while columns are inserted to the left of the current column. You may also insert rows or columns by right clicking the row or column and selecting the appropriate option from the menu.

When you check the Table menu commands, you will see that many more are possible once you have a table in your document such as changing the width or height of a row, selecting a row or column, or deleting grid lines. If you decide to delete the table, highlight it, and choose Cut.

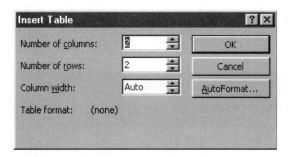

FIGURE 5–10.
Table Dialog Box (2x2 Table)

Creating Merged Documents

You can use Word to create envelopes and form letters and print a personalized copy for each person to whom you are writing. Word replaces merge fields from a main document with information from a data source.

Style is Simple 1 shown under Formats.

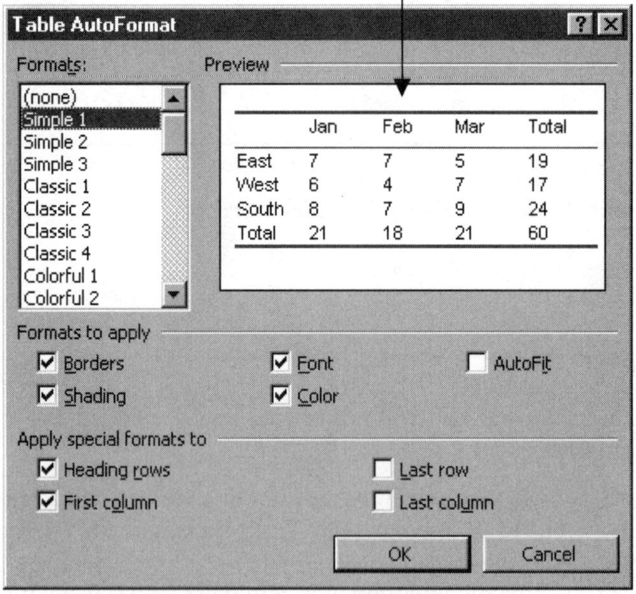

FIGURE 5–11.
Table AutoFormat Dialog Box

Insert Table Icon.

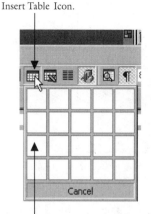

Highlight number of squares for rows and columns.

FIGURE 5–12.
Selecting the Table Icon from the Standard Table

You will create two documents:

1. A *data source* contains the name and addresses (and whatever else you wish to individualize) for each letter. You can set up a series of subdocuments that Word could also merge into your text. Your data source can be an Outlook address book, an Access database, an Excel spreadsheet with column headings, or a Word table. We will use a Word table that you create. Every data document consists of three parts: records, fields, and field headers. Each paragraph in a data document is a record and each column is a field. You need to plan your data document carefully so that it does what you want it to do.

2. A *main document* contains the same text that you want in each letter and the field code from which to insert the personalized data from the data source.

Creating the main document

Click **New** ⬜ or **Open** 📂 button for the main document. This document can be a new one or a letter you have already typed. For practice, just do the essentials of the letter or document; you can finish the rest later.

Select **Tools, Mail Merge.** You will see the Mail Merge Helper screen.

Click **Create** under **1 Main Document**, which is the document you have open.

Choose **Form letters.** See Figure 5–13.

Click the **Active Window.** On the next screen under the Create button you see the type of merge it will perform and the name of your main document.

Next step is to create a data source. Click **Get Data** under **2.**

Choose **Create Data Source,** as shown in Figure 5–14.

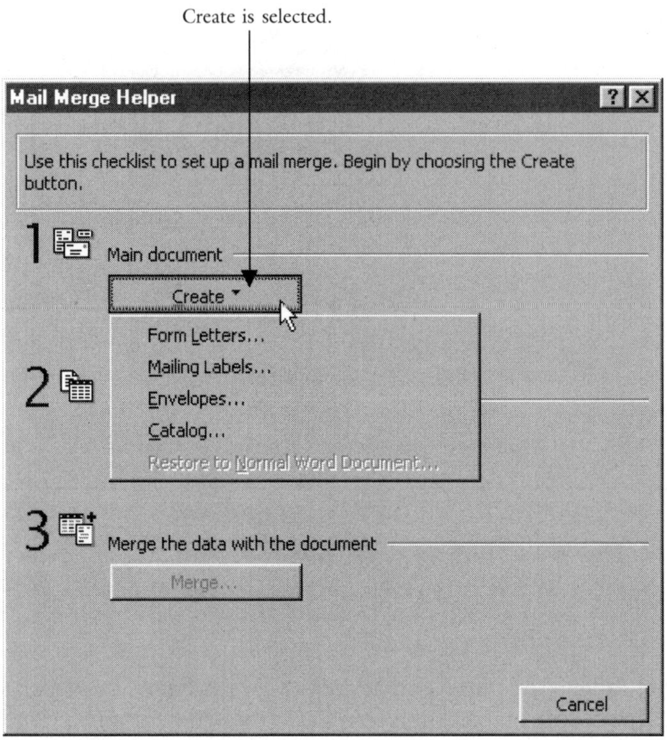

Create is selected.

FIGURE 5–13.
Mail Merger Helper

Preparing a Data Source Document Under the **Create Data Source** screen you see a box for Field name and the Field names in Header Row on the right. You will want to delete the field names that you *won't use.*

Highlight a **Field name**.

Click the **Remove Field Name** button.

From the data form shown in Figure 5–15, you will need to delete **Job Title, Company, Address2, Country, Home, and Work Phone** (these fields could also be left blank).

Click **OK** and Word asks you to name the document to save it.

Type **Data Source 1.**

Click **Save** or press **Enter.** Word asks you if you want to edit the Data Source or the Main Document.

Choose **Data Source.** You will see a window like Figure 5–16, only the fields will be blank.

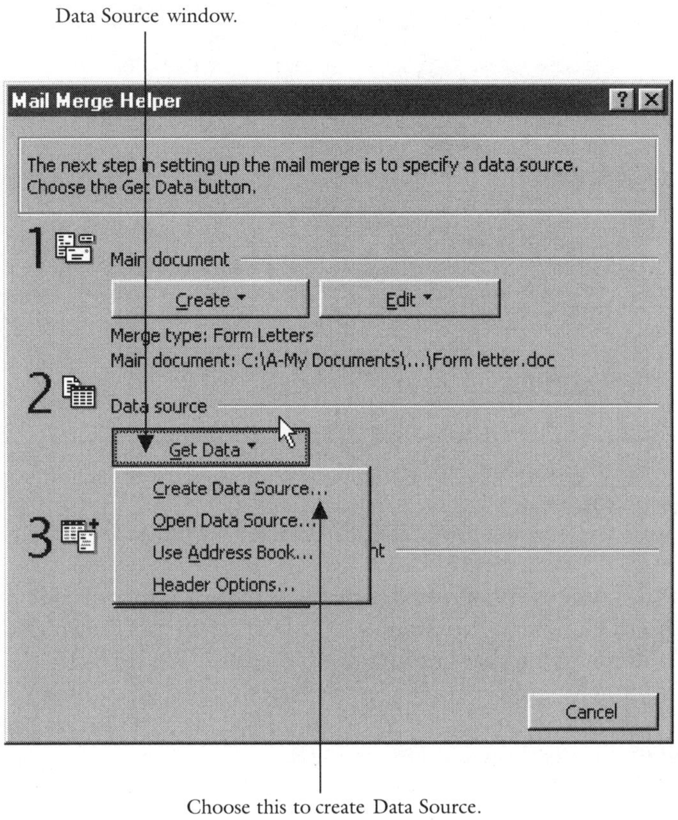

Data Source window.

Choose this to create Data Source.

FIGURE 5–14.
Mail Merge Helper: Create Data Source Window

Type the **Title, First name, Last name** and so on, for each of your records. (Use the names and addresses in Exercise 3 at the end of this chapter.)

You can move ahead in the dialog box by pressing the **Tab** key; you can move back with **Shift+Tab**. Be sure to use the correct case for your entries, such as two capital letters for State. Note that in Figure 5–16 this is record **1**.

When you click **Add New** you will be given Record **2** to fill in the data. Use this screen to add, remove, or edit records in the Data Source. If you click **OK** and the screen closes before you are finished, simply go to the **Tools** menu, choose **Mail Merge**, and select **Edit** under option 2. Also remember that every data record (each name and address) must contain the same number of fields. If the individual does not have a street address then leave that field blank.

When you finish adding records to the Data Source, click **OK.** You will be asked to return to the main document.

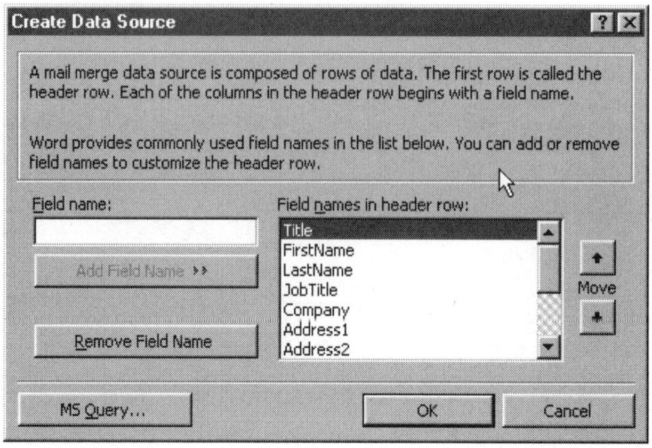

FIGURE 5–15.
Create Data Source Window

Editing the main document Now you are ready to refine your main document. You create, edit, and format this document as you want it to appear in the final form. Note that the document toolbar looks different and has another toolbar added, Figure 5–17.

This toolbar is a function of the Mail Merge Helper screen. Each time you come to a place where you want to insert information from the data source, click the **Insert Merge Field** button on the Mail Merge toolbar as shown in Figure 5–18.

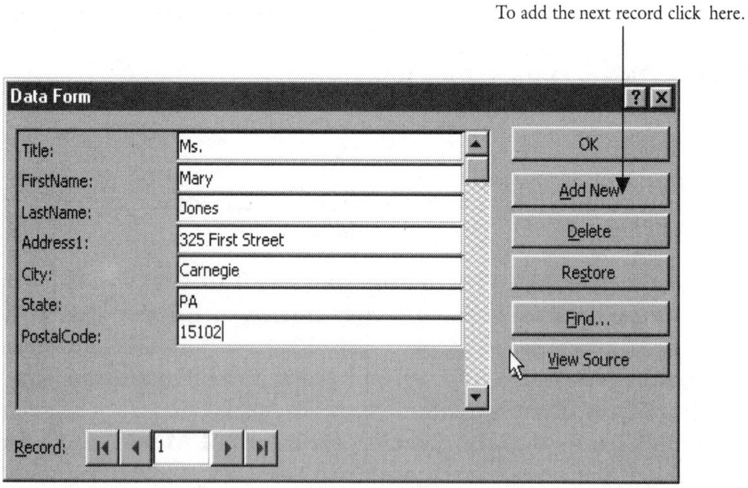

FIGURE 5–16.
First Record in Data Source

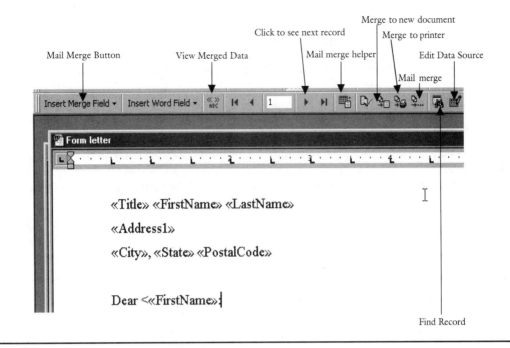

FIGURE 5–17.
Mail Merge Toolbar

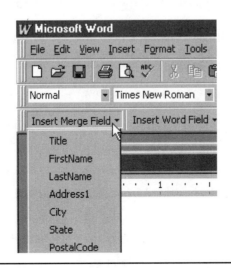

FIGURE 5–18.
Insert Merge Field Menu

To add fields to this document:

Select **Insert** and choose **Insert Date and Time**.

From the dialog box, choose the **Style** you wish.

Position your cursor where you want to add the name of your first category of addressee information as is shown in the document in Figure 5–17.

Choose **Insert Merge Field** and click **Title**.

Repeat the process to insert the remaining fields—**First Name**, then **Last Name**. Leave a space after each word where you want a space when the address is typed in the letter. The heading in your letter should look like the example below and that in Figure 5–17.

July 1, 2000

<<Title>> <<FirstName>><<LastName>>

<<Address1>>

<<City>><<State>><<PostalCode>>

Dear << FirstName>>:

(Put body of letter here.)

Signature

Type your name here.

After editing the Main Document, choose **Save** from the File menu or press **CTRL+S**.

Type a name that reflects the nature of the document like **Form Letter**.

Merging data with the main document Check to make sure that you typed all the addressee information correctly into each record. Then make sure that your main document is the way you want it. Now you are ready to merge the main document with the data source.

Have the main document in your active window.

Click the **View Merged Data** ABC button on the Mail Merge toolbar. See Figure 5–17. You will see your first letter with the merged fields.

To view the second record, click the **Arrow** ▶ to the right of 1.

To review the first record, click the **Arrow** ◀ to the left of 2.

Click the **Merge to New Document** button. Word places all the form letters in a single document, separating the letters with section breaks (double dotted lines). Each section starts a new page. You can then insert additional comments into the letters to personalize them.

To go back to your Form letter, select **File, Main document File name** at the bottom of the menu.

To print the letters, click the **Merge to Printer** button or choose **File, Print** from the menu bar.

SUMMARY

There are unlimited possibilities for creating documents in Word. We have only described a few of the basics. Some of the possibilities include outlining, creating an index, generating a table of contents, inserting clip art, making newsletters, addressing envelopes, and customizing and optimizing Word. Use the documentation from the software company or purchase a book that introduces Word or that is published through Microsoft but sold separately from the program. It will take time and diligent work to take advantage of all of the program's features.

EXERCISE 1: BASIC MS WORD FUNCTIONS

Objectives

1. Perform selected word processing functions.
2. Explain basic word processing terms and functions.

Activity

1. Start Word. (Note: you can complete most of this exercise using any word processing program.)

2. Create a document.

   Type the following text. Type it as fast as you can. Do not correct mistakes and do not hit the enter key. Do not pay attention to spelling errors.

   Using word processing software for your documents can save you many hours and much pain. It can also be very exasperating if you don't follow a few simple rules. If you choose to ignore these rules, disaster can strike. These are a few of the simple rules: 1. Periodically, save your work. 2. Pay attention to the warnings given. 3. Always keep a second copy of your work on another disk, in another place.

   Not pressing the enter key will cause _____ and this is called _____.

3. Save your document.

   Select **File, Save** or press **CTRL+S**.

In the Save in Text box, select the **3½"** Drive A by clicking the **Down arrow** ▼ button and selecting **3½" drive** option. See Chapter 4 if you need further help.

Highlight the **Text** in the **File name** textbox and type **Rules for wp** and press **Enter**. Word will periodically save it—every 15 minutes.

You can also click on the **Save** 🖫 button on the toolbar (next to the Printer icon) to save your document. When the document has a name and location, it will just update the file and not display the Save as dialog window.

4. Move around the document.

   Practice moving around the document.

   Use the **Arrow** keys, and **Page Up** and **Down** keys.

5. Edit text.

   Highlight the **Text**. (Press **CTRL+A**.)

   Select **Edit** and **Copy**.

   Position the **Insertion point** two or three lines below the original paragraph. Press **CTRL+End**, press **Enter** twice.)

   Select **Edit** and **Paste**. You will now have two copies of the text.

   Select **Edit** and **Undo**.

   Try doing the same things using the **Cut** ✂, **Copy** 🗐, and **Paste** 📋 buttons on the Formatting Toolbar.

   Finish with one copy of your text on the page.

   Go back to **Edit** and choose **Repeat Paste**; your text returns.

   If you choose to make another copy of different text, or if you choose to cut a section, the first text that was saved will be gone from the clipboard. You can undo the last few commands, however. Remember you can also use keyboard commands to cut (**CTRL+X**), copy (**CTRL+C**), and paste (**CTRL+V**). End this task with two of the same paragraphs.

6. Align text.

   Highlight the **second copy of the text.**

   Click **Right Align** ▤ button.

   Note what happens. Now click both Right and Left Justification or **Full Justification** ▤ button. Note all sentences are flush at both margins except for the last one.

   Click **Left Justification** ▤ button.

7. Edit the document.

   You can delete one copy of the text if you wish.

Using the tab and enter keys, create the following looking document:

> **Using word processing software for your documents can save you many hours and much pain. It can also be very exasperating if you don't follow a few simple rules. If you choose to ignore these rules, disaster can strike.**
>
> **These are a few of the simple rules:**
>
> 1. **Periodically, save your work.**
>
> 2. **Pay attention to the warnings given.**
>
> 3. **Always keep a second copy of your work on another disk, in another place.**

Press **CTRL+Home** to place your insertion bar at the beginning of the paragraph.

Select **Tools, Spelling** and **Grammar** to correct your errors.

When the dialog window appears it will highlight misspelled words and offer corrections.

Click the **Change** button if the highlighted selection is correct, the **Ignore** button to ignore a correctly spelled word.

Word will tell you when it has completed checking the document.

8. Format the document.

   Type a **Title** for the above text. (Press **CTRL+Home**, type **Word Processing Rules**, and press the **Enter** key twice.)

   Highlight the **Title**, click the **Bold** **B** button, click the **Center** button.

   Click in your text to deselect the title.

9. Print the document.

   Press the **CTRL+P** keys or click the **Printer** button.

10. Close and save your document.

    Click the **Save** button to save your document. This will update the file you already saved.

    Click the **Close** **X** button on Word application or go on to Exercise No. 2.

EXERCISE 2: SEARCH, REPLACE, AND PARAGRAPH BORDERS

Objectives

1. Use a search and replace function.
2. Create a document with a paragraph border.

Activity

1. Create the document.

   Type the following text in the new document window:

   A descriptive survey was used to elicit information concerns of new moms as part of an evaluation of single room maternity care (SRMC) at a small midwestern hospital. The investigators developed a list of concerns common to new moms. New moms were asked to check as many of the 16 concerns listed that they would like the nurse to help with or discuss following the birth of their baby. Following a pilot study of 10 new moms, the survey was mailed to all new moms who delivered a live infant during a 12-month period.

2. Search and replace all occurrences of moms with mothers.

   Press **CTRL+Home** to go to the top of your document.

   Select **Edit**, then **Replace** from the menu bar.

   In the Find what box, type **moms**.

   Press the **Tab** key or click on the **Replace With** text box.

   Type **mothers**.

   Click the **Replace All** button. What happens? Click **OK** button.

   Make sure you use Replace All with caution as it will change all words that have the sequence of letters moms in them.

   Change dialog boxes again and reverse your directions.

   Type **mothers** in the Find what box and **moms** in the replace with box.

   Click the **Replace All** button. Your document will return to normal.

   Click **Close** button to close the replace dialog window.

3. Create paragraph borders.

   Go to the end of your document and press **Enter** twice.

   Select the **Above paragraph**.

   Click the **Outside Border** button on the Toolbar. If the picture on the button does not have a black outlined box, click the down arrow to the right of it, and select the black outline button.

   Type **Another paragraph** at the end of the document.

Highlight the **new Paragraph.**

Select **Format**, and **Borders and Shading.** Click the **Borders** tab if not selected.

Click **Box** button. From Style choose the **Double line.** From width, choose **$1\frac{1}{2}$ pt.** Click **OK.**

Your box should look like the following box:

A descriptive survey was used to elicit information concerns of new moms as part of an evaluation of single room maternity care (SRMC) at a small midwestern hospital. A list of concerns common to new moms was developed by the investigators. New moms were asked to check as many of the 16 concerns listed that they would like the nurse to help with or discuss following the birth of their baby. Following a pilot study of 10 new moms, the survey was mailed to all new moms who delivered a live infant during a 12-month period.

Save your document and **print** your boxed paragraph.

Tip: Always leave a paragraph mark (press **Enter**) below the text you will box or below a table so that you can type below the box or table. If the last paragraph mark is within the box, pressing **Enter** will only enlarge the box or table.

EXERCISE 3: MERGE AND SEARCH FUNCTIONS

Objectives

1. Create main, data, and merged documents.
2. Use the search and replace function.
3. Print created letters.

Activity

1. Create the documents.

   Create the main and data source documents like those at the end of this exercise. Use the directions earlier in this chapter on creating the Mail Merge documents.

2. Use find and replace function and replace all occurrences of:

   DM with Diabetes Mellitus

   April 25, 2000, with April 25, 2001

   medications with insulin

3. Merge the documents.

Use the merge (mail merge) feature to generate and print the individual letters.

Check them for accuracy.

Note: How these fields appear depends on the word processor. They may be the name of the field, a number with a ~, etc.

Primary Document

<<Title>> <<FirstName>> <<LastName>>

<<Address1>>

<<City>> <<State>> <<PostalCode>>

(Use the automatic DATE function to place date with this style Month Day, Year here.)

Dear <<FirstName>>:

We invite you to attend a patient education program on adult onset DM. The date of the program is April 25, 2000. The program time takes place from 1–3 pm in the Patient Education Conference Room, 4th floor, Computerville Hospital.

We designed this program for newly diagnosed diabetics. The program will address adjusting to diabetes, diet and exercise, and medications. The guest speaker is Nellie Netscape, Nurse Practitioner.

Please notify us at 624-3333 if you plan to attend. There is no charge for this program. We look forward to seeing you.

Sincerely,

Mary Data, PhD, RN

Data Source

Title	FirstName	LastName	Address	City	ST	ZIP
Ms.	Mary	Jones	325 First Street	Carnegie	PA	15102
Mr.	Robert	Tutor	4456 Software Ave.	Melford	PA	15102
Dr.	Susan	Master	8997 Default Lane	Eagan	MN	55123

ASSIGNMENT 1: PREPARING A RESUME

Note: This assignment can be done with any word processing program.

Directions

A resume is usually needed when you apply for a new job to summarize your educational and professional accomplishments. Assignments 1 and 2 both ask you to prepare a resume but each asks for a different format. Look over both assignments before completing them and think through how you can use what you create for one for the other.

1. The nonscannable resume:
   - Obtain a want ad from the paper (preferably in the health field).
   - Compose a resume using a word processing package.

2. Your resume should include:
   a. Information about the person
      Name
      Address (city, state, zip)
      Telephone, fax, and email address
   b. Job/work objective (not always included)
   c. Summary of qualifications (use the job description in ad as a guide)
   d. Education (school, degree, date, major)
   e. Professional experience as a nurse
      Begin with most recent and include year, name of position, type of unit.
   f. Other information—licensure, honors, professional organizations, publications, grants, special skills, projects, etc.

3. When formatting this resume, make it pleasing to the eye.
   Bold categories.
   Use upper and lower case.
   Use tabs, center, spell checker as appropriate.
   Justify on left only.

4. Compose a cover letter applying for the position.

5. Run the cover letter through a spell and grammar checker.

6. Make appropriate revisions in the cover letter based on results of the spell and grammar checker (if available).

7. Submit ad, letter of application (original and revised), and resume.

ASSIGNMENT 2: A SCANNABLE RESUME*

Directions

In today's health care organizations, computerized resume scanning is becoming more and more common. A scannable resume increases your chances of being selected for an interview since it is an "unbiased" way of matching applicants with available positions. In these resumes it is important for you to match the skills you have with the words in the position ad. The rules for a scannable resume differ from the rules by which you would prepare the resume you did for Assignment 1.

Basic rules for a scannable resume:

- Set margins at: 1.25 left; 1.5 right.
- *Do not* use bold, italics, underline, or bullets.
- Use a laser printer, standard font and size, for example, Times Roman 12 pt. (It might be a good idea to check with the Human Resource department to see what they prefer.)
- Use CAPITAL LETTERS for each separate heading.
- Use white space to emphasize headings.
- Use hard carriage returns (hrt) or Enter *at end of each line.*
- Use an asterisk (*) to set off each item under a heading. For example, each job you have had, each degree, or each specific responsibility in a position.
- Do not use headers or footers. (Put your name on the top of each page, but not in a header.)
- Avoid any misspelled words as the scanner can misinterpret them.

It is important to repeat key words from the position qualifications in your resume. Scanning also combines and condenses key words into skill sets so it helps if you can describe your qualifications in matching terms.

Prepare a scannable resume.

Hand in the scannable resume with the nonscannable one.

---

*Note: The authors gratefully acknowledge Teresa Casino, RN, MS, Rochester, MN for the information regarding preparation of a scannable resume.

ASSIGNMENT 3: MERGE FUNCTION

Directions

1. Write a procedure or policy for some aspect of your practice. It can be something that exists, but requires revision; or it can be a new one that requires development.

   Use the following document format:

Margins	left	2″
	right	1.5″
	top	2″
	bottom	1″
Header	Flush right, procedure/policy number on each page	
Footer	Pagination centered - 38 -	
	Last page to have your initials	

2. Merge function. Create a form letter to send to the five procedure/policy members that includes an explanation of the attached, a due date for review, and the person to contact if they have questions. Set it up to use the merge function. Embed the field codes in the form letter. Create the data source with the following information: name (first and last), title, and hospital location.

3. Turn in the procedure/policy, letter with merge fields, and a copy of the merged letter.

Chapter 6

Introduction to Presentation Graphics

OBJECTIVES

1. Define basic terminology related to graphics.
2. Describe selective uses of presentation graphics software.
3. Develop a PowerPoint presentation.

INTRODUCTION

Presentation Graphics software programs are among the fastest growing applications used by computer consumers and MS PowerPoint is one of the most commonly used. Many software programs contain some graphics capabilities. For example, word processing packages, with a wide variety of fonts, now permit creation of overheads and limited graphics; spreadsheets permit creation of pie, line, and bar graphs; and some database programs can also be used to create limited graphs.

Graphics programs include presentation software, draw programs, and computer-aided design. Most presentation programs include text handling, outlining, drawing, graphing, clip art, and special effects. They allow you to produce high-quality presentation slides, transparencies, handouts, or electronic slide shows. Draw programs help produce clip art and images used in presentation programs or other applications where images enhance the message. Computer-aided design programs assist draftsmen, engineers, and architects to produce their design plans and drawings.

The focus of this chapter is presentation graphics using PowerPoint. The main use of presentation graphics programs is to present information in a pleasing visual fashion to facilitate decision making and to communicate a message. Visuals that sustain interest, highlight content, and disseminate information enhance presentations. They create an impression.

SLIDE OR CHART TYPES

Slide or chart types refer to the appearance of the content; how you display the content. Each program has many choices including the following:

Area   Area charts present or emphasize total quantities (volume) of several items.

Bar	Bar graphs show the changing nature of data over time or compare data. We sometimes refer to bar charts as column charts. Many variations of the bar graph exist. For example, there are horizontal or vertical bars, stacked bars, overlapping bars, and paired bars.
Drawing	Drawing graphs can create a diagram, map, or flow chart. For example, if you want to show a process or flow of some content, use the drawing features to create the boxes and arrows to show the direction or flow of the process. Use the draw options to import clip art.
High/low	High/low graphs show changes for data within a specific time period or to show the changing nature of data over time.
Line	Line graphs present a lot of data when you want to show trends over time.
List	Lists help organize the presentation content, to cover the main points of the topic. Often a bullet or number precedes each item on the list.
Organization structure	Organization structure graphs show relationships of people or positions within an organization.
Pie	Pie graphs compare parts to a whole or several values at one point in time. They also help to emphasize a particular part or to show relationships between sets of items.
Scatter	Scatter graphs show trends or statistics such as average frequency, regression, or distribution.
Table	A table presents text information in column form. Use it when you want to display two or three items and some related information about those items. For example, when you want to show the elements of three concepts.
Title	Title charts introduce the presentation and to separate sections within the presentation. It is helpful to orient the audience to the topic and its parts.
Text	Text charts contain textual information and sometimes clip art. Use it to show the main points of the presentation and to help orient the audience to the topic.

PRESENTATIONS

The first step in preparing a presentation is to clearly define the purpose or message. The second step is to outline or organize the content. Many presentation programs offer an outliner feature to help with this step. Next, decide the best medium to present the message given the time allowed. This requires knowledge of both the environment where the presentation will occur, and the equipment that will be available. Some common media used for presentations are:

Handouts	Sometimes we provide the audience with handouts that outline the presentation, define selected terms, or present complex information. Use the presentation program's handout feature to prepare the handouts if you want copies of the slides or speaker notes. It is easy to develop appropriate hand-

outs and notes that go with the presentation. If you want to give details not covered in the presentation or reference lists, use your word processing program.

Slides   Many presenters use 35mm slides. Slides focus the audience on key points and present data in a pleasing and helpful manner. They generally require a dark room and large enough letters to be seen by all.

Slide shows   Connecting the computer to a data projector enables PowerPoint slides to be projected on a large screen. You create slides in PowerPoint, add special effects that control how the slide content appears, and touch it off with sound. Save the presentation as a slide show to the hard drive, diskette, or zip disk. This makes it easy to adapt your presentation to different audiences and time slots without going to the expense of making new 35mm slides. Data projection systems are increasingly available in educational and health care institutions as well as at convention centers. Newer models are portable and project high-quality images that are easily seen in regular lighting.

Transparencies   Some presenters opt for transparencies because they are easy to prepare and use and the equipment is readily available. One advantage of transparencies is that you can use them in rooms with normal lighting. This facilitates note taking. Transparencies can be easier and cheaper to produce than slides and may work better in less technologically developed places. Laser and color printers also add to the effectiveness of transparencies. Transparencies, however, are not as easily revised as are electronic slide shows.

KEY POINTS OF CREATING A TRANSPARENCY

With computer-generated visuals, there is a tendency to produce crowded charts that detract from the message. The following are some key points for creating quality text charts.

1. Limit your text to no more than seven lines per transparency and five to seven words per line. If the information does not fit, divide the chart into two logically separated ones and use only key words or phrases. Keep it simple.
2. Use upper and lower case as normally seen in print. All upper case letters are harder to read. Reserve upper case for titles or to emphasize a word.
3. Limit the use of italics. Italic print looks pretty, but is harder for the audience to read.
4. Select large print of an easy-to-read font. It is better to have it too large and simple, than too small and fancy. Minimum size for text is $\frac{1}{4}$"; in PowerPoint this is 24 or 28 points. For titles, the default size is 44 points.
5. Use boldface. Boldface makes transparencies easier to read.
6. Center titles but left justify text. We normally see titles centered and text left justified. We read the English language from left to right.
7. Use bullets or numbers to emphasize key points.
8. Use symbols and images as appropriate. Symbols should enhance the content, not detract from it.

9. Accent charts with color, but do not overdo it. Many people have color printers available that print on laser transparency film. Make sure the color adds something to the transparency. If you do not have access to a color printer, use transparency pens or color transparency film to add interest. Generally, transparencies should have a light background with dark print while slides are the reverse—a dark background with light print.

KEY POINTS OF CREATING AND PROCESSING 35MM SLIDES

The same information presented with creating transparencies also applies to creating slides. The following are a few additional pointers.

1. Limit colors to three or four per slide except for special applications like pie charts or graphics.
2. Shadow text. This creates crisper or sharper looking text and gives a more professional appearance.
3. Use a color theme for the total presentation or to separate parts of the presentation. For example, use a blue background with white letters and yellow titles throughout the presentation. Avoid red letters as people find them hard to read.
4. Some fonts used in graphics programs don't produce nice slides. Obtain information on acceptable fonts from your slide processing center. Use upright block type fonts.
5. If using a film recorder, be sure the color palette is the same as that used by the film recorder. If not, change the palette in the graphics program. This decreases surprises with the final product.
6. Make sure the slide developer supports or can develop slides from the graphics programs you use. Tell the developer the name of the program, version number, and system platform. If not supported, ask for acceptable file formats. File format means how the program stores the file. Save your files in that format.

Once you create the presentation you need, process it to produce the 35mm slides. The following are some common ways of processing them.

Film recorder	Some computer labs have a computer with a film recorder attached to it. You create the graphics files and then the recorder, loaded with 35mm film, snaps a picture of the chart. The film is then taken to a developer for processing.
In-house	Many schools provide in-house slide development services. With these services, you submit slide files on a diskette or over a modem for processing. The service returns processed slides.
Commercial slide service	Many commercial slide services exist. These services operate like the in-house slide developers, but are usually more expensive. The service accepts files over a modem or by mail. Many will promise 24-hour turnaround time. Often you can submit your slides electronically.

KEY POINTS OF CREATING POWERPOINT PRESENTATIONS

Most of the preceding information also applies to PowerPoint presentations since you can create transparencies and 35mm slides in PowerPoint as well. So keep those ideas in mind in addition to the following ones.

1. Keep text concise; six to seven words maximum per slide. Use phrases to highlight the major points.
2. Use a consistent format as far as design templates, font style, and color.
3. Include graphics and images for emphasis as appropriate.
4. The best fonts are Times, Palatino, and Helvetica. Whatever you choose, be consistent.
5. Keep special effects to a minimum unless they add to your presentation.
6. Design and use an image for wait times (waiting to begin the presentation, breaks, etc.). If this is a conference where people might not be familiar with your school or organization, import a picture of it and/or a map locating it in the city.
7. Use a catchy logo or cartoon to add to the presentation or provide a humorous break from difficult material.

PRESENTATION GRAPHICS TERMINOLOGY

Here are additional terms used with presentation graphics.

Analytic	Analytic graphics present data in graph form for analysis, understanding, and decision making. You can use presentation graphics, spreadsheet, or statistic programs to create these graphs.
Bitmapped	Bitmapped refers to graphics images stored and represented by pixels or tiny dots. It is a common form for photo images. Examples are PIC, PCX, and TIF.
Bullet	A bullet is a graphic to the left of the text list. Different symbols represent the bullet such as a dot, arrow, block, or check.
Clip art:	Clip art is a library of symbols (images) prepared by others for use with specific graphics programs.
DPIs	DPIs (density per inch) represent pixel density or the number of dots (pixels) per inch. The larger the DPIs the better the resolution.
File format	File format is how the program stores the graphic or image. The file format is important for importing data and developing slides.
Handles	This is the term used to describe the squares that surround a selected image or block of text. Use them to move, enlarge, or shrink the image.
Labels	Labels refer to the groups that represent the content of graph slides. They help the user understand the graph. For example, the names given to each pie wedge or bar.

Landscape   Landscape refers to the orientation of the slide in a wide or horizontal view. Use this orientation to produce 35mm slides.

Pixels   Pixels are tiny dots or picture elements. The more pixels you have, the sharper the image or resolution.

Portrait   Portrait is the orientation of the slide in an upright or vertical view. Use this view for overhead transparencies.

Presentation   Presentation is the group of slides or charts that make up the actual material you want to present.

Resolution   Resolution is the number of pixels on the screen.

Slides   Slides are the individual screens you create.

Symbols   Symbols are the clip art or images available or importable into the presentation program.

Template   A professionally designed format and color scheme for a presentation. Some programs call this the presentation style.

Vector graphics   Vector graphics is an image created with lines, arcs, circles, and squares. This file format stores images as vector points. Some examples are CGM and PGL.

X-axis   X-axis is the horizontal reference lines or coordinates of a graph.

Y-axis   Y-axis is the vertical reference lines or coordinates of a graph.

INTRODUCTION TO POWERPOINT

PowerPoint comes with Office 97 for Windows' computers and with Office 98 for the Macintosh. You operate it very much the same on each system. This section is written using the Windows version. PowerPoint helps you design, create, and edit presentations. These presentations can be presented to your target audience in several ways: as transparencies, using computer screens; as Web pages, as 35mm slides, as handouts or notes, and even as a workbook.

You will discover that the PowerPoint screen has many similarities to Word and Excel, especially when you look at the menu and toolbars. For a quick overview go to Help, Choose Content and Index, and search for Create. You will see several possibilities under Create. Choose "creating presentations." When you have questions, remember the Help button, and be sure to use any documentation provided, or purchase your own at a local bookstore.

To start PowerPoint:

Click the **Start** button on the Taskbar, select **Programs**, then highlight **Microsoft Power-Point**. OR

Click the **PowerPoint** icon on the MS Office shortcut bar OR

Double click on a previously prepared **PowerPoint** presentation.

The main PowerPoint menu and toolbars are shown in Figure 6–1.

FIGURE 6–1.
MS PowerPoint Menu and Toolbars

As in Word and Excel, you can customize the toolbars. If you compare Figure 6–1 with Figures 5–1 (Word) and 7–1 (Excel), you will see how similar the menus and toolbars are. When you position your pointer over one of the toolbar buttons, a box appears telling you the name of the button. These floating toolbar button descriptions are called ToolTips.

PowerPoint has a Draw Menu, instead of a Table Menu (Word) or a Chart Menu (Excel). Even the menu commands are similar to Word and Excel, except many involve *Slides* in Power-Point. *Slide* refers to an overhead or slide. Here is a brief description of the PowerPoint menus.

PowerPoint Menus

File	These commands are similar to those in other Microsoft applications for New, Open, Save, and Print.
Edit	Contains the Select, Undo, Cut, Copy, Paste, Clear, Duplicate text or objects, Find, and Replace commands.
View	From View you choose Slide, Outline, Slide Sorter, Notes Pages, Slideshow, Master, Speaker Notes, Toolbars, and Zoom.
Insert	Allows you to insert a New Slide or add Date, Time, Slide Number, or import a Picture or Clip Art from other programs.
Format	Deals with font size, bullets, text, background, and alignment. You can adjust line spacing, case of text and change layout, template, or color scheme. The commands for "Presentation Template" and "Pick a Look Wizard" are here as well.
Tools	Contains commands for spelling and style and dialog boxes for building transitions and customizing your presentations.
Slide Show	Here is where you make settings for how your presentation will run if displayed on the computer screen. You can add sounds, animation, and special effects for transition between slides.

Window and Help are similar to the menus in other Office 97 programs.

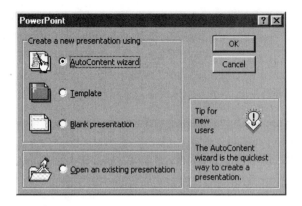

FIGURE 6–2.
Start PowerPoint Screen

Create a New Presentation

Start **PowerPoint**.

You will see the dialog box Create a New Presentation as shown in Figure 6–2. You are asked to chose between AutoContent Wizard, Template, Blank Presentation, or Open an existing presentation.

Choose **AutoContent Wizard** and click **OK**. When you create a new presentation using the AutoContent Wizard, you will be given help to develop your presentation by answering a series of questions.

The Start, or first, screen explains AutoContent Wizard. Click **Next**.

Select **One** of seven categories and click **Next**. Here you choose from all types of presentations (Figure 6–3).

The Wizard asks how the presentation will be used: for Presentations or for the Internet or a Kiosk. Select **Presentations** and click **Next**.

You are asked to choose between an On-screen presentation, Black and white overheads, Color overheads, or 35mm slides. Select **One**. You are also asked if you will Print handouts. Click **Yes** or **No** and then **Next**.

On the next screen you enter information for your title slide. Type **Title of Presentation, Your name, Title**, and **Institution** and click **Next**. A screen appears where you select Finish to view the document. Click **Finish**.

After you complete the AutoContent Wizard you are shown a sample outline with a default design. See Figure 6–4.

You can use this outline as a guide or highlight it and type in your own.

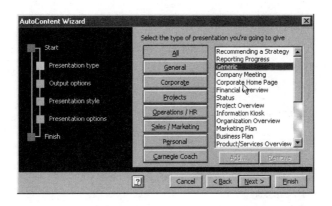

FIGURE 6-3.
Second Screen of AutoContent Wizard with Generic Presentation Selected

If you are already using PowerPoint and want to create a new presentation with the Auto-Content Wizard,

Click **File**, **New**.

Click the **Presentations** tab.

Double click the **AutoContent Wizard** and continue as above.

If you do not want to use the AutoContent Wizard but want to create a new presentation, select one of the other options—template or blank presentation.

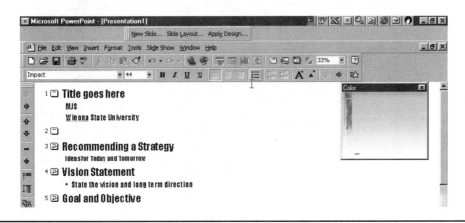

FIGURE 6-4.
Outline Screen That Appears After Finishing AutoContent Wizard

For a template:

> Click **File, New**.
>
> Click the **Presentation Design** tab.
>
> Double click a **Design**.
>
> Double click an **AutoLayout**.
>
> Type your **Content**.

When you select a blank presentation, you will skip the Design screen.

Developing Your Presentation

Usually you will want to choose either Blank Presentation or Template from the Start Power-Point Screen (Figure 6–2). When you click Template you will be given several templates from which to choose. After you choose one, you will see the New Slide screen with AutoLayouts as shown in Figure 6–5. This screen also appears when you choose Blank Presentation or if you choose New under the File menu.

AutoLayouts bring together five basic slide elements—charts, tables, titles, body text, and objects—in various combinations (Figure 6–5). Begin by choosing the **Title Slide**. It is shown in Figure 6–6. You can see that in Figure 6–6 there is no design applied to the slide.

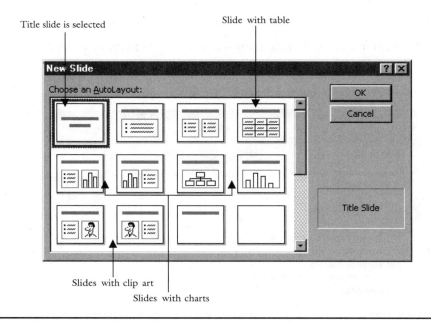

FIGURE 6–5.
New Slide Screen with Autolayouts

New Menu Bar

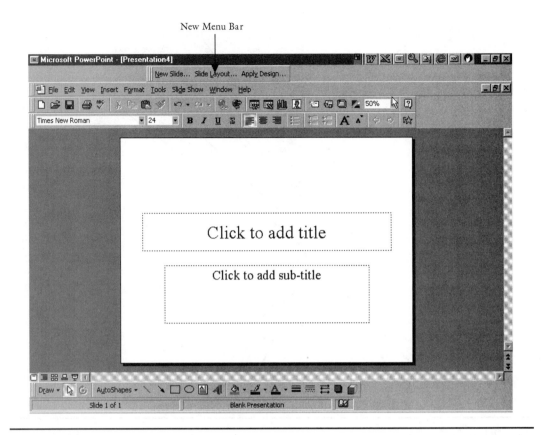

FIGURE 6–6.
New Slide Layout

Note the new Common Tasks Control Toolbar on top of the Standard Toolbar above the menus in Figure 6–6. (If you don't have this toolbar on your screen, go to **View, Toolbars,** and add the **Common Tasks Control** Toolbar.) It contains three choices: N̲ew Slide…Slide L̲ayout…Appl̲y Design…. You can click on Apply Design and review the many design examples that PowerPoint gives you. When you click on a design, it appears on your slide. If you were in the outline view a sample slide would appear at the right of the screen. When you choose a design always consider whether you are preparing transparencies or slides.

Once you have chosen the design for your slides, you can begin typing the presentation. You can type directly on the actual slide or go to the Outline View. Outline View works well for organizing your presentation and ensuring a logical flow to your ideas. It is easy to add or delete parts of the outline. If you work in the outline mode you will see the toolbar shown in Figure 6–7. The arrow buttons help you easily promote bulleted items to titles or demote something to a lesser part of the outline. Note that objects on the slide do not appear in Outline View; text created as an object or with TextArt does not show in Outline View. The only text that shows in this view is text in text place holders.

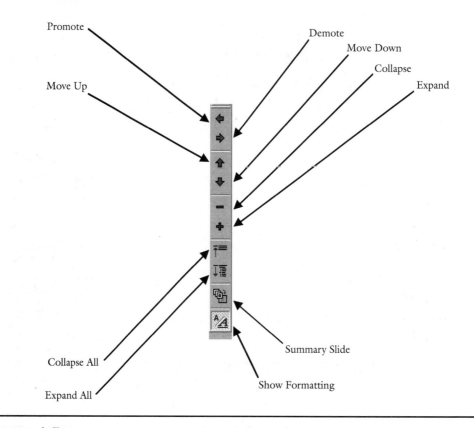

FIGURE 6–7.
Outline Toolbar

As you work on your presentation you may find the need to use the table, chart, or graphic template. Go to **New Slide** or **Slide Layout** on the **Common Tasks Control Toolbar**. You will get the screen shown in Figure 6–5. Pick the one you want and proceed from there to prepare the slide.

You can always move back and forth between the outline and slide. In fact, after you type an outline segment go to the slide show and review your slide. View buttons will help you do this.

View Buttons

Figure 6–8 shows you the View buttons you use to scroll through the different views of your slide presentation. The View buttons are located just above the status bar at the bottom of the screen. You will find these same choices under View in the menu bar. You can go between these views anytime during your work by clicking on one of the View buttons.

Slide View   Lets you see each slide as the audience will see it, one at a time, and modify it as needed. The double-arrow keys at the bottom of the right scroll bar allow you to go back and forth between slides.

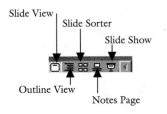

FIGURE 6–8.
View Buttons

Outline View	Lets you edit and see all your presentation text in one location. It helps you organize your ideas.
Slide Sorter View	Displays the whole presentation so that you can move slides around. It allows you to preview your presentation. To move a slide, simply click on it and drag it to a new location. After you have outlined the presentation, look at each slide in the slide view. This is the time to make format changes and decide if you want to add clip art or animation.
Notes Page View	Lets you create and edit notes for the presentation's speaker. Click the notes section, go to the zoom box, and choose a larger percent (80 or 100 percent). Then you can see what notes you type. You can also access Speaker Notes under the View menu.
Slide Show	This is the best way to view your slide show. You can check transitions from one slide to another or any special effects or sounds. Press the Esc Key or right click the mouse to end the Slide Show.

Adding Clip Art

More than 500 clip art pictures are included with PowerPoint. There is a Find feature that helps you find a particular piece of clip art. You can also add pictures to the Art Gallery from CD collections, from the Web, or even scan in a photo.

Click **New slide** button.

Select a **Slide with a graphic** on it from the AutoLayout template.

Double click the **Picture image** and the Clip Art Gallery opens.

From the slide view, you can also select **Insert, Picture**, from the menu bar and choose Picture from Clip Art or a picture from a file. If you use the Clip Art Gallery for the first time, PowerPoint must create a clip art database, so click **Yes** in the dialog box if it comes up. This will take some time. When the art is loaded you will get a dialog box like the one shown in Figure 6–9.

Click a **Category**, scroll through it, and click a **Picture**.

Click **OK** and you will see the clip art in your slide.

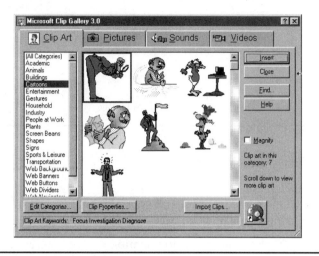

FIGURE 6–9.
PowerPoint Clip Art Gallery

Click inside the box and handles will appear so that you can move the art to the best position in the slide.

Use the handles (little squares) around the picture to change the size. This works just like sizing a window. When you have the double-headed arrow, drag the mouse to enlarge or reduce its size.

You will also see the Picture Toolbar shown in Figure 6–10. It is used to modify inserted pictures. It appears automatically when you insert a picture if you have Picture checked under View, Toolbars, Picture.

If you want to insert a picture from a CD collection, go to **Insert** menu.

Choose **Picture**, then **From File**.

Choose the **File location**, select the **file**, and click **Insert**.

You can also find many images on the Internet. A free, general clip art site is: http://www.barrysclipart.com.

Go to a category and browse until you find an image. Right click the **Image**. Select **Save Target As...**; a menu will appear asking where you want to save the graphic.

Specify a **Folder** and a **File name**.

You may want to set up an Image folder on your hard drive for images so you know where to find them. If you are using a lab computer, use a diskette specifically for images. Refer to Chapter 3 for creating folders.

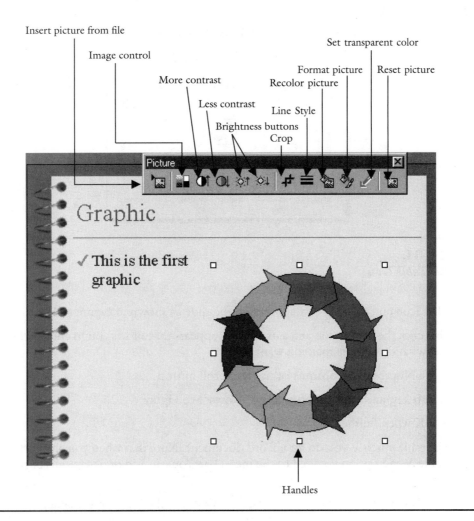

FIGURE 6–10.
Slide with Graphic Showing Handles and Picture Toolbar

Adding a Table

Tables are used to summarize data, categories, research results, or to help the reader make comparisons between things.

To add a table:

Click the **New Slide** button on the toolbar or **Insert, New Slide** from menu bar.

Double click the **Table AutoLayout**.

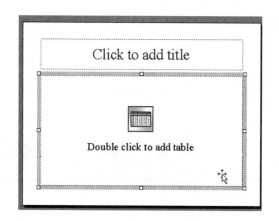

FIGURE 6–11.
Slide with Table Icon

A **Table** icon and a dialog box appears on the slide as shown in Figure 6–11.

Double click the **Table** icon and a dialog box appears that allows you to choose the number of rows and columns that you want.

Type the **Number** of **Columns** or use the scroll button.

Press **Tab** key, and type the **Number** of **Rows**. See Figure 6–12.

Click **OK** when finished.

Prepare the table much as you do for a Word document. Note that when you are working in the table, a Table Menu option is added to the menu bar. You can add or delete cells or rows as you can in Word.

When you complete the table contents, click **Outside** the table on the slide.

Select the **Title** place holder.

Type the **Title** of the slide.

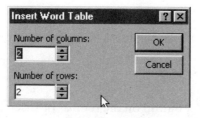

FIGURE 6–12.
Insert Word Table Dialog Box

Remember, however, that you have a limited amount of space on a slide. You can also import a table that has been prepared in Word.

Adding a Chart (Graph)

To add a chart or graph:

Select **New** **button**.

Double click **Chart slide** from AutoLayout. A chart slide has a chart icon showing as in Figure 6–13. There are several versions of chart layouts—one with a chart to the left of bullets, one to the right of bullets, and one full slide chart.

Double click the **Graph** icon on the slide (AutoLayout) or click the **Insert, Chart** from the menu bar.

The graph application program starts and you get a Standard Toolbar at the top of the screen. A new datasheet is displayed with a chart object behind it. It has a set of default values with a 3-D default chart behind it.

Highlight (select) the **Cells** and press the **Delete** key to clear the datasheet or go to **Edit** on the menu bar, and select **Clear, All**.

Select **Chart** from the menu and choose **Chart Type**. You will get a list of chart types on the left with pictures of subtypes on the right.

Click **One** that fits your data and click **OK**.

Pie charts are good for one set of data values to compare to a whole. Bar and column charts compare different items over time. Line charts show progress over time or multiple data sets.

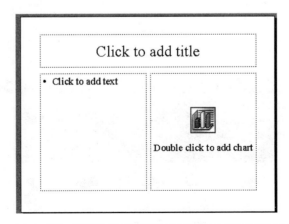

FIGURE 6–13.
Slide with Chart Icon

Filling in the data sheet is much like doing an Excel spreadsheet. Once you enter the data, if the data sheet has too many columns, clear the ones you don't need. You can also add rows and columns. Since we cleared the sample data sheet, you are ready to type your data. Figure 6–14 shows a highlighted data sheet overlaid on a slide.

Type the **Numbers** and **Labels**.

Click **Your slide**. The data sheet disappears and the graph appears.

Single click the graph and it can then be moved or changed as you wish. Double click it and the data sheet returns.

Under the Insert menu you will see commands for inserting a text box if you need a caption. Even the color of the graph can be changed. Under Format, choose Slide Color Scheme. You

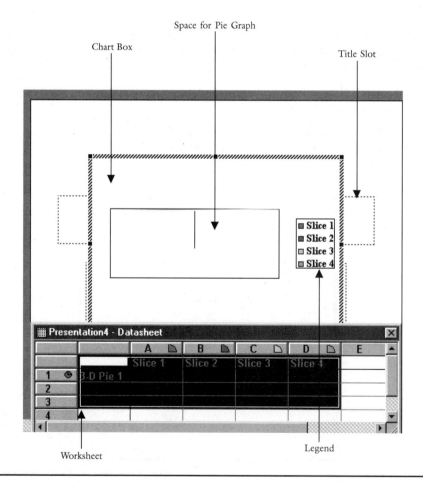

FIGURE 6–14.
Datasheet for Preparing a Pie Chart

get a dialog box that allows you to choose different colors. At this point you can change the type of graph if you find that the one you selected isn't as clear as you would like it. You can also prepare the data sheet in Excel and import the graph into your slide by using the Insert command.

There is much more to learn about graphs and charts so be sure to look at the documentation that comes with PowerPoint and keep experimenting.

Adding Transitions to a Slide Show

When you do your presentation as an electronic slide show, you can add transitions to parts or all of the slide show. Figure 6–15 shows the Selection screen for adding transitions to a presentation and the Help instructions available to you.

Click the **Slide Show** menu.

Click **Slide Transition**.

As you select the different transitions available, you see them in the box on the screen. You can apply the transition to all slides or to selected ones. Be sure to view your transitions with Slide Show.

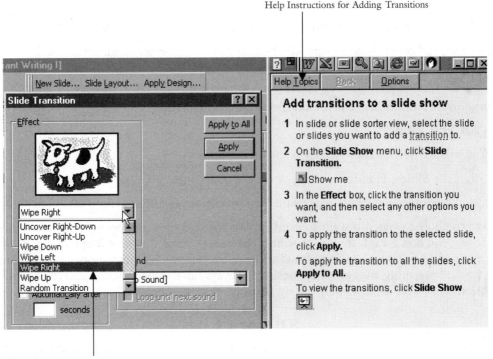

FIGURE 6–15.
Slide Transition Selection Screen and Help Instructions

Changing a Presentation Design

You can always change the design of a presentation. When your presentation is open,

> Select **Format** and **Apply Design** OR click **Apply Design** button on the Common Tasks Control Toolbar.

> Choose **Another** design.

To change text or objects for all the slides in the presentation use the Master Slides. This is the template used for all slides in the presentation and is where you add things such as corporate or university logos to all your slides. It is also the place to change the text properties of all slides.

> Select **View, Master, Slide Master**.

> Select the **Text** or **text holder** on the Slide Master that you want to change.

> Change the **Text** properties. For example, bold, shadow, 30 points.

Sometimes you will need to change the font size on only one slide.

> View the slide in **Slide View**.

> Select the **Text** that needs to be changed.

> Change the **Text** properties with the format toolbar or Format, Font menu.

Color, style, and other characteristics can be changed with Format menu command.

Printing with PowerPoint

To print overheads, audience handouts, notes, or a presentation outline:

> Click **File, Print**.

> You will see the Selection Screen as shown in Figure 6–16.

> Select the **Slides, Handouts** (2, 3, or 6 per page), **Notes page**, or **Outline**.

> Check the other settings to make sure they are correct and click **OK**.

Be sure to choose what you want to print or you will end up with copies of all your slides or something you don't want. If you are printing handouts, print 1 page of 3 or 6 to a page to see which one will work the best for your audience. Avoid printing handouts until you are sure you have finished preparing and revising your slides. Always run the spell checker and consider using AutoCorrect to handle misspellings along the way.

SUMMARY

PowerPoint is a powerful presentation program that will help you produce presentations that are professional and make your points with the audience. This introduction is only a start in getting acquainted with all the things you can do with PowerPoint. There are many more things you can do with PowerPoint, such as audio or motion clips, or putting a presentation on the Web. You will have much more to learn as you continue to prepare presentations using PowerPoint.

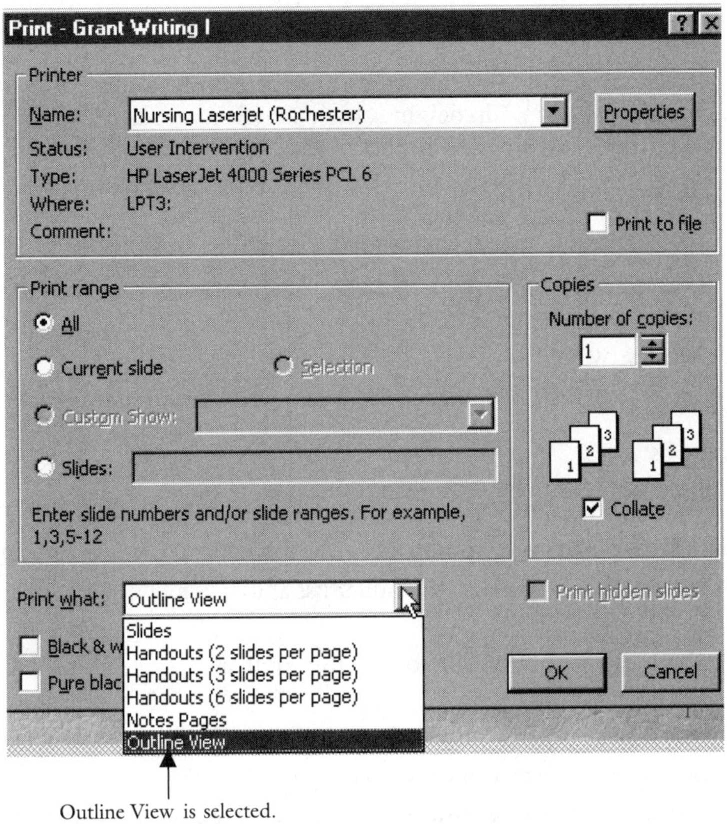

Outline View is selected.

FIGURE 6–16.
Print Selection Screen

EXERCISE 1: CREATE A TEXT AND IMAGE CHART WITH A WORD PROCESSOR

Objectives

1. Create a computer-generated overhead using text and an image.
2. Save and print the image.

Activity

1. Start **Word**.
2. Select font and font size.

Click the **Font Down arrow** ▼ button on the Formatting Toolbar and select **Times New Roman**.

Click the **Size Down arrow** ▼ button on the formatting toolbar and select **40** points. The letters should be about $\frac{1}{4}$" in height. Other serif fonts are also OK. Serif fonts have the little feet on the letters and are used for body text.

3. Create the title.

   Type **Tips on Creating Transparencies** for the title.

   Click the **Center Justification** ▤ button to center it.

   Press the **Enter** key twice.

   Does it all fit on one line? If not, center the title on two different lines.

4. Create a bullet list.

   Click the **Left Justification** ▤ button if it is not selected.

   Click the **Size Down-arrow** ▼ button on the formatting toolbar and select **22** points.

   Type **Limit text to 7 lines** making the bullet list about $\frac{1}{4}$ inch in height.

   Click the **Bullet** ▤ button on the formatting toolbar.

   Click the **Print Preview** ▤ button. Does it look OK? If not, correct it.

   Click the **Close** button to exit Print Preview.

   Press the **Enter** key and type **4 more points** about creating transparencies pressing the **Enter** key after each item.

   Press **CTRL+A** to highlight all the text.

   Click the **Bold** **B** button.

5. Save your document.

   Click the **Save** 🖫 button on the standard toolbar.

   Select the **3½" floppy disk (Drive A)** in the Save in text box.

   Highlight the **Text** in the **File name** text box, type a **Name**, and press **Enter**.

6. Check for spelling errors.

   Right click any **Red wavy** line and make the appropriate selection.

   Right click any **Green wavy** line and make the appropriate selection.

   Note: If you don't have the spell checker turned on, then select Tools, Spelling and Grammar checker and follow the directions.

7. Add a symbol.

Place the Insertion point at the end of the document and press the **Enter** key twice.

Select **Insert, Picture,** and **Clip Art**.

Double click an appropriate image.

Most programs come with a limited number of symbols or clip art. Make sure you place and size it so it is pleasing to the eye.

8. **Save** and **Print** the document.

Click the **Save** 💾 button.

Click the **Printer** 🖨 button.

EXERCISE 2: CREATING AN OVERHEAD WITH POWERPOINT

Objectives

1. Create a computer-generated overhead using text and an image.
2. Save and print the image.
3. Explain or describe what happens when menu commands are issued.
4. Use the screen menus to complete the transparency.

Activity

1. Start **PowerPoint**. What options do you see in front of you?

2. Create a presentation.

Choose **AutoContent Wizard** and click **OK**. Click **Next**.

Click **Generic** for type of presentation and **Next**.

Click **Presentations** and **Next**. Click **On screen** and click **Next**.

Type **To Your Health** for the title, **your name, title, institution,** and click **Next, Finish**.

3. Enter and edit the content.

Click the **Slide sorter** ⊞ button on the bottom left of the screen (in the middle). Hold down the **Shift** key while clicking on slides **5** through **9**.

Press the **Delete** key.

Double click **Slide 1.**

Click **Your name text** place holder and drag to the **bottom right** screen.

Click the **Next slide** ⊻ button.

Click **Title place holder** and highlight **Introduction**. Type **Diet and Exercise**.

Click the **Bullet text holder** and highlight **All bullets.**

Type **Balance exercise with diet.** and press **Enter.**

Type **Don't overdo either one.** and press **Enter.**

Type **Select food and activities you enjoy.** Click **Next slide** ⊻ button.

Click **Slide layout** option on the Common Tasks Control Toolbar.

Double click **Clip Art and Text** option.

Click **Title place holder** and highlight **Title.**

Type **The Food Pyramid.**

Double click the **Clip Art** icon, select **Food and Dining category**, and double click the **Chef**.

Click the **Clip Art** and use the **Handles to resize it.**

Highlight the **Bullet** text and type **Fats—2–3 per day** and press **Enter.**

Type the remaining bullets pressing **Enter** after each one but the last one.

> Milk & Meat—**2–3 per day**
>
> Vegetables & Fruits—**2–5 per day**
>
> Bread & Cereal—**6–11 per day**

Click **Next slide** ⊻ button.

Click **Title place holder** and highlight **Title.**

Type **Have Fun!** If you still have a bullet text holder, click it and click **Cut** button.

Click the **Clip Art** icon on the toolbar, select **People category**, and double click the **Man lifting weights**.

Click the **Clip Art** and use the **Handles to resize it**. Make it much larger.

4. How do you use the spell checker? Go to the top of your slides and run the the spell checker.

5. How do you alter the font size, change the font, and alter the bullets?

6. View each slide individually using **Slide view**. Do you need to make changes?

7. Now view the whole slide presentation.

Click the **Slide Show** 🖥 button.

Does it look OK? If not, what can you do to change it?

8. Save your presentation. Give it a name that makes sense. Save your file on your diskette in the A drive using the Save as command. Close PowerPoint.

9. Open the presentation again.

10. Now add a slide to it. (Go to the end and click the **New slide** button.)

11. Save the presentation. Print the outline and slides.

EXERCISE 3: TABLE, LINE, PIE, AND BAR GRAPHS

Note: You can do this exercise with PowerPoint or Excel, but we prefer you to practice with PowerPoint. The table can also be done in Word.

Objectives

1. Create a computer-generated table, bar, pie, and line graphs that you can use to create transparencies or use in a PowerPoint presentation.
2. Save and print the slide/transparency.

Activity

1. Create a line chart and table using the following data.

    Create a **New** presentation and select the **Chart** option.

    Select the **Title text** and type **Projected FTE Requirements and Supply of RNs in the US**.

    Double click the **Chart** icon in the middle of the slide.

    Type the following data.

Year	Requirements (A)	Supply (B)
2000	1,969,000	1,987,000
2005	2,095,000	2,128,000
2010	2,232,000	2,214,000
2015	2,391,000	2,277,000
2020	2,575,000	2,284,000

Click the slide and look at it. Now, change it to a line chart.

Double click the **Chart**, click the **Chart type** button down arrow and select **3-D line**.

Click the **Slide**, **Save** and **Print** it.

Now create a new slide with the same data in a **Table**.

Which one presents the data in the clearest manner?

2. Create a pie chart using the following data.

    Follow directions above but create a **pie** chart.

Title:	Medicaid/Medicare Expenditures Fiscal Year 1997	
Items:	Home Care	14 %
	Physician	18 %
	Hospital	43 %
	Skilled Care	24 %
	Others	1 %

    Save and **Print** it. What alterations can be done on this pie to enhance it?

3. Create a line chart using the following data.

Title:	Present and Future Sales of Computers	
Data:	X-axis	Y-axis
	1992	4 billion dollars
	1994	5.5 billion dollars
	1996	10.5 billion dollars
	1998	20 billion dollars
	2000	36 billion dollars
	2002	50 billion dollars

    Save and **Print** it.

ASSIGNMENT 1: CREATE PIE, LINE, AND BAR CHARTS

Directions

1. Create a pie chart with the following data using PowerPoint.

   Title: 1992 Racial/Ethnic Background of Nurses in US

   Types: White: 1,984,175

   Black: 90,911

   Asian/Pacific Islanders: 75,785

   Hispanic: 39,441

   American Indian/Alaska Native: 9,988

   (Total 2.2 million—add this figure using the text box.)

   Move the legend to the bottom of the slide.

   Enhance the title of the slide.

   Try different styles of the pie charts. Pick the one that most clearly shows the data.

   Save and **Print** the slide.

   Under what conditions would you use a pie chart?

2. Create a stacked bar graph from the following data:

   Title: Projected types of graduates from collegiate nursing education programs

	Generic	Post RN Baccalaureate	Post RN Masters
1999–2000	26,492	13,175	9,946
2004–2005	29,481	12,542	7,415
2009–2010	32,905	12,929	9,681
2014–2015	34,007	13,306	10,202
2019–2020	33,352	13,518	10,373

You may need to use just the last part of the year. Use a slide with only a title on it so you have more room for the bar graphs and legend.

Save and **Print** the slide.

3. Create a line chart using the following data:

   Title: Labor and Delivery Payroll Hours

Month	Actual	Budget
January	3,377.04	2,800.90
February	2,708.70	2,537.49
March	3,175.72	2,800.90
April	3,303.97	2,702.37
May	2,906.58	2.800.90
June	2,887.66	2,702.37
July	2,768.17	2,800.90
August	3,101.77	2,800.90
September	2,725.11	2,702.37
October	2,871.03	2,800.90
November	2,835.76	2,702.37
December	2,860.37	2,800.94

Save and **Print** it. Under what conditions would you use a line graph? Submit this sheet along with your printouts if so instructed.

ASSIGNMENT 2: PREPARATION A POWERPOINT PRESENTATION

Directions

1. Prepare a PowerPoint presentation on a topic related to technology in health care that you will present using a computer and data projector. Use your creativity and knowledge gained from this chapter to produce quality slides following the good design tips given throughout the chapter.

2. Include a minimum of 15 slides with at least one title slide, one table, one chart/graph, and some clip art. Use some variety in the layout of the slides. You should not have more than three bullet list slides in a row. Use some of the shapes to enhance the slide.

3. Use a transition between slides.

4. Print an outline and a handout with three slides to a page. Prepare at least one "Notes" page. Turn in the papers if so instructed.

Chapter 7

Spreadsheet

OBJECTIVES

1. Identify uses of the spreadsheet in general as well as for health care applications.
2. Define basic terminology related to spreadsheets.
3. Review selected functions for using Excel 97.

INTRODUCTION TO SPREADSHEETS

Spreadsheets do for numbers and charts what word processing does for writing. Though their strength is their function as numeric calculators, most spreadsheets also have a database management component for organizing, sorting, and retrieving information, and a chart component for creating and printing graphs. In this chapter, you will learn how to use the spreadsheet as an electronic calculator. Advantages of computerized spreadsheets include accuracy and speed. Spreadsheets also have the capacity to automatically recalculate formulas when any numbers used in the calculation are changed. Spreadsheets have many uses; they can be used for inventories, tax returns, patient records, grade records, personnel files, budgets, and quality assurance information.

COMMON SPREADSHEET TERMS

Rows	Rows run horizontally across the spreadsheet, numbered beginning with 1 down the left side of the spreadsheet. Though the maximum number of rows varies with different spreadsheets, they may have as many as 65,536 rows.
Columns	Columns go vertically down the spreadsheet, labeled from left to right, A to Z. After Z, labeling continues with AA to AZ, BA to BZ, and so on, usually for 256 columns.
Cell	A cell is a place holder for data. Each cell occurs at a specific intersection of a row and column. Cells are labeled by the column letter followed by the row number, for example, A1 or T112.

Cell Address or Cell Reference	The label for each cell is called the cell address or cell reference.
Active Cell	The active cell is the cell currently being used; it is outlined or highlighted so it can be quickly seen on the spreadsheet. The address of the active cell appears in a designated location on the spreadsheet screen.
Range or Block	A group of cells in a rectangular pattern defined by the top left and bottom right corners is called a range or block of cells. For example, a range of cells from A1 to E6 would include all the cells in columns A, B, C, D, and E in rows 1, 2, 3, 4, 5, and 6. When you are working with a block of cells on a spreadsheet, they are identified as a dark rectangle. Blocks of cells may also be noncontiguous.
Workbook or Notebook	A workbook or notebook is a collection of spreadsheet pages. In some spreadsheet programs, pages in a notebook are numbered; in others they are labeled by a letter. All the pages are saved together in one file.
Worksheet	Spreadsheet pages are also called worksheets in many programs. In some programs when the worksheet is blank, they are called sheets. When they contain data, they are called worksheets.
Template	This is a spreadsheet formatted with labels and formulas but no specific data; it is helpful when multiple uses of the same spreadsheet are needed. Use a template for a yearly budget for yourself or your health care unit. The labels you use and the way you calculate your figures remain stable from one year to the next, only the figures change.

SPREADSHEET SCREEN DISPLAY

The screen displays for most spreadsheets are similar. Spreadsheets look like a page from an accountant's ledger with many rows and columns. A series of letters, denoting columns, goes horizontally across the screen and a series of numbers, denoting rows, runs vertically along the left hand side of the screen. As with other Windows programs (previously discussed in Chapters 3 and 4), the menu bar and any additional toolbars are located across the uppermost part of the screen; scroll bars appear along the right and bottom of the screen. Features specific to the spreadsheet screen display include the current cell address, formula bar or input line, and the message area. See Figure 7–1.

Current Cell Address	This indicates the active cell and is usually located near the top left of the screen.
Formula Bar or Input line	The data or formula you are entering appears in this location on your screen.
Message Area	This shows what actions will occur when a function or button is activated. It may also show error messages. It is usually located in the lower left corner of the screen.

Input Line/Formula Bar

Cancel Button
Enter Button

Cell Address

Edit Formula

Temporary
File Name

Active Cell

Worksheets

Message Area

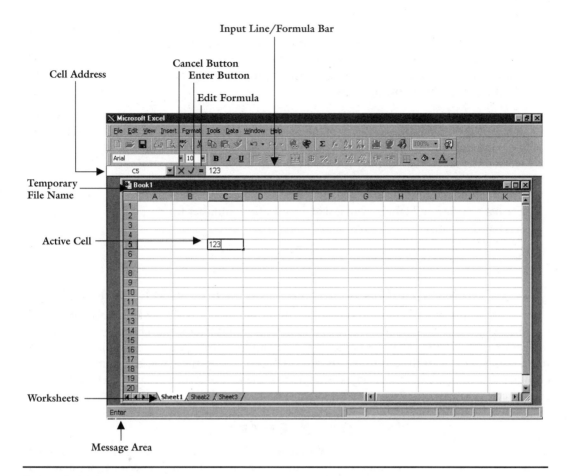

FIGURE 7–1.
Excel Screen Display

GETTING READY TO USE A SPREADSHEET

Prior to beginning spreadsheet use, it is important to carefully consider the goals of your project so that you can develop a spreadsheet that is optimally useful. Consider the following:

1. What type of data do you want to put in the spreadsheet, e.g., text such as labels for individuals or inventory supply information, or numbers for income or expenses?
2. Are time intervals going to be used, e.g., monthly, quarterly, or yearly?
3. Do you want to be able to make comparisons, e.g., between units or across time periods?
4. How much data do you have? Can you use one worksheet or would it be better to divide data into several?

It is often most logical to place categories of data in columns since the width of columns can be customized to the data. The specific data for each record, situation, or individual can then be entered in each column under the category headings.

Once you have determined the goals of your project, the general process for creating the worksheet includes the following steps:

- Enter spreadsheet-identifying information on the first few rows. This includes data such as name of the organization, department or division, the project (quarterly budget, inventory), and spreadsheet originator.
- Next, enter labels that identify the columns and rows.
- Enter data.
- Enter formulas and functions.
- Format the data and labels (fonts, size, justification, number format, etc.).
- Format the worksheet (borders, shading, etc.).
- Create charts or graphs.
- Print worksheets, and/or charts.

ACCOMPLISHING TASKS IN THE WORKSHEET

Moving about the worksheet is accomplished using the mouse or arrow keys alone or in combination with other keys on a keyboard (more details on this later in the chapter). As you move, the active cell is highlighted and noted as the cell address. In order to accomplish a task, you select commands from the menu bar or click on icons. Using the scroll bar to move does not change the active cell; it only changes your view of the spreadsheet until you click in the worksheet area.

DATA ENTRY

Spreadsheets allow the user to enter two types of data, *constants* and *formulas*. Constants include dates, numbers, text, logical values, and error values. Formulas perform mathematical operations such as calculating the mathematical relationships between the constants on the worksheet. When you change the constants, the formulas are still there, and the results on the spreadsheet are recalculated to keep your spreadsheet up-to-date.

To enter data:

Click the **Cell** in which the data will be entered. The cell address will be displayed and the cell will be highlighted or outlined.

Type the **Data** into the cell.

Press **Enter,** click in another cell, or press an **Arrow** key.

When typing the data, you will see your data in the input line. You can see an example of this in Figure 7–1 where data has been typed into C5, the active cell. While there are a variety of ways to enter data into the cell, the most common is by pressing **Enter** or clicking the mouse. In some programs, data is entered automatically when you move to another cell. If you enter data into a cell that already has data, you will overwrite the original data. Typically in spreadsheets, text is aligned to the left and numeric values are aligned to the right.

When you enter data, the numbers 0 to 9 and certain characters are treated like numbers unless you indicate otherwise. Other characters commonly treated as numbers include:

$- +. ( ) \$ \% / *$

Any number is treated as positive (+) unless you place a negative sign (−) in front of it. When you place a % after a number, it may be displayed differently. For example, 45% will appear as .45. Some spreadsheet programs automatically convert any numbers you begin with a $ to a decimal. For example, if you type $12, it will be displayed as $12.00. In other spreadsheets you control the way the percentages and dollars are displayed through format functions.

The following numeric operators commonly are used in formulas:

Symbol	Meaning	Symbol	Meaning
^	exponentiation	=	equals
*	multiplication	/	division
+	addition	−	subtraction
<	less than	>	greater than

When multiple numeric operators appear in a formula, the formula is calculated using certain ordering rules. Most often the standard rules of precedence are used. The first operator evaluated is exponentiation, followed by multiplication and division, lastly addition and subtraction; if there is a tie, calculation proceeds from left to right. Calculations enclosed in parentheses will always be calculated before other operations.

Example: 5*4+3 would calculate as 20+3 or 23

5*(4+3) would calculate as 5*7 or 35

SAVING WORKSHEETS

Each spreadsheet program has specific conventions for saving. Like word processing programs, spreadsheets replace newer versions of a worksheet or notebook by overwriting older versions. The cautions that relate to saving word processing documents are equally important with worksheets and notebooks. Save often and before you try something new!

USING CHARTS

One of the last tasks you complete when creating worksheets is the chart. Since the data in a spreadsheet can be more easily understood in graphic form, all spreadsheets come with the ability to create charts. A good chart lets the reader instantly see the point being made by the data. It graphically displays the data.

To create a chart:

Select the **Data** to be graphed.

Choose the **Chart** type.

Select and orient the **Data range and series**.

Type chart options—like **Title** and **Labels** for X- and Y-axis.

Choose a **Location** for the chart—this worksheet or a new one.

Some new terms related to charts are defined here:

Axis	The horizontal (x) and vertical (y) plane or line on which the data is plotted is the axis. It provides a comparison or measurement point.
Categories	Categories are labels given the X- and Y-axis.
Chart Type	This refers to the way the chart will display the data. Some examples are pie or bar charts.
Data Series	A data series is a group of related data points on a chart that originated from rows and columns in the worksheet. These values are used to plot the chart.
Legend	The legend is a box that identifies the pattern or color of a specific data series or category.

While the Wizard makes it easy to create the charts, only the person knowledgeable about the data knows the best type of chart to use in displaying the data. For example, if you are comparing parts to a whole, such as the department's budgets to the total budget, then you might use a pie chart. Some questions you might ask yourself when creating a chart are:

1. Is this the right chart to convey the data in the worksheet?
2. How would you expect to see this data displayed?
3. Does it add to understanding the data and help the audience make decisions?
4. What questions or solutions does the chart suggest?

INTRODUCTION TO EXCEL

There are a number of spreadsheets available for use. This chapter focuses on Excel 97. Excel is available for both the Macintosh and Windows operating systems. Although this chapter provides specific information about the Office 97 version of Excel for Windows, the Office 98 version of Excel for the Macintosh is very similar. Since Excel operates in a Windows environment, the features common to Windows and outlined in Chapters 3 and 4 also apply to Excel. Starting Excel is done just like starting other Windows programs. Click the **Start** button at the lower left of the screen, select **Programs**, then highlight and click **Microsoft Excel**. If there is an MS Office

Shortcut toolbar with the Excel icon on your screen, you may click on this and save a step. See the toolbar in Figure 4–6. Ask your lab assistant if you are unsure how to access the program.

The Menu Bar and Commands

Refer back to Figure 4–1 and you can see how similar the menu bar for Excel is to that of Word. Only one menu item is different; Excel has *Data* whereas Word has *Table*. Many of the icons in the toolbar below the menu bar are also the same. Like Word, you can use the menu bar and mouse to select commands and options. For basic spreadsheet use, File, Edit, View, and Help operate as previously described (Chapter 4). Uses specific to spreadsheets for the other commands on the menu are outlined here.

Insert	Use this for adding rows or columns or page breaks. The chart and function wizards are also located in this menu option.
Format	Use this menu to format cells, rows, columns, and worksheets. You can control how numbers are displayed and aligned, such as in currency or percent. You can also choose the font style (bold or italic), add a border or pattern, protect a cell, or make a column width narrower or wider. The AutoFormat command for selecting predesigned spreadsheets and the sheet command for renaming sheets are also located in this menu option.
Tools	Use this menu for spelling, auditing, and sharing your worksheet. The option command is also located here. Use it to customize Excel.
Data	Use this to sort or filter data when you set your spreadsheet to function as a database or access data from an external source.
Window	Use this to split your window into several parts. When working with long spreadsheets you may want to see selected parts of the spreadsheet. Use the Freeze Panes with larger spreadsheets to keep the labels displayed on the screen when accessing rows and columns that exceed the width of your screen. Remember this is also the command to use when switching from one spreadsheet to another.

The Toolbars

There are many icons in the toolbars that are similar to those in Word. The menu and toolbars are also essentially the same for the Windows and Macintosh versions of Excel. On the Standard Toolbar, from left to right, icons similar to Word are Open a New Workbook, Open Another Document, Save, Print, Print Preview, Check Spelling, Cut, Copy, Paste, Format Painter, Undo, Redo, Add a Hyperlink, and Access the Web toolbar. At the far right, like Word, the last icon is the Help button and the one to the immediate left is the Zoom control. Other icons between these are specific to spreadsheet functions and provide shortcuts for Excel commands. These buttons are AutoSum, Function Wizard, Sort Ascending, Sort Descending, Chart Wizard, Map, and Drawing Tool (see Figure 7–2). Use the mouse to move the arrow slowly just inside the icon, and Excel will show you the command function of the icon. These icons allow you to perform the following functions in Excel.

AutoSum

This button automatically sums a selected series of numbers and puts the total in a designated blank space. It looks to the cells above first. If no values are there to sum, it looks to the cells to the left. You can override the cell range to sum.

Function Wizard

This button opens a dialog box that allows you to select functions such as mathematical or statistical formulas or date functions, and assists you to complete the formula for that calculation.

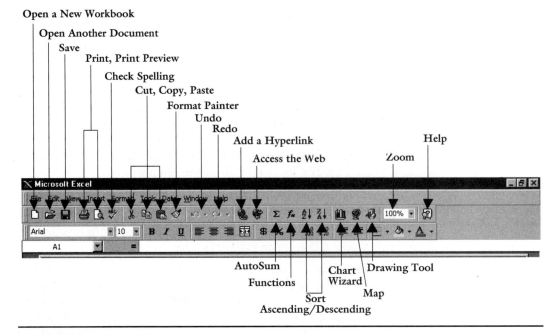

Open a New Workbook
Open Another Document
Save
Print, Print Preview
Check Spelling
Cut, Copy, Paste
Format Painter
Undo
Redo
Add a Hyperlink
Access the Web
Help
Zoom

AutoSum
Functions
Chart Wizard
Drawing Tool
Map
Sort Ascending/Descending

FIGURE 7–2.
Excel Standard Toolbar and Icons

Sort Ascending

This button sorts according to ascending numbers or letters, i.e., beginning with the letter closest to the beginning of the alphabet or the smallest number used.

Sort Descending

This button sorts according to descending numbers or letters, i.e., beginning with the letter closest to the end of the alphabet or the largest number used.

Chart Wizard

This button opens a dialog window presenting commonly used graphs such as bar, line, or pie and helps the user develop the selected graph.

Map

This map button is a special function to represent data with geographic maps. This component usually must be added by custom installation before use.

Drawing Tool

This button provides a toolbar with tools for drawing lines, shapes, creating text art, or changing colors.

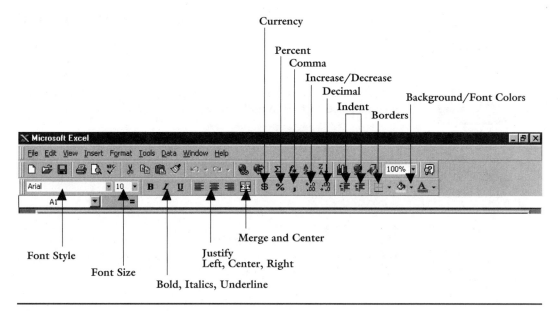

FIGURE 7–3.
Excel Formatting Toolbar

Like the **Standard Toolbar**, the Formatting Toolbar contains many features that are the same as those in Word. (See Figure 7–3.) Beginning on the far left are Font Style and Size, Bold, Underline, and Italics icons, and Justification options. As in Word, these are used to change the format of text and its placement (left, right, or center) in the cell. Next you see the icons unique to Excel: Merge and Center, Currency, Percent, Comma, Increase and Decrease Decimals, Increase and Decrease Indent, Borders, and Colors icons. To use most of these, you merely select the cell or cells to which the command will apply, click the icon, and where presented with a dialog window, click the selection desired.

Merge and Center

When a single cell with data is selected, this button centers the data. When a cell range is selected, it merges the selected cells and centers them across the columns; if the cells include multiple rows and have data, some data will be lost.

Currency

This button automatically formats selected cells in currency format, e.g., 4 becomes $4.00.

Percent

This button automatically formats selected cells in percent format, e.g., 5 becomes 500%.

Commas

This button automatically inserts commas in appropriate places and adds two decimal places.

↑ and ↓ Decimals

For selected cells, the first button adds and the second subtracts one decimal place with each mouse click.

↑ and ↓ Indent

For selected cells, the first button adds and the second subtracts one indentation, usually five spaces.

Cell Border

Clicking the arrow beside this icon presents a dialog window for you to select the border you wish to place around selected cells. If you want the border showing on the button, click it.

Cell and Text Color

These work like the Word buttons, and allow change of color for text or cell background. The first button fills the cell with that color; the second changes the text color. Click the arrow to change the color from that which is displayed to one of your choice.

Additional toolbars can be placed in your spreadsheet and left in place or opened and closed as you use them. You may access these easily in one of two ways:

1. Click **View** and choose **Toolbars**; then click the **Desired Toolbar** or
2. Place your cursor on **Any Toolbar** and right click.
   Click the **Desired Toolbar** in the dialog window.

If you wish to move the toolbar to another location on the screen, move it like you would any other window.

Place your cursor in the **Title** bar.

Drag the toolbar to the **Desired location**.

When you wish to remove the toolbar from your screen, click the **Close** ⊠ button in the upper right of the toolbar.

Underneath the toolbars is the address of the current active cell and the input line or formula bar. When you enter data into the active cell, that data also appears in the formula bar. As you enter data, three buttons ⊠✓= appear to the left of the formula bar. Clicking the X cancels your data entry. Clicking the checkmark has the same effect as pressing the Enter key; it finalizes your entry. Clicking the = or Edit Formula button enters the = sign into the cell and designates the data as a formula.

The Title Bar

The title bar is similar to the one you saw in Word. You can see it in Figure 7–1 with the temporary filename, Book 1. You may name the file using the conventions for Windows. Excel will automatically add an extension so that the file is recognized as a spreadsheet document. The extension varies for different versions of Excel; Excel 97 adds the three letters *xls*. You can see an example of this in Figure 7–4 in the workbook window. By dragging the title bar you can move the worksheet window around the screen. The standard buttons for minimizing, full screen display, and close file are found at the right of the title bar.

Entering Data and Correcting Errors

Notice in Figure 7–1 the message area at the bottom left of the screen. This says "Ready" when you can enter data. After you type your data and are ready to enter it, the message area says "Enter." You may enter data several ways; the most common is to:

1. Press **Enter** or
2. Use the mouse or an arrow key to move to another cell.

If you notice an error after entering data, you may change it in one of three ways:

1. **Retype** the data and press **Enter**. It will automatically overwrite the error.
2. Place the cursor in the **Input** line where the error occurs, press **Delete**, type the correction, and press **Enter**.
3. Place the cursor on the **Cell** to be changed, **Double click** and make appropriate **Changes** to the cell.

Moving in the Worksheet

Moving in the worksheet may be done with the mouse, arrow keys, or key combinations. The simplest way to move is to place the mouse in the desired cell and click. Other ways to move include:

Arrow keys	move one cell in the direction of the arrow key used
Tab key	moves one cell to the right
Shift Tab	moves one cell to the left
Ctrl Home	moves to the beginning of the worksheet, or A1
Page Up/Down	moves to the cell one screen up/down in the same column
Alt Page Up/Down	moves left/right one screen in the same row
Ctrl End	moves to the intersection of last row and column containing data

If you wish to go to a specific cell:

1. Type the **Address** in the cell address area and press **Enter** or
2. Press **F5** for the Go To dialog window, type your desired **Cell address** in the reference box and press **Enter**.

Viewing the Worksheet

You may also change your view of the worksheet in several ways. Note that this does not change the location of the cursor, just the part of the worksheet you see. Clicking the arrow keys on the scroll bars will move the worksheet one cell at a time in the direction of the arrow. For example, if you click the down arrow on the vertical scroll bar, the spreadsheet will be moved down one cell; if you click the right arrow you will move one cell to the right. Clicking in the gray area between the scroll bar and the arrow moves the display by a whole screen, either vertically or horizontally depending on the scroll bar you select.

Common Commands

Create a New Worksheet	Select **File, New** or click **New** button. Note that File, New gives you a dialog window and templates from which to choose. Selecting the new page icon assumes you want a new blank worksheet.
Access an Existing Worksheet	Select **File, Open** or click **Open** button, then access the **Drive** and/or **Folder** where the file is stored and click the desired **File**.
Selecting Cells	To clear cells, cut, copy, and change cell formats or to apply formulas to a series of cells, you first select the cells.

To Select	Do This
A single cell	Click the **Cell**.
A range of cells	Click a **Cell** at one end of the series and drag the mouse to **Highlight the desired range** of cells. Make sure that your pointer is the white plus sign when you hold down the mouse button to drag. If it is a left slanted arrow or a black plus sign you will be moving or autofilling respectively.
Entire rows or columns	Click the **Row** or **Column Heading** (the gray horizontal or vertical area containing row numbers or column letters). Drag to include more than one row or column.
Multiple cells columns, or rows not contiguous	Hold down the **CTRL** key while clicking all **Desired cells, Columns or Rows**, then release **CTRL**.
Entire worksheet	Click the **Rectangle** at the left of the columns just under the title bar.

Clear	Clear acts as an eraser and eliminates information or formats from a worksheet. You can clear a cell or several cells. The cells are left on the worksheet and retain a value of zero. Select **Edit, Clear,** and **All** to clear both format and content, **Formats** to erase cell formatting features, or **Contents del** to erase the data.
Delete	The **Del** key erases cell contents.
Changing Column Size	At the top of the worksheet along column letters, place the cursor on the **Vertical** line to the right of the column you want to widen or make smaller. The cursor will appear as a vertical line with arrows pointing left and right. Drag the **Column lines** to the size desired. You may also double click to use the size to fit option. If you see a column filled with **####**, this means you need to widen the column to show the numeric data there.
Insert Row/ Column	Place the cursor where you desire the new row or column, click **Insert**, then **Row or Column** or right click on the **Row or Column header** and select **Insert**. Rows are inserted above the current row and columns to the left of the current column.
Delete Row/ Column	Place the cursor on the row or column heading where you wish to delete the row or column, click **Edit, Delete** or right click the **Row** or **Column header** and select **Delete**.

Save, Save As, Print, Cut, Copy, and Paste functions work the same as in all Office 97 programs. See Chapters 3 and 4 for a review of these functions.

Numbers and Formulas

Cell entries are considered as either labels or values. Values can be numbers or formulas. The first character you type determines the type of cell entry you are making. In addition to the numbers 0–9, Excel treats the following characters as values:

– + / * . E e ( ) $ and %

Formatting Numbers. The default for numbers is general numbering. Any numbers entered into Excel appear exactly as typed. Number formatting can be changed to reflect decimals, percents, currency, or other types of numbers. As different selections are made, examples are presented in the dialog window so you can visualize the format.

Highlight the **Cells** you wish to format first.

Select **Format, Cells**.

Click the **Number** tab. The dialog window presents the various numbering formats available.

Select the **Desired** format.

Note that in the formatting toolbar (see Figure 7–3) there are shortcut icons for changing the format of numbers to currency, percents, adding commas, and changing the number of decimal places. To make these changes simply highlight cells to be formatted and click the desired formatting icon. When you are formatting currency, use the same method for formatting throughout your spreadsheet. The two formatting methods create a slight difference in placement of the dollar sign ($) and using both in the same spreadsheet will give an uneven look to currency cells.

Formulas and Function. Formulas help you analyze the data on a worksheet. With formulas you perform operations such as addition, multiplication, and comparison and enter the calculated value on the work sheet. A function is a preprogrammed formula. An Excel formula or function always begins with an equal sign (=).

To build a formula:

- Type an = sign in the cell where the formula will be placed.
- Enter the **Formula** by typing cell addresses or selecting cells by clicking on them with the mouse and including the desired math calculation symbol where appropriate (e.g., + – * /).
- Press **Enter** or click the enter box (green checkmark) in the formula bar.

When using formulas in Excel, the standard rules of precedence listed earlier in the chapter dictate how the mathematical calculation proceeds. Note in Figure 7–4 the formula to add the cells appears in the formula line.

The AutoSum ∑ function is the most commonly used function. It automatically adds a series of numbers in either rows or columns.

Highlight the cells to be summed and include a blank space at one end of the series.

Click the **AutoSum** icon and the sum will be displayed.

Another way to use this function is to:

Click an **Empty** cell where your sum will be displayed.

Click the **AutoSum** icon.

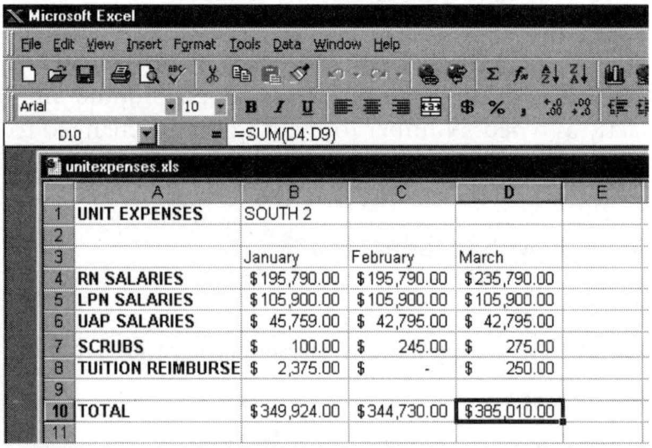

FIGURE 7–4.
Numeric Formulas: Note formula for the total in cell D10 appears in the formula bar

Confirm the **Range of cells** to be added by highlighting them.

Click the **AutoSum** button again.

Some commonly used formulas have been included in numeric functions; this eliminates some of the steps of writing a formula. There are several hundred functions built into Excel, including financial, date and time, mathematical, statistical, and lookup functions. To access these you click the **Function** f_{κ} button on the toolbar or click **Insert, Function**.

Commonly used functions include:

Function Name (cell/range)	Purpose
=AVERAGE(range)	averages the values indicated
=COUNT(range)	counts numbers within a range
=MAX(range)	returns the largest value within a range
=MIN(range)	returns the smallest value within a range
=STDEV(range)	computes the standard deviation for the range
=SUM(range)	sums the values indicated
=VAR(range)	determines the variance for the range

Absolute Cell Addresses. Cell addresses in formulas that are designed to change when copied to other cells are called relative addresses. Absolute addresses are cell addresses in formulas, which remain the same despite other changes in the worksheet. These are indicated by a $ prefixing the part of the address that is to remain absolute. For example, if you always wanted to use the number in C5 as your divisor in a formula, no matter where the formula was moved, you would indicated that address as C5. The following are various combinations for keeping certain parts of an address constant.

CR   Both row and column address always remain the same.

$CR   Row changes, column address always remain the same.

C$R   Column changes, row address always remain the same.

Creating Charts

Charts or graphs allow you to visually display your data. Excel has a Chart Wizard that guides you through the procedure to make your graph. First, highlight the data you wish to include in the chart. Include labels for the x- and y-axis as well as the numerical data. Click the Chart Wizard button to access the first page (see Figure 7–5), and then follow the four steps.

1. Click the **Type of graph** you want (pie, bar, etc.). Select **Next**.
2. Select **How you wish your data to be displayed** on the x-axis by indicating a series in columns or rows. You can visualize the variations on your screen. Once you are satisfied, click **Next**. If you want to try a different chart type, go back.
3. Add **Legend** and **Axis Titles** here. Type those in the appropriate dialog window and click **Next**.

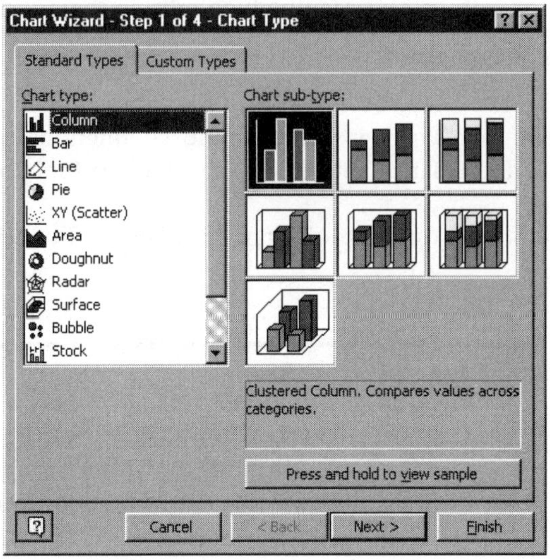

FIGURE 7–5.
Chart Wizard for Selecting Type of Chart

4. Select the **Location** for the chart. Select **Finish**.

You will then see your graph. If you elect to put your chart on your spreadsheet, it will have an outline around it so you can move it to the desired location on the spreadsheet.

SUMMARY

Spreadsheets can make things such as budgeting, inventory tracking, quality assurance documentation, and many other tasks involving numeric calculations much easier and more accurate. This chapter provided information about using spreadsheets at a basic level, building simple formulas, using common functions, and developing charts to visually represent data. While this chapter focused on Microsoft Excel, other spreadsheets are similar.

EXERCISE 1: CREATE AND PROJECT SALARIES

Objectives

1. Create a simple spreadsheet.
2. Use simple formulas and functions.
3. Format a worksheet.
4. Print, save, and retrieve a spreadsheet.

Activity

1. Access Excel.

   Click **Start**, **Programs**, and **Microsoft Excel**.

   Once you see the spreadsheet on your screen with "Ready" in the message area, you can begin. Be certain you are in the correct cell for performing designated actions that follow.

2. Practice moving the cursor.

   Practice moving from one cell to another using the mouse and the arrow keys.

   Move from cell **A1** to cell **C5**. What happens to cell **C5** when you moved your cursor there _____

   What shape does the pointer assume when it is inside the worksheet? _____

   Look for the current cell address in the top right corner of your screen. What do you see?

3. Practice entering data.

   Type **Your First Name** in cell **C5** using small letters.

   Then place the cursor in cell **C6** and type **Your Last Name** and press **Enter**.

   While still in cell **C6**, press the **space bar**, and then press **Enter**.

   What happens? _____ Now erase your name from cell **C5**.

4. Enter spreadsheet ID information.

   Click cell **A1**. Type **UNIT BUDGET** and press **Enter**.

5. Enter labels. Click each cell indicated below and type the appropriate data. Do not worry about making it look nice at this point. Formatting comes after the labels and data are entered.

   Highlight the range of cells **A3:G3**.

   Press the **Cap Lock** key.

   Type **Last Name** in cell **A3** and press **Enter** (**A3** will look white, **B3** to **G3** will be black).

   Type **First**, press **ALT+Enter**, type **Name** and press **Enter**.

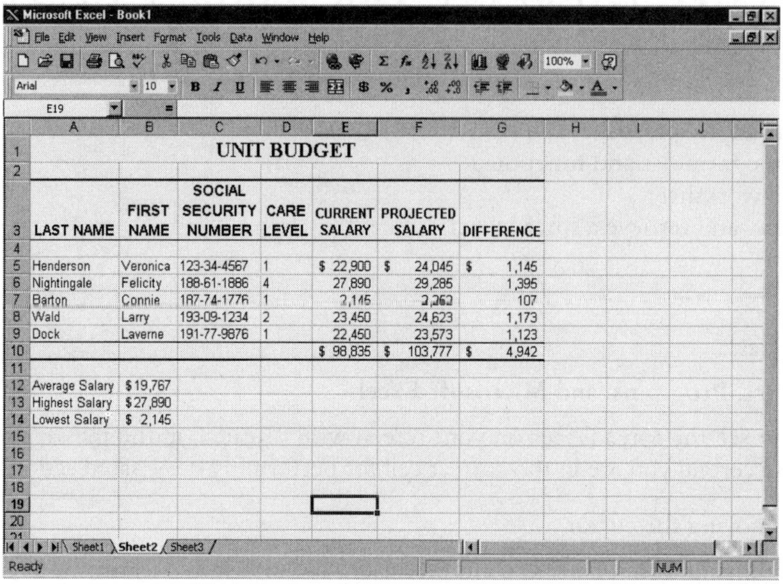

FIGURE 7–6.
Exercise 1 Labels and Data Unit Budget

Type **Social**, press **ALT+Enter**, type **Security**, press **ALT+Enter**, type **Number**, and press **Enter**.

Type **Care**, press **ALT+Enter**, type **Level**, and press **Enter**.

Continue typing the labels as shown in Figure 7–6. Be sure to press **ALT+Enter** after each word entered and **Enter** for the last word to move to the next cell.

6. Enter the data.

Press the **Caps Lock** key to turn off caps lock. Click cell **A5**.

Type the following data in the cell as indicated and press enter after each name:

ROW	COLUMN A
5	Henderson
6	Nightingale
7	Barton
8	Wald
9	Dock

Complete the rest of the data as shown here and continuing on Figure 7–6. **Do not type numbers for columns F and G or totals in row 10.** Those are formulas. Enter only data for columns B through E and rows 5–9. Do not worry about the $ or commas now, you will format them later.

A	B	C	D	E
5	Veronica	123-34-4567	1	22900
6	Felicity	188-61-1886	4	27890
7	Connie	187-74-1776	1	2145

7. Create formulas. Project a salary increase of 5% for each health care worker.

   Click cell **F5**, type =(**E5*1.05**) and press **Enter**.

   Click cell **F5**.

   Place pointer at bottom right of cell until it turns to a **Black plus** sign, **drag through cell F9** and release.

   What formula appears in cell **F7**? _____

   Click cell **G5**, type =, click cell **F5**, type – sign, click cell **E5**, and click **Green check** on formula toolbar.

   Place pointer at bottom right of cell until it turns to a **Black plus** sign, **drag through cell G9** and release.

8. Use functions. Use the sum function to total the salaries and differences in your budget.

   Click cell **E10**.

   Click **AutoSum** button twice. What total do you get? _____

   Place a sum in cell **F10** and **G10** to total the projected salaries and differences.

   Add the following labels in the designated cells:

   A12 **Average Salary**

   A13 **Highest Salary**

   A14 **Lowest Salary**

   In cell **B12** type =**average(E5:E9)**.

   In cell **B13** type =**max(E5:E9)**.

   In cell **B14** type =**min(E5:E9)**.

   Change Nightingale's salary to 28000 by typing **28000** in cell **G7**. What total do you see now in cell **B13**? _____ Now change it back.

9. Format labels, numbers and worksheet.

   Click cell **A1**.

   Click **Font down arrow** [Arial ▾] [10 ▾] and select **Times New Roman**.

   Click **Size down arrow** and select **16**. Click the **Bold** button.

   Select the range **A1:G1**, click the **Merger and Center** [▦] button.

Select the range **A3:G10**, select **Format, Autoformat, Simple** format from the menu bar.

Select range **E5:G5**, hold down the **CTRL** key, and select range **E10:G10** and **B12:B14**.

Click the **Currency** **$** button on the formatting toolbar.

Click the **Decrease decimal** button twice.

Select range **E6:G9** and click **Comma** button.

Click the **Decrease decimal** button twice.

Drag Columns A:G header highlighting these columns.

Place your pointer on the **vertical line between F and G** and **double click** to use the autofit feature. If you still need to make adjustments, use the manual column sizing command.

The last formatting you need to do is to center your labels. Think about how you do this using Word. What will you do? _____. Do it now.

If you have completed all steps above correctly, your spreadsheet should look like the one in Figure 7–6

10. Save your worksheet.

Click **File, Save** on the menu bar or click the **Save** button.

Be sure you have a diskette in drive A: if you are in a public lab.

Tell the computer where to store your file and what to call it. In the dialog window, click the folder icon until you see the drive and directory listed where you wish to save your file.

In the **File name** box at the bottom of the screen type your initials followed by budget and click **Save** button.

11. Exit Excel.

Click **File, Exit** on the menu bar or click the **Close** **X** button in the upper right of the screen.

12. Reopen Excel and find your file.

What steps will you use to see where you stored your budget file? _____

What is the full filename of the budget file? _____

Retrieve your worksheet. Click **File, Open**.

Make sure the Look in text box says **A drive**. If not, change it.

Highlight the **Budget file** with the mouse and click **Open** button.

Click the **Printer** button or select **File, Print** to print your spreadsheet.

Be sure you have access to a printer and that it is turned on.

Exit the program. Be sure to fully exit windows and turn off your equipment as instructed.

EXERCISE 2: CREATE A SIX-MONTH BUDGET

Objectives

1. Create a six-month budget using selected spreadsheet commands.
2. Use selected functions and simple formulas.

Activity

1. Create the identifying information.

   In row 1, type the heading for your spreadsheet: **6-MONTH BUDGET**.

   In row 2, column B type **BUDGET**; in column C type **ACTUAL**; in column D type **DIFFERENCE**.

2. Add the labels.

   Type **JAN** in cell **A3**.

   Use autofill to fill the labels through cell **A8**. (Place the cursor in the lower right corner of cell **A3**. With the black plus sign, drag through cell **A8**.)

A3	A4	A5	A6	A7	A8
JAN	FEB	MAR	APR	MAY	JUN

3. Enter the data. For each month under the headings enter the data as indicated here:

MONTH	BUDGET	ACTUAL
JAN	850	743
FEB	850	695
MAR	825	789
APR	875	849
MAY	850	778
JUN	875	834

4. Add functions. Use the sum function for finding sums in row 9, columns B and C.

5. What formulas would you use to compute the differences between the budgeted amounts and the actual amounts for JAN?

   BUDGET: _____

   ACTUAL: _____

   Enter this in column D.

6. What feature would you use to copy the formula to compute differences for each month? _____ Copy the formulas to the appropriate cells.

7. How would you write the function to determine the average for the six-month BUDGET and ACTUAL amounts? _____ In row 11, enter that function to determine those averages.

8. Format your spreadsheet by using AutoFormat and selecting the Classic 1 style.

9. Print your spreadsheet.

EXERCISE 3: CREATE A CHART

Objectives

1. Use the Chart Wizard to create several chart styles.
2. Print several chart styles.

Activity

1. Create a spreadsheet representing your expenses for three months. Include the following categories: utilities, rent, food, car expenses, and personal expenses and use the figures below or fill in your own.

Expense	JAN	FEB	MAR
Utilities	175	145	124
Rent	350	350	350
Food	234	245	275
Car Expenses	45	85	75
Personal Expenses	145	176	143

2. Using the Chart Wizard, create a chart showing how your expenses are divided for the month of January. What standard chart type would work most effectively for this? _____ (If you are not sure what chart would be best, open the Chart Wizard using step b. below. Click each type of chart and read the description provided under each pictured version of the chart.)

   a. On your spreadsheet, highlight the **Labels and Data** for expenses for the month of January.

   b. Click the **Chart Wizard** ▥ button on the standard toolbar.

   c. *Step 1.* The first step in the Wizard allows you to select the chart, that will best display your data. Click the **Chart** you desire from the list; then click the **Chart Subtype** you want. Preview it to ensure this chart will indeed show the data as you desire—click on "press and hold to view sample" and hold the mouse button down until you see the sample displayed. If this chart is not what you want, go to some of the others and preview them until you find the desired chart. Once you have selected your chart and chart subtype, click **Next**.

Step 2. Since you already highlighted the range of data and labels, you should see your chart here and can go on by clicking **Next**.

Step 3. Label your chart by typing **January Expenses** in the box under Chart title. Click the tab labeled **Data labels**, If you choose a pie chart, click **Show percent**, and click **Next**. If you choose a bar or column chart, click **Show value** and click **Next**.

Step 4. Click to show your chart **As a new sheet**. Click **Finish**.

d. Print your chart by clicking the printer icon.

3. Using the steps you learned above, create and print a column chart (any subtype) that shows a comparison of all of your expenses for the three months.

ASSIGNMENT 1: CREATE A SIMPLE SPREADSHEET

Directions

1. You may create a spreadsheet for any of the following:

   a. A unit budget that includes last year's costs, this year's cost to date and projections for next year if costs increase 5 percent.

   b. A drug worksheet that lists the dose by weight for a class of drugs (e.g., emergency drugs for preemies or for cardiac arrest, a comparison sheet for safe doses of narcotics) and formulas for calculating the drugs for individuals of different weights.

   c. A personal budget of your living costs for the past year, current year, and projected for next year if all costs increase by 3 percent.

   d. Special topic approved by faculty.

2. Submit both your printed spreadsheet and a diskette showing what happens with formulas and "what if" questions.

ASSIGNMENT 2: CREATE A GRADE SHEET

Directions

1. Using the spreadsheet of your choice, create a grade sheet that includes headings for first and last name, ID number (social security number), and the test scores for a midterm, a project, a final exam, and the final grade.

2. Enter the data under the headings as it appears below:

ID	Last Name	First Name	MIDT	PROJ	EXAM	FINAL
123-45-6789	Titmouse	Martha	95	98	87	
125-12-4534	Finch	Jerry	87	75	90	
124-65-9087	Cardinal	Sam	65	70	67	
124-65-9087	Robins	Sally	85	80	90	
125-65-1234	Nuthatch	Jamie	85	90	95	
127-12-1234	Wren	Timothy	90	95	90	

3. The midterm and project are each weighted 30 percent and the final exam is weighted 40 percent of the final grade. Enter formulas to calculate the final grade for each student.

4. Using the appropriate functions, enter formulas to calculate the highest and lowest grade and the average for the midterm, project, and final exam grade.

5. Adjust columns so the spreadsheet is visually pleasing.

6. Print the spreadsheet. Turn in your spreadsheet and a diskette.

ASSIGNMENT 3: CREATE A CHART

Directions

1. Using the data from Assignment 2, create a chart that compares all five students' grades on each of the three different parts of the grade they earned for the course.
2. Print your graph. On the back of the paper indicate why you selected the chart you did.
3. Turn in your graph.

Chapter 8

Introduction to Databases

OBJECTIVES

1. Define terms related to database applications.
2. Identify data types best managed through databases.
3. Describe database design process.
4. Interpret basic directions for operating a database program.

INTRODUCTION

Health care institutions use a variety of database programs to meet their needs. These include mainframe and PC-level programs. This chapter introduces you to basic database concepts and terms as well as some introductory keystrokes for completing the exercises. For more detailed information, consult the application program manual or any related reference book.

Database management systems help us organize, store, and retrieve data. These programs permit the user to create table structures, modify the structures, store data, and retrieve it in a variety of ways. They act as efficient file systems; they are, however, only as effective and efficient as the accuracy and structure of the data.

The main advantages of electronic databases are:

- Reduction in data redundancy (duplicate data in a variety of places)
- Reduction in data inconsistency (data stored differently in the same file. For example, how do you store a person's name? Full name, including first and middle, or first, middle initials, and last name?)
- Increased data access

Some people treat data security as an advantage. They believe with centralized data, control over access is much easier. Others believe data security is a disadvantage because increased access to data results in increased security concerns. To counter this disadvantage, you must make decisions about who has access to what data and at what level. Should everyone have the ability to correct and add data? Do some need only access to viewing it, but not changing it? In the health care arena, should the receptionist in the lobby have access to the patient's diagnosis and physician's name or do they only need access to the patient's name and room number fields? Should the supervisor have the ability to chart medications on all patients or should only the nurses on the unit have that ability? These are the types of issues that a centralized database raises.

DATABASE MODELS

There are three main database models. Each model structures, organizes, and uses data differently. Hierarchical and network models are commonly used on mainframes and minicomputers. Most PC database programs use a relational model. The model underlining the design of the database program influences or limits the searching permitted. It also influences the maintenance of the database.

Hierarchical

This model is like a tree or organizational chart. During searching, the program searches sequentially each root and branch, and checks for a match. This is commonly called traversing the tree. Some common terms associated with this model are root, parent, and siblings. When designing the database, each child in the hierarchical model can have only one parent.

Network

The network model was developed to solve problems caused by the hierarchical model's inability to store certain types of data easily. The network model permits more than one parent per child. However, it requires multiple links to the various fields making it much more difficult to revise or edit.

Relational

A relational model relies on so-called flat tables for its structure. Designers use only one data element per field. This means you must reduce tables to their simplest form. The term used for this process of reduction is normalizing the table. For example, a parent with two children would become two tables that you link on a common field.

An alternative database model that you see on the Internet or on intranets is the Hypertext design. This design relies on objects linked to other related objects. The object may be text, pictures, data files, or sound files. This structure is particularly useful for organizing large amounts of diversified data. The disadvantage to this set up is that you can't perform numerical analysis on the data nor can you be sure how people will access each part of the database.

COMMON DATABASE TERMS

These terms describe the structure of a database from smallest unit to largest:

Data	Raw facts consisting of numbers, letters, characters, and dates are data. They are the contents of fields. Other names for data are data items or elements. Some examples of data are Jones, 200-23-1234, and Chicago.
Data Types	Data types refer to the description of what data to expect in a field. They are software dependent; each program defines them. Most programs include alphanumeric (characters and numbers), numeric (numbers), short numeric (short, whole numbers), currency (money), character (letters), date and time, logical (equal to, greater than, or less than), memo (comment), and object (pictures or objects) data types.

Field	A field is a space within a file with a predefined location and length. Another name that describes a field is attribute. Use only one data item in each field. For example, place temperature, pulse, and respiration in separate fields; do not place them together in one field such as a vital sign field. Examples of field names are last name, first name, city, state, diagnosis #1, systolic B/P, pulse, and height. Use a field name that reflects the data you intend to store in it.
Record	Collection of fields related or associated with a focal point is a record. For example, a patient is a focal point around whom we collect and store certain data. A patient chart is a record. Your college transcript is a record. Each row of a table, in most programs, is a record.
File	Files are collections of related records. For example, all the patients in St. Luke's Hospital make up a file. Many people compare a file to the file drawer in a filing cabinet. Related data are kept in the same drawer.
Database	A database is a collection of files and is like a file cabinet; it holds related drawers of records. It is organized in such a way that a computer program called a database management system can quickly retrieve the data you want.
Database Management System	Database management systems (DBMS) are the programs that enable you to work with electronic databases. They permit you to store, modify, and retrieve information from the database.

The following are descriptions of additional database concepts:

Key Field	One or more fields with a unique identifier are key fields. Having key fields ensures that there are no duplicate records in this database because a key field accepts only one record with that combination of text and/or numbers. One of the most commonly used key fields is your social security number.
Link	A link is a logical association between tables based on the values in corresponding fields. This is a connection between two tables in a relational database program. This is what permits you to query or ask questions of multiple tables and extract only the data you want from these tables. The linked field must be of the same data type.
Table	The table is the structure used to store the data. It consists of fields and records. The vertical columns are fields, and the horizontal ones are records.

COMMON DATABASE FUNCTIONS

Common database functions allow you to create table structures, edit data or records, search tables, sort records, and generate reports.

Creating the Database

There are two steps to creating the database: designing the structure (sometimes called the schema) and entering the data.

Designing the Structure. Designing the structure of the file requires identifying the field names, field types, and field widths. This structure design is generally stored in a data dictionary, which is a file that defines the basic organization of a database. It lists all the files associated with the database as well as the names and types of each field. Many times it also includes comments about the range of acceptable data.

Entering Data. Enter data using the designed structure. Sometimes this involves redesigning the structure to facilitate entry of all data. Most databases provide options for verifying accuracy of the data entered. These utilities or tools permit you to set data ranges and data images to help ensure the accuracy of the data entered.

Editing Data or Records

Editing data or records involves adding records, deleting old records, or changing data in active records.

Add	The add function permits placement of additional records into the database.
Delete	Delete permits the user to remove records from the database.
Change	Change permits the user to alter the contents of a record.

Searching the Database

Searching is the process of creating data subsets or locating specific records in the database. Some terms used to describe this process are search, query, find, and ask. The power of the database lies in the search function and the ability to extract data. Described here are additional terms related to searching.

Answer Table. In some databases, the answer table is a temporary table where the program stores search results. It is overwritten when you conduct a new search or deleted when you exit the program. In other databases, the answer tables or results are automatically saved in the Queries tab.

Boolean Searching. This is using specific strategies to expand or limit the search. Three of the most often used Boolean operators are AND, OR, and NOT. It is one of the most commonly used features for searching any database; that is the ability to narrow or expand your search as well as eliminate some records. You will have more on searching in Chapter 11, Information—Access, Evaluation, and Use.

AND	This strategy provides records that include both terms on either side of the AND. For example, computer and health elicits only records that include both terms. If one term is missing, that record does not show in the search results. And the match must be exact. If a record has computers and health, it does not show in the search results. Computer is not the same term as computers.
OR	This strategy provides records that have either term. For example, computer OR computing finds records that include either the term computer or the term computing.

NOT   This strategy provides records that exclude the term following NOT. For example, computer NOT bedside elicits records containing the word computer and eliminates records that have the word bedside.

There are some additional operations such as NEAR and ADJACENT that you may use, but they are not as common as these three. What is important is that you refine your search strategy to be the most efficient for eliciting the information you want.

Exact Match   This search finds only entries that are an exact match for the word you are searching. Any minor difference results in exclusion of that entry from the results. For example, when searching for child, it finds only child and not children, infants, or teenagers.

Pattern   This type of search permits the use of wild cards in place of a character. For example, nur* would match the string nur and any word with nur as the beginning string. Thus, it would find nurse, nurses, nursing, nurture, and nurturing.

Range   These are operators like greater than, less than, equal to, or some combination of them. We call this the logical operator. It returns records that fit the operator such as all patients with pulses greater than 110.

Select Fields   This refers to selecting the fields you want to display in the search results. This involves using some mark to identify the fields to display in the results. You may display all the fields or selected ones. For example, you may choose to display only the patient name and room number in the results or you may choose to display additional fields like diagnosis, doctor, primary nurse, and lab test results.

Sorting the Database

This function permits the user to arrange records in a variety of ways and to work with some subset of them. Many times you might want to see the list of names in alphabetic order or all the zip codes together in numeric order. This feature lets you arrange the data in the order that makes sense for what you are doing. Two terms used when sorting are ascending and descending. Ascending sorts in alphabetic or numeric order from A or 1 to Z or NN. Descending is the reverse going from the highest value to the lowest.

Generating Reports

Another powerful feature of databases is the ability to generate multiple reports from the same database or data subset. Most programs permit multiple report formats on the same data.

A FEW DATABASE DESIGN TIPS

The most difficult task in developing databases is creating the database structure. This is a time-consuming task and requires the designer to pay attention to detail. Below are some questions you must answer before creating the table structures.

1. What output do you desire?
2. What search questions will you ask?

3. What fields do you need to produce the desired output and answer the search questions? What do you need to define the record accurately?
4. What do you want to name the fields?
5. What data type will you place in each field?
6. What serves as the unique identifier for each record?
7. How do you want to relate this table or file to other tables or files? What are the relationships?
8. Do you have any redundant (duplicate) data in this table? Should you normalize it?

COMMON USES IN HEALTH CARE

There are many uses of databases in health care systems. Examples of some common uses are listed next. Additional databases are discussed in Chapter 11, Information—Access, Evaluation, and Use.

Administration	This area includes databases such as staffing, scheduling, personnel records, quality assurance (improvement), and inventory control.
Clinical	Two clinical database uses are patient records and drug files.
Education	Educators use databases for test banks, student experiences, and student records.
Research	Research related databases include literature access, data collection, data storage, and data retrieval.

ADDITIONAL TERMINOLOGY

As things change in the computer world, new terminology develops. Discussed here are three terms that you might hear related to database concepts.

Data Mining

This concept refers to database applications that look for patterns in already created databases. Do not confuse it with software that presents data in new ways. Data mining software actually discovers new relationships between the data items that were not previously known. This class of database software has great potential for discovering new patterns of patient responses, who responds to what type of treatment, and who is at greater risk for developing certain conditions or side effects.

Data Warehouse

This concept refers to a collection of data designed to support decision making. The purpose of a data warehouse is to present a picture of the general conditions of the entity at a particular time. Software extracts data from operating systems and places it in a warehouse database system. This means that many different databases from the institution are collectively scanned for the data relative to support decision making. Generally a warehouse supports summary, not detail, data. It does not deal with the day-to-day operations of an institution. This data supports analysis of trends over time.

Data Mart

A subset or smaller focus database designed to help managers make strategic decisions is a data mart. Sometimes it is a subset of a data warehouse. Like data warehouses, it combines aspects of many databases within the institution, but with a focus on a particular subject, department, or unit.

INTRODUCTION TO ACCESS

The remaining part of this chapter describes a relational database program called Access. Basic information to help you begin using Access is presented here. Remember to use the help system when you want to learn additional functions or refer to the many full Access books available at most bookstores.

Starting Access

There are many ways to start this program. Some of them are listed here.

Double click on the **Microsoft Access** icon.

Click the **Start** button, **Programs, Microsoft Access.**

Double click an **MS Access** file.

Click **New Office Document** icon on the MS Office Shortcut bar, click **New Blank database** icon.

You will now be directed to either create a new blank database or to retrieve an existing one. The exception is if you double click an actual database file. You will also be asked to name the database if you are creating a new one.

Closing and Exiting the Database

Once you create and use the database you will need to close it and exit the program. Make sure when you do this you respond to the prompts to save your data and the related forms and reports. Note that there are two close buttons—one for the database and the other for the application.

To close the database:

Click **Database close** button. Make sure you click the close button for this database and not the application one.

Respond to any prompts regarding saving any unsaved data, forms, and reports.

To close the application:

Click the **Application close** button. Again make sure you respond to any prompts.

Creating and Opening an Existing Database

Each database you create is stored as a separate file containing the structure (tables), data, reports, forms, macros, and queries. A tab in the database window represents each separate component in the database. See Figure 8–1 for the look of the basic screen in Access. Listed in the Table tab are all the tables containing the data that are associated with this database. Note that in this figure, you can see the two different close buttons—one for the application and the other for the database.

To open an existing database:

Start **Access** (see above).

Confirm the Open Existing Database is selected and click **OK**. See Figure 8–2.

Select the **Location** and **Database File** and click **Open**.

To create a new database:

Start **Access** and click on the **Blank Database** option and **OK**.

Click the **Down arrow** ▼ button in the Save in text box, and the **A drive** icon to switch to A drive.

Highlight **Db1.mdb** in the name text box and type **Database Name**, press **Enter**.

Click the **Table Tab** if not already selected, and click **New** button on the right side.

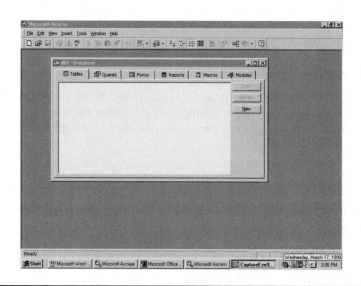

FIGURE 8–1.
Typical Access Screen

FIGURE 8–2.
Access Database Screen

Select **Design View** and click **OK**.

Type **Field names**, press **Tab**.

If not a text field, click the **Down arrow** ▼ button, click the **Data type** for this field.

If a text field, press **F6**, type **Length of field**, press **F6**. Pressing F6 toggles you to the screen at the bottom so you can type the length of the field. By default the text length is 50 characters.

Press **Tab**, type **Description of the field**.

If this is a key field, click the **Key** 🔑 button on the toolbar or go to the **Edit** menu and select **Primary Key**, press **Tab**.

Continue typing the field names, sizes, and description until you have the structure complete.

Click **Table close** ✕ button. Make sure you click the close button on the table window to close this table not the application.

Click **Yes** to save the table, type **Table Name**, and press **Enter**.

Note you are now back at the database window.

When naming files you will find it helpful to label them as:

Table:Name

Query:Name

Form:Name

Report:Name

This helps when you base queries on tables, forms, etc. When a list pops up of what you want to base a query on, you will know what files are tables, forms, and so on. It serves as a reminder to you regarding the nature of the file.

Moving Around the Database

There are two main views for working with your database: datasheet and form views. When you open an existing database the data are displayed in Datasheet view. That is they are in rows and columns just like a spreadsheet. If you want to view your data one record at a time, then you need to switch to Form view. To switch from one view to the other click the **New Object button down arrow** ![icon] for the change view menu. Select **Autoform.** This presents you with a view that shows you all the fields for one record at a time. (To switch back to Datasheet view, click **View** ![icon] button, and select **Datasheet view**.)

Use the following keys or buttons to move through tables in **Datasheet and Form views.** Figure 8–3 shows use of the movement toolbar.

Tab	to go to the next field in the record
Shift Tab	to go to the previous field in that record
Click Next Record	to go to the next record in the database
Click Previous Record	to go to the previous record in the database
Last Record	to go to the last record in the database
First Record	to go to the first record in the database
Double Click Specific Record, Type Record Number	to go to a specific record in the database

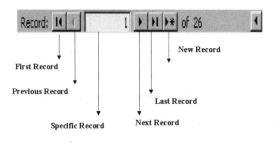

FIGURE 8–3.
Movement Toolbar in Access

Entering and Editing the Data

Once you create the structure, you are ready to enter data. Entering data is straightforward. Type the data in the appropriate field and press the tab key to go to the next field.

To enter data:

Click **Table Name** in the main Access screen and click **Open**.

Type the **Data** in each of the appropriate fields.

Press **Tab** to go to the next field.

If you make mistakes while entering the data, use the backspace key to erase it and then retype it. Another way to edit the mistake is to place the cursor in the field, click the field, use the cursor keys to go to the place of the mistake, type the correction, and delete the extra letters with the delete key. Use the tab key to move to the next field.

To add another record to a table:

Highlight **Table Name** and click **Open** button.

Click the **New Object button down arrow** for the change view button.

Select **Autoform**.

Click the **New Record** button.

Type the **New Data** in the appropriate fields.

Click the **Close** button, click **Yes**, click **OK**.

To change the contents of a field:

Highlight **Data to replace**.

Type **New Data** and click the **Close** button. The change is automatically saved.

To delete a record from a table:

Click the **Record selector** for the record your want to delete. See Figure 8–4.

Press the **Delete** key, click **Yes** to confirm deletion of this record.

Click **Close** button to close the table.

Note you may also click the **Delete Record** button on the toolbar.

Sorting and Finding Records

When you use a database and open a table, the records may not be in the order in which you want to view them. For example, you might want to review the records by job positions or

Social Securit	Lasrt
168-33-1700	Mains
197-56-4378	Kiminsl
200-34-2314	Smith
212-45-4556	Quinn
213-45-6789	Jones
235-34-5612	Wish

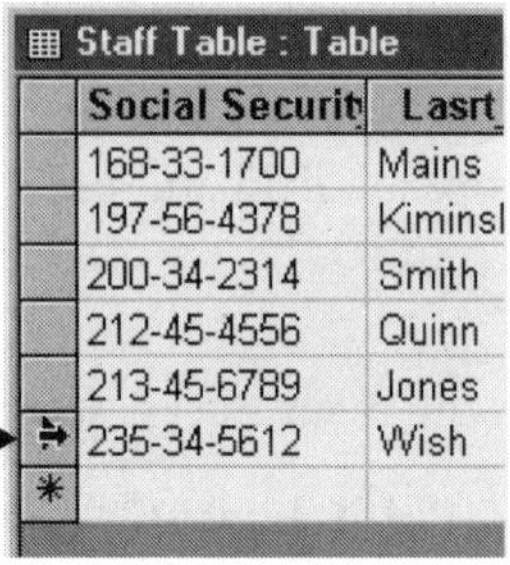

Staff Table : Table

Record Selector ⟶

FIGURE 8–4.
Record Selector

patient diagnosis or date. It is easier to sort the records than it is to scroll through them to find the ones for which you are looking. You can rearrange or sort the records by using the sort button on the toolbar. There are two types of sort—ascending and descending. Ascending sort arranges the records in order from the lowest value to the highest value in the field on which you tell it to sort. Descending reverses the order going from highest value to lowest value.

To sort records in a table:

Open the **Database** and **Table** you want to sort.

Click the **Column** heading of the field on which you want to sort.

Click the **Sort Ascending** or **Sort Descending** 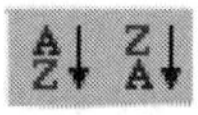 button.

Sometimes it doesn't matter what the order is because what you want to do is find a specific record to either verify some information or to update a record. Note that the find feature searches in only the field you select. It does not have the same power that the query feature does.

To find records:

Open the **Database** and **Table**.

Click in the **Field** that you want to search. The field column does not need to be highlighted.

Click the **Find**  button.

Type a value in the **Find What** Box.

Select a **Search** option, and select a **Match** option.

Click **Find First**.

When you find the first record you want to change, click the close button, and make the change. With the field still selected, click the Find button, then Find Next and repeat the process until all records are found and updated. When all changes are made, click the close button.

Searching or Querying the Database

The reason you create databases is for the ease of searching for specific information or records. Searching, however, is an exacting process and requires you to have some knowledge of the database and data. The power of any relational database is the ability to also link multiple tables together and pull only the data needed from each table. Described below are directions for searching a single table and for linking two tables for a search. Note that you only save the query if this is one you use all the time. Do not save queries if they are one-time searches.

There are several types of searches. You might want to search all records but display only selected fields from one or more tables. You might want to combine two or more tables and display selected fields from them. You might want to create a subset of records meeting specific criteria.

To start the search:

Start **Access** and open the **Database**.

Click the **Query tab,** click **New** button, select **Design View**, and click **OK**.

Select **Table** you want to query, click **Add** button, and click **Close** button.

The query design screen appears. See Figure 8–5.

Adjust windows so all fields in the **Query Table** are displayed. Refer to Chapter 3 if you don't remember how to size windows.

Double click **Each field** listed in the table at the top to display the field in the query table at the bottom.

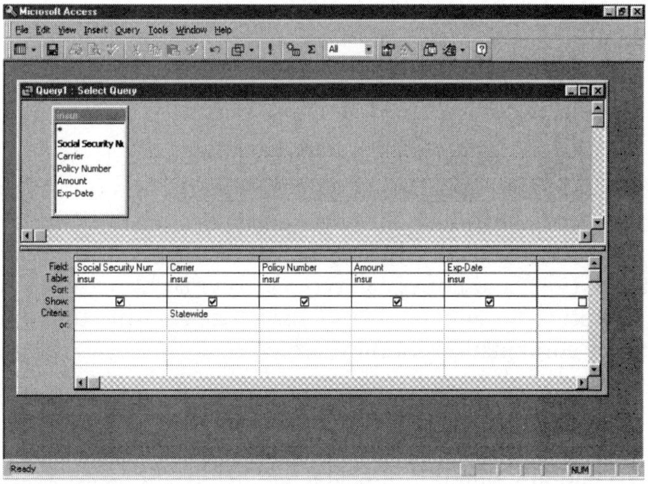

FIGURE 8–5.
Query Design Screen

Set the **Search criteria**.

Click the **Run** [!] button.

To search one table but selected fields:

Start **Access** and open the **Database**.

Click **Query tab**, click **New** button, select **Design View**, and click **OK**.

Select **Table,** click **Add** button, and click **Close** button.

Adjust windows so all fields in the table are displayed.

Double click the **Selected Fields** you want to display.

Set the **Search criteria**.

Click the **Run** [!] button.

To search two tables with selected fields:

Start **Access** and open the **Database**.

Click the **Query** tab, click **New** button, select **Design View**, and click **OK**.

Select **Table**, click **Add** button.

Select **Second table**, click **Add** button, and click **Close** button.

Adjust windows so all fields in the table are displayed.

Double click **Selected Fields** from both tables.

Set **Search criteria**.

Click the **Run** [!] button.

You might also want to refine a search to a specific group of records. You can use a single criterion, like city, or multiple criteria like city and state. You set the criterion by typing the condition in the Criteria cell for the field to which the criterion applies. You can search by using the comparison operators like equal to (=), less than (<), greater than (>), less than or equal to (<=), greater than or equal to (>=), and not equal to (<>). You may also use wild card characters like the asterisk (*) to substitute for any number of characters and question mark (?) to substitute for one character. Some combinations of these are:

Heart*   .   To find any number of characters after heart like heartburn, heart attack, heart condition, etc.

*Heart   To find any number of characters before the word heart like ace of hearts, coronary heart, etc.

??art   To find two characters in that location ending with art like chart and heart.

You may also use AND and OR queries. The AND search means that both conditions in both fields must be true to return the record. To search using the AND, type the criteria on the same criteria line for each field. The OR condition means that one or the other has to be true to return the record. To search using the OR condition, type in the related OR row.

To search using specific search criteria:

Start **Access** and open the **Database**.

Click the **Query** tab, click **New** button, select **Design View**, and click **OK**.

Select **Table**, click **Add** button.

Adjust windows so all fields in the table display.

Double click the **Selected Fields** that you want to be in the display.

Type the **Criteria** on the Criteria line in the related Field name column.

If using an OR search, type the **Criteria** on the OR line.

Click the **Run** button.

Generating a Report

Once you search and create your data subset, you will want to create a report of the results. This is one of the primary reasons for creating and maintaining a database. You also may want to report the total contents of a table. You can generate multiple reports for each table; each report gives the user a different view of the data. Access has both an AutoReport and Report Wizard feature to help you create your reports.

Since this is an introductory chapter, forms are not covered in this book. The major difference between forms and reports is that reports are intended for printing only and not for display in a window. Forms are for displaying in a window on the screen. Reports are designed to report some result and, unlike forms, not for changing values of fields.

There are six basic types of Access reports. They are single-column, tabular, multicolumn, grouped, mailing labels, and unbound reports. Which report type you choose depends on the data and how you want them displayed. We will create simple column and grouped type reports in this chapter.

Creating a Simple Report:

Select the **Table or Query** tab.

Highlight the **Table or Query**.

Click **New Object** button down arrow.

Select **AutoReport**.

Click **View** button down arrow. Select **Design View**.

Make whatever changes to the report you need by dragging the objects to their new location. To move a field name or field separately, click the top left corner of the field box and move it to its new location. Once you complete the design, toggle to the Preview. Use properties to change fonts, add colors, and so on. You can toggle between the two views until the report is like you want it.

Creating a Grouped Report. Grouped reports let you organize your data in a particular fashion by grouping like records together. For example, you could group the records by department or diagnosis or health care provider. The example below uses the Report Wizard to help you design and layout your report.

Select the **Table or Query** for the report.

Click the **New Object** [icon] ▾ down arrow button. Choose **New Report**.

Select **Report Wizard** and click **OK**.

Add the **Fields** your want to the report and click **Next Button**.

Select the fields to **Group** the report by, click **Next Button**.

Set the **Sort** order. Click the **Next Button**.

Select a **Layout** and a **Style** for the report. Click **Next Button** after each selection.

Click **Finish**.

Modifying and Formatting a Report. You can modify your reports using some of the design tools available with the program. Remember reports contain fields and field labels that you can rearrange. You can also add descriptive text to the data as well as headers and footers.

To modify and format a report:

Select the **Report to modify**.

Click the **Design Button**.

Make the **Modifications**.

SUMMARY

This chapter presented basic database concepts necessary to understanding the world of databases. The database structure and related terms were discussed. Specific directions for using Access as an example of one database then followed. Much of what we do and access is stored in a database and learning how to use them increases your ability to retrieve and use information to help with decision making.

EXERCISE 1: CREATE TABLE AND ENTER DATA

Objectives

1. Create two tables with a linked field.
2. Enter and save the data.
3. Edit fields and add records.

Activity

1. Start the program.

   Insert your diskette into Drive A. You will be creating the tables on your diskette.

   Double click the **Access icon**. Note you may need to access the program by selecting Start, Program, and Microsoft Access OR by using the Microsoft Office shortcut toolbar on the desktop and selecting Access.

2. Create the table structure.

   Click **Blank Database** and **OK** to open a new blank database. See Figure 8–2 for the dialog screen.

   Click the **Down arrow** ▼ button in the Save in text area, click **3½" floppy A drive** icon to switch to A drive.

   Highlight **db1.mdb** in the name text box and type **Staff Insurance**, press **Enter**.

   Click the **Table tab** if not already selected, and click **New** button on the right side.

   Select **Design View** and click **OK**.

   Type **Social Security Number**, press **Tab**, press **F6**, type **11**, press **F6**, press **Tab**, type **Unique Identifier, Separate numbers by dashes**. Pressing F6 toggles you to the screen at the bottom so you can type in the length of the field. By default the length is 50 characters.

   Click the **Key** 🔑 button on the toolbar to make this a key field and press **Tab**.

   Continue typing the field names, sizes and descriptions as outlined below.

Last_Name	Text	10	Staff person's last name with first letter capitalized
First_Name	Text	10	First name
Street_Name	Text	20	Street Address
City	Text	15	City
State	Text	2	State, use 2 letter all cap abbreviation
Zip_code	Text	5	5 digit zip code
Phone#	Text	12	Phone number including area code
Dept	Text	2	Depart 2 letter code

When finished your screen should look like this (Figure 8–6).

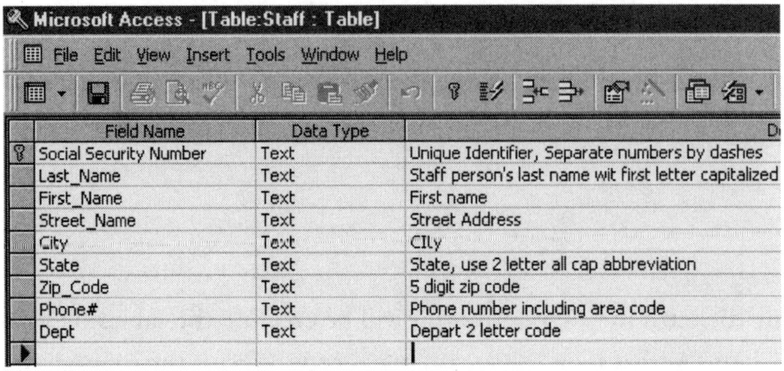

FIGURE 8–6.
Staff Table Structure

Click **Table close** ☒ button. Make sure you click the second one down to close this table, not the application.

Click **Yes** to save the table, type **Table:Staff** and press **Enter**.

What type of data does the program accept in the field Zip_code?

What other data types can you use in Access?

Where can you find this information?

3. Create a second table. Use the directions from above to do this. Call this one **Table:Insur.** Enter the following field names and data types:

Field Name Data	Type	Value	Description
Social Security Number	text	11 key	Unique Identifier, Separate numbers by dashes
Carrier	text	30	Insurance carrier
Policy_#	text	11	Individual's policy number
Amount	currency		Policy value amount
Exp_Date	date		Expiration date of policy

Make sure to save this structure.

4. Enter data. Enter data into both of the tables created above. If you make a mistake while entering the data, use the backspace key to erase it and then retype it. Another way to edit the mistake is to place the cursor in the field, click on the field, use the cursor keys to go to the place of the mistake, type the correction, and delete the extra letters with the delete key. Use the tab key to move to the next field.

Click **Staff** table in the main Access screen and click **Open**.

Type the following data in each of the appropriate fields.

Table: Staff

200-34-2314	213-45-6789	197-56-4378
Lisa Smith	Mary Jones	Robert Kiminsky
34 Terry Blvd.	5997 Irish Place	99 Moonlight Lane
Pittsburgh	Bethel Park	Forest Hills
PA 15267	PA 15102	PA 15343
412-675-3333	412-833-7659	412-635-3557
PT	4W	6S
412-33-5690	235-34-5612	212-45-4556
Pat Holmes	Jan Wish	Anna Quinn
45 White St	7886 Center Ave	912 Modern St
Carnegie	Greentree	Moon City
PA 15106	PA 15106	PA 15111
412-276-1122	412-355-5195	412-567-3227
4W	OR	ER

Click the **Printer** 🖶 button on the toolbar to print a copy of this data.

After entering the data, click the **Close** ⊠ button for that dialog window.

Select **Table:Insur** and repeat the process to enter the data below. Remember to provide a **print** of this data too, and close this window.

Table: Insur

200-34-2314	213-45-6789	197-56-4378
Allstate	Statewide	Mutual Care Provider
A20034231	2345612	M197564378
1,000,000	500,000	2,000,000
2/12/00	6/20/00	4/10/00
412-33-5690	235-34-5612	212-45-4556
Statewide	Fireman's	Statewide
4562340	F345612	8976002
1,000,000	500,000	1,000,000
10/1/99	12/5/99	11/18/99

5. Edit records.

   Add another record to the **Staff** *table.*

   Highlight **Staff** table and click **Open** button.

   Click the **down arrow** 📇 ▾ for the change view button. Select **Autoform**.

   Click the **New Record** ▶✳ button.

   Type the following data: 168-33-1700, Mains, John, 123 Irish Place, Whitefish, PA 15261, 724-333-1234, ER.

   Click the **Close** button, click **Yes**, click **OK**. Close the **Staff** table.

   Change the contents of one record.

   Open the **Staff** table.

   Highlight **333-1234** in the phone number field of the John Mains record.

   Type **345-1234** and click the **Close** button. The change is automatically saved.

   Delete a record.

   If necessary, open **Table:Staff**.

   Click the **Record selector** for Mains record. See Figure 8–4.

   Press the **Delete** key, click **Yes** to confirm deletion of this record.

   Click the **Close** button to close the table. You should now have six records in the table.

6. Close Access.

   Click the **Close** button to close the application.

   Remove your diskette from the A drive.

EXERCISE 2:
CREATE SEARCH, SORT, AND GENERATE REPORT

Objectives

1. Search (Query) the database using one table, two tables, all fields, and selected fields.
2. Sort the database.
3. Prepare and print a report.

Activity

1. Preliminaries.

   Start **Access**. Place your **diskette into Drive A**.

   Open the **Staff Insurance** database. Make sure you change the Look in to the A drive.

2. Search. You are now ready to search. First we want to know the answer to the question "Do any of the staff have an insurance policy with Statewide?" If yes, how many?

To start the search:

Click the **Query** tab, click **New** button, select **Design View**, and click **OK**.

Select **Table:Insur**, click **Add** button, and click **Close** button.

The query design screen appears. See Figure 8–5.

Adjust windows so all fields in the Insur table display. Refer to Chapter 3 if you don't remember how to size windows.

Double click **each field** listed in the Table:Insur to display the field in the query table.

Type **Statewide** in the cell that is the intersection for carrier and criteria.

Click the **Run** ![Run button] button.

Click the **Printer** ![Printer button] button on the toolbar to print a copy of this query.

Do any of the staff use Statewide as their insurance carrier? _____ If so, how many staff use Statewide as their insurance carrier? _____ HINT: You should have three records. If you don't, check your query table to make sure it is correct, then check your data in the tables to make sure your data is correct. This was an example of a simple search displaying all the fields from a single table.

Click the **Close** button for the query window.

Click **No** to not save this query.

Now, we want to conduct a search displaying all records but selected fields.

Click the **Query tab,** click **New** button, select **Design View**, and click **OK**.

Select **Table:Staff**, click **Add** button, and click **Close** button.

Adjust windows so all fields in the Staff table display.

Double click **Social Security Number, Last_Name, First_Name and Dept** fields listed in the Table:Staff to display the field in the query table.

Click the **Run** ![Run button] button.

Click the **Printer** ![Printer button] button on the toolbar to print a copy of this query.

Click the **Close** button for the query window.

Click **No** to not save this query.

Now, we want to do a more complex search on two tables.

The question to answer this time is "What staff have liability policies due to expire in October, November, or December, 1999?" A reminder to renew and provide current information on their policies will be sent.

Click the **Query** tab, click **New** button, select **Design View**, and click **OK**.

Select **Table:Insur**, click **Add** button.

Select **Table:Staff**, click **Add** button, and click **Close** button.

Adjust windows so all fields in the **Staff** table are displayed.

Double click **Social Security Number, Last_Name, First_Name and Dept** fields listed in the **Staff** table to display the field in the query table.

Double click the **Exp_Date** field of the Insur Table.

Type **>=10/1/99 AND <1/1/00** in the cell of the intersection of Criteria and Exp_Date field.

Click the **Run** button.

Click the **Printer** button on the toolbar to print a copy of this query.

How many have insurance policies that are about to expire? (You should have three.)

What departments are they in?

Click the **Close** button for the query window.

Click **Yes** to save this query. Type **Query:expdate** and press **Enter** or click **OK**.

3. Sort the data. Some times you want to place the records in a different order from that in which they are displayed.

Open the **Table:Staff**.

Click the **Last_Name column** heading. That is click over the words Last_Name. The total column is now highlighted.

Click the **Sort Ascending** button.

Click the **Printer** button on the toolbar to print a copy of the data in this order.

Click the **Close** button of the table window.

Click **No** to not save the sort changes.

4. Find a specific record. Sometimes you want to find a specific record for the purpose of checking some information in it.

Open the **Table:Staff** if needed.

Click in the **City** field. The field column does not need to be highlighted.

Click the **Find** button.

Type **Carnegie** in the Find What box.

Select **All** in Search option, and select a **Whole Field** in the Match option.

Click **Find First**. Click **Find Next** and click **OK** to the prompt for no more records found.

Click the **Close** button in the Find window.

Sometimes you want to find a record to update it.

Click in the **Last_Name** field. The field column does not need to be highlighted.

Click the **Find** 🔍 button.

Type **Smith** in the Find What box.

Select **All** in Search option, and select a **Whole Field** in the Match option.

Click **Find First** and click **Close** button to close the find window.

Press the **Tab** key until you are at the phone number field.

Highlight the **3333** and type **1234**. Click the **Close** button.

5. Generate reports.

   Select the **Query** tab.

   Highlight the **Query:expdate**.

   Click **New Object** 🗎 ▾ button down arrow.

   Select **AutoReport**.

   What is wrong with this report? HINT: Look at the location of the date.

   Click **View** 📝 ▾ button down arrow. Select **Design View**.

   Click the **Date place holder**, and then click the **Left** justify button. Click the **Label** 🅰 button on the toolbox bar, click in the **Page Header** band, and type **Prepared by Your Name**. If the toolbox bar is not displayed, select **View** from the menu and click **Toolbox**. Figure 8–7 shows you what the form should look like.

   Click the **Close** button, **Yes** to save it, type **Query:expdate**, and click **OK**. If prompted to replace the Query:expdate report, click Yes.

   Click **Report** tab, highlight **Query:expdate**, and click **Preview** button.

   Close **Report Preview** window.

   Using the Table Wizard.

   Click **Table** tab.

   Select **Table:Staff** table.

   Click the **New Object** 🗎 ▾ down arrow button. Choose **Report**.

   Select **Report Wizard** and click **OK**.

   Click the >> button to place all the fields in the Report window.

   Click **Next**, select **Dept field**, click >, and click **Next, Next**.

Select **Block** and **Landscape**. Make sure Shrinks to fit is selected.

Click **Next**, select **Corporate**, click **Next**.

Type **Staff Report** and click **Finish**.

Click the **Printer** 🖨 button, click **Close** button, and click window **Close** ☒ button. Exit **Access**.

EXERCISE 3: DESIGN A SMALL CLINICAL DATABASE

Objectives

1. Design a record structure to use in generating a reminder or work list for caring for a group of patients.
2. Enter data for ten patients.

Activity

1. Use the following table to outline the data structure for the database. Develop the database for data you need to provide patient care. Consult a reminder sheet, worksheets, and patient plans or progress notes from your clinical facility for ideas of data to include.

Field Name	Field Type	Field Size	Description Data

Field Name	Field Type	Field Size	Description Data

2. Enter the data for ten patients.

3. What problems did you encounter?

4. Save the data.

5. Search for an individual patient.

6. Search for all patients with a specific diagnosis.

7. Add two more records.

8. Generate a work list or reminder sheet for a group of patients.

ASSIGNMENT 1: CLINICAL EXPERIENCE DATABASE

Directions

1. Construct a table structure(s) to use for monitoring your clinical experiences. Attach a sheet of paper that identifies the fields, data type, and field size.

2. Explain the rationale behind the table(s). What questions were you trying to answer? What experiences were you trying to monitor?

3. Create the table and enter records for ten of your experiences. Provide a print out of the table structure as created and the data in the table.

4. Conduct a search to answer one of your questions. Print the results.

ASSIGNMENT 2: DATA CLASSIFICATION, TAXONOMY, AND DATA SETS

Directions

1. Read two references on the Nursing Minimum Data Set or any other Clinical Minimum Data Set.
2. Answer the questions below.

Questions

1. Define classification systems, taxonomies, and data sets. Review an article or two about one of those below. You can use:

   International Classification of Diseases, 10th Clinical Modification (ICD-10 CM)

   The Physicians' Current Procedural Terminology (CPT-4)

   Diagnostic and Statistical Manual of Mental Disorders (DSM-III)

   Systematized Nomenclature of Pathology (SNOP)

   Systematized Nomenclature of Medicine (SNOMED)

   Nursing Intervention Classifications (NIC) (McCloskey and Bulechek)

   International Classification of Nursing Practice (ICNP) (Working paper on international classification)

   Home Health Care Classification (HHCC) (Saba)

   North American Nursing Diagnosis Association (NANDA)

   Omaha Visiting Nurses Association System

   Nursing Minimum Data Set (NMDS) (Werley)

   Nursing Lexicon (Grobe)

2. What are the major advantages/disadvantages of doing this type of work?

3. What are the database and automation implications of this work?

4. Design table structure(s) using elements from any of the above.

Chapter 9

Using the World Wide Web

OBJECTIVES

1. Describe the Internet and the World Wide Web.
2. Define related Internet terms.
3. Describe the meaning of components of World Wide Web addressing.
4. Identify the hardware and software needed to get connected to the Internet.
5. Use browsers to explore the World Wide Web.
6. Download various files from the Internet.
7. Evaluate and create Web pages.

INTRODUCTION

This chapter focuses on the fastest growing use for a computer—accessing the Internet. Computer users access the Internet for the purpose of communicating with others, obtaining information and files, and purchasing products. A brief definition and description of the Internet and a discussion of the World Wide Web begin this chapter. This is followed by a discussion of the services available on the Internet, how one connects to the Internet, browsing for and locating information, and downloading files. A brief discussion of creating Web pages is also included. Additional information on Internet communication (e-mail, newsgroups, list services, etc.) and informational resources (searching and search engines) is included in Chapters 10 and 11 respectively.

THE INTERNET

The Internet, sometimes referred to as the information or global superhighway, is a loose association of thousands of networks and millions of computers across the world that all work together to share information. It is a true global network providing us with quick access to information from all over the world.

No one source foots the bill for the Internet. Everyone pays for their part. For example, colleges and universities pay for their connection to some regional network. This regional network in turn pays a national provider for access. Many institutions and companies donate their computer resources in the form of servers and computer technicians to hold up some part of the Internet. Other companies own and operate components of the Internet in the form of communication lines and related switching equipment. The main lines that carry the bulk of the traffic are collectively known as the *Internet backbone*. In the US, there are four main network access points (NAPs), each owned by a different company. They are PacBell in San Francisco, AmeriTech in Chicago, MFS in Washington, DC, and Sprint in New York. These companies sell access to the Internet to organizations and businesses. In turn, additional companies are in the Online and Internet Service Provider (ISP) business. This will be discussed in more detail later in the chapter.

By connecting to each other, these networks create high-speed communication lines that crisscross the United States. These high-speed communication lines also extend to Europe, Great Britain, Australia, Japan, Asia, and the rest of the world. Note, however, that all points along the route may not be as equally well developed as the network in the United States and some other countries. In the United States the backbone has many intersecting points. If one point fails or slows down, data is quickly rerouted over another part. This redundancy was one of the key points in its development. In some parts of the world, the network may have less redundancy making it more vulnerable to slowdowns or breakdowns.

While no one entity owns or controls the Internet, there are a handful of organizations that are influential in its development and maintenance. Here are a few of them.

- The Internet Society (ISOC) is a supervisory organization made up of individuals, corporations, nonprofit organizations, and government agencies from the Internet community. It holds the ultimate authority for the direction of the Internet.
- The Internet Architecture Board (IAB) is responsible for defining the overall architecture of the Internet (the backbone) and all the networks attached to it. It approves standards and allocation of resources like Internet addresses.
- The Internet Engineering Task Force (IETF) focuses on operational and technical issues related to keeping the Internet running smoothly as a whole.
- World Wide Web Consortium (W3C) works with the standards for HyperText Mark-up Language (HTML) and other specifics as they relate to the Web part of the Internet. Documents displayed in Web browsers are coded through the use of HTML.
- Backbone ISPs, cable and satellite companies, regional and long-distance phone companies, and various agencies of the US government contribute to the Internet telecommunications infrastructure.
- The Internet Assignment Numbers Authority (IANA) and the Internet Network Information Center (InterNIC) are the two organizations responsible for assigning IP addresses and domain names, respectively.

What makes this network work is a network communications protocol called Transmission Control Protocol/Internet Protocol (TCP/IP). This is a communications protocol that is the basis for computers talking to each other over the Internet. Every computer on the Internet must use and understand this protocol for sending and receiving data. This protocol uses what is called a packet-switched network that minimizes the chance of losing data sent over the transmission medium. The TCP part of the protocol breaks every piece of data into small chunks called packets. Each packet is wrapped in an electronic envelope that contains the Web addresses for both the sender and the recipient. Once the packets are created, the IP protocol determines the best route for getting the packet from one point to another point. Each packet may arrive at its destination by a different route. Routers examine the destination address and then send the packet to another router until it finally reaches its destination. The router sends the packet by the best route available at that time. When the packet arrives at its destination, TCP takes over. Its function now is to identify each packet, to make sure it is intact, and to reassemble the packets into the original data.

SERVICES ON THE INTERNET

There are many services available to you on the Internet. Most people, when using the term Internet, use it to mean the World Wide Web. The Web is just one part of the Internet albeit the fastest growing one. Basically the services available to you can be placed into three categories. These are electronic communications, information services, and information retrieval.

Electronic Communications	These services permit the users to communicate with other people on the Internet via electronic mail, bulletin boards, chat rooms, list services, and news groups. These are discussed in Chapter 10.
Information Services	Information services are commonly referred to as remote login. These services permit the user to login to other computers from their computer for the purpose of obtaining information. Some of these services include telnet, gopher, and the Web.
Information Retrieval	These services permit you to obtain files from other sites and bring them to your computer. This is commonly referred to as file transfer. Ftp (file transfer protocol) is the most commonly used protocol for transferring files from one computer to another.

One thing that is happening regarding services on the Internet is that all of them are becoming easier to use. For example, when transferring a file you do not need to know all the earlier commands for getting and putting files or for activating the file transfer protocol (ftp). Most of the time you click on a download hyperlink and respond to prompts. You may even download a graphic by right clicking on the graphic and selecting save target as from the shortcut menu. The user is isolated from the background commands necessary to use these services.

Another trend regarding services on the Internet is the closing of some sites that use telnet and gopher protocols. Telnet sites permitted you to login to a computer at another site for the purpose of accessing its information. Many of these sites permitted anyone to use them. Gopher sites were hierarchically based menus for accessing information available on the Internet. The user selected from the menu and submenus until the information was found. Now, the Web and search sites make it easier to find and access this information by using search engines, directories, and hyperlinks. The services that were once provided by telnet and gopher sites are now being replaced by Web sites and searching facilities.

WORLD WIDE WEB

Some consider the World Wide Web (WWW) the easiest of the Internet services to use. This part of the Internet is the graphical portion that stores electronic files, called Web pages, on servers that you access from your computer. Keywords in a document are highlighted. Selecting a keyword takes the reader to another part of that document related to that word, to another document at that site, or to another site. In addition, some graphics and buttons are also hyper-linked permitting the user to go to different sites or obtain more information at this site.

Presented here are some of the terms related to the World Wide Web.

Client-server Client is your Web browser software that knows how to communicate with a Web server. Your personal computer is the client. The server is the remote computer that stores the Web page files and communicates with the client. The computer you are communicating with is the server.

Hyperlinks   Hyperlinks are text or graphics linked to other parts of a file or to other files at this site or other sites. You know you are on a hyperlink when your pointer turns to a hand ( ).

HTML   HyperText Markup Language. The tagging that is used to code the Web page files so they display on a variety of computers. Included in these tags are commands for linking text and graphics.

HTTP   HyperText Transfer Protocol. The communications protocol used for access-ing and working with the World Wide Web. Do not confuse it with HTML.

Web Browser   Software, like Internet Explorer and Netscape Navigator, used to access Web pages on the Internet and to interpret HTML code into readable form.

UNDERSTANDING ADDRESSING

When you connect to the Internet, you are identified by a unique address. This address allows you to access information and have others send information to you. While humans like words and graphics to communicate, computers like using numbers to communicate. In this section we discuss the IP address, Domain Name, and URL, which are all terms used to locate and dif-ferentiate your computer and files from all other computers and files on the Internet.

IP Address

The IP or Internet Protocol number is a unique identification number for each computer on the Internet. No two computers can have the same number. It uses a four-part number from 0 to 255 for each part of the four-part number. This number may be something like 208.34.242.17. The same thing going on with our phone system is now going on with the IP address system. Just like we are running out of phone numbers with the growth of the cellular phone business, we are fast approaching the 4.2 billion possible addresses for the IP system. Work is proceeding on finding alternative numbering systems that do not require major hardware or software changes.

Domain Name

A domain name is an address, similar to that used by the postal service, that points to a com-puter with a specific IP address. It is a description of a computer's location on the Internet. Domain names create a single identity for a series of computers used by a company. A special Domain Naming System (DNS) computer looks up the name and matches it with its assigned number. Remember computers like numbers, people prefer names.

Examples of domain names are www.adobe.com or webopedia.internet.com.

The domain name contains a few components, separated by a period. It goes from left, more specific name for the computer, to right, category that describes the nature of the organization. The first item is the name of the host itself (www or webopedia). The next item is the second level domain name (adobe or internet). An organization or entity with INTERnet Network Information Center (InterNIC) registration services registers it. This is the part of the domain name that is registered. The last item (com) is a top-level domain name and describes the purpose of the organization or entity who owns the second level name.

com   Business or other commercial enterprises

edu   Post-secondary institutions

gov   Government agency or departments

mil   Military

net   Network service provider or resource

org   Organizations, usually nonprofit or charitable

Additional top-level domain names are currently proposed. Some of these are *.shop* for businesses that sell products or goods and *.arts* for cultural and entertainment activities. A domain may contain other components between the host and second level domain; these are called subdomains. Subdomain names are used by large organizations that support many Internet servers. For example, the US government and its many agencies differentiate one agency from another through use of the subdomains.

Anyone can register with the InterNIC for a second level domain name. However, there is a fee for having one's own second level domain name. To see who owns specific domain names go to http://rs.internic.net/rs-internic.html. Some enterprising people have registered a variety of names of big corporations and now make money selling the rights to these second domain names to those organizations.

Understanding the domain names will help you identify the type of information you are likely to receive from a certain site. For example, knowing that the site is a government agency like the IRS (http://www.irs.ustreas.gov) means that the forms and instructions for the forms provided there are legitimate. Obtaining health information from the National Library of Medicine (http://www.nlm.nih.gov) or Centers for Disease Control and Prevention (http://www.cdc.gov) means you are probably accessing information that is accurate and reliable. However, accessing information from someone's personal home page could mean you are accessing information that may or may not be accurate or reliable.

Uniform Resource Locator (URL)

URLs help a computer locate a Web page's exact location on the Web server. Note that while IP addresses and domain names locate the computer, they do not locate the Web documents on the server. The URL helps the computer find the actual Web pages.

Here is a sample URL http://www.dept.institution.edu/path/toa/webpage.html

The first part http:// identifies the communications protocol the computers are using to talk to each other. Other examples are ftp, gopher, news, and telnet.

The second part www.dept.institution.edu is the Web server or host computer where the page is located. Remember the first part of this address describes the local host site and the second part describes the domain name that is registered to that institution. The institution can decide how it wants to set up its local host. For example, the local host might be www or www.healthschools or www.dept.

The third part /path/toa/ tells the server where the file is found. The slashes represent folders, just like those on your computer. This provides the computer with the information about the location of a Web page file.

The last part webpage.html is the actual filename you are trying to find. Most of the time it will be a HTML or HTM file. This is the actual file the browser displays on your screen.

Most of the URLs you will be using start with http:// because you are accessing WWW. Remember when typing these URLs in the location or address box, there are no spaces between the parts, they always use forward slashes, and you must type them in exactly. If you type a one (1) for a lower case L (l), the computer will not be able to find the site and will return an error message. If you have the URL in electronic form, highlight the URL and use the copy and paste feature to place it in the **Address** or **Location** text box to avoid typing errors.

CONNECTING TO THE INTERNET

This section provides a brief outline of the equipment and software needed to access the Internet. Depending on what you want to do on the Internet, you may need more or less equipment. For example, using the Web and accessing multimedia files requires a higher level computer than accessing a Pine e-mail program on a Unix computer. In addition, you need software for each type of service you want to access. To make things easier software-wise, most Internet Service Providers and browser programs now come with many of the features you need bundled into one easy to install program.

As discussed above, you will also need an IP address for your computer and a host domain name. The university or service provider assigns these to you. You might have a fixed IP address that needs to be configured with your software or a dynamic one that works behind the scenes like with an Internet Service Provider (ISP). You will also need to obtain a user ID and password for signing onto the Internet. Your user ID and password may be chosen by you or assigned by the institution using their user naming standards. For example, some institutions use the users last name, first letter of first name and middle initial; others use last name, first letter of first name and a number. So a user name might be joosir or joosi1. Many ISPs let you choose your user ID as long as someone else on the system does not have that ID. So you may decide to be ngtcrawler, nurseJane, or hojo. What is important is that each user on that system must be uniquely identified in the system. No two users can have the same user ID.

While the user ID is public knowledge, your password is private. You should safeguard your password as you do your PIN from your ATM account. You should not give it to anyone or write it down where others can see it. In addition, each system has criteria for what are acceptable passwords. For example, many systems require a minimum number of characters and a combination of letters and numbers. So, your password might be bri811. You should not use any word found in a dictionary or that is common knowledge about you such as your spouse's first name. These are too easy for someone to break. Many suggest you use nonsense combinations that make sense to you. An example might be gcle95 where g=green, cle=camry le, and 95=year of the car.

Computer

While the computer requirements are not very demanding, you do need a computer with sufficient RAM, a fast processor, and free hard drive space. To use the Web and take advantage of its graphics capabilities, you need a computer manufactured in the last three years. At the least, it needs to run Windows 95 or Macintosh OS 8. The operating system then dictates some of the hardware specifications. For example, you will need a minimum of 8-16 MB of RAM, at least a 486 processor, and 1 GB hard drive. While Windows 95 is the minimum, you might consider Windows 98 or Windows 2000, Pentium level processors with 300, 400, or 500 MHz speed, and multi-gigabyte hard drives. It really depends on what you want to do on the Internet. Remember that hardware requirements change rapidly as our expectations and demands grow, so chances are great that you will own more than one computer in your lifetime. Every few years you purchase another computer as your needs and the technology change. If you expect full multimedia information to appear on the computer instantly, you need a higher level computer with higher speed connections and full multimedia capabilities—sound cards, speakers, and good graphics. If you expect to use primarily e-mail, a basic computer will do.

Network Connection

From home, your computer needs to have a connection to the host computer. This is generally accomplished through your phone line, however, there is growing interest and availability of connecting through your TV cable or a one-wire-fits-all connection for your phone, cable, and the Internet. When connecting on campus through your dorm or office, the connection is done through the campus network connections.

Modem From home you need a phone or cable modem. On the sending end of the communication process, a phone modem converts a digital signal from your computer to an analog signal that can be transmitted over a telephone line. Remember that at present most of our phone lines to homes are analog connections. On the receiving end of the process, the phone modem converts an analog signal from the telephone line to a digital signal that can be interpreted to the computer. The phone modem needs to have access to the phone jack since it uses the phone line to establish a connection with the Internet host computer.

The cable modem is designed to work with your cable TV line and is specified by your cable provider. It provides faster access to the Internet than traditional phone modems. A cable modem typically has two connections, one to the cable wall outlet and the other to the computer via an Ethernet card.

As the price of digital phone connections comes down, you might be connecting through an ISDN (Integrated Services Digital Network) or DSL (Digital Subscriber Line) modem. As phone lines are converted to digital rather than analog signals, more users have access to digital phone services. Both of these technologies are presently out of reach cost-wise for most users. In either case, you need special modems to make these types of connections and generally an Ethernet card.

Network Card and Cable This is a card and related cable installed into a computer that enables a direct connection to the network. This is the typical connection from college dorms, labs, and offices. This type of connection does not need a modem, but requires a special cable and active network port. You will need either the modem or network card.

Access Providers

Access providers are organizations that provide access to an Internet host computer. These access providers often supply the software needed to connect to the Internet. There are several different types of access providers as outlined below. You need to choose the type of access that is appropriate for you.

Internet Service Providers Two types of ISPs are online providers who give you access to a variety of special services and databases as well as Internet and e-mail access, and Internet service providers who give you access to the Internet and e-mail, but no other special services or databases. Some examples of this first group are America Online, Microsoft Network, AT&T WorldNet, and Prodigy. Examples of the second group are USA OnRamp, EarthLink, and MindSpring.

When selecting your ISP, you will want to consider the following points:

- Local access phone numbers or 1-800 numbers with national access
- Flat rate that covers all connecting time
- The latest version of the standard browsers like Netscape or Explorer
- Fast, reliable connections—not just at off peak hours
- Reliable and responsive technical support
- Space on the server for your home pages
- Services that you want to use such as e-mail, Web and related multimedia files, ftp, newsreader, gopher, and telnet

Free-Net Access These are generally community-based computer networks designed to help the local citizens access and share information and resources. One of the resources is access to the Internet. Funding to support this type of access is generally done through local libraries, government funds, and interested local businesses. Some areas offer free net access through the local libraries and other types of organizations; others charge a small fee for access. This type of service is generally restricted to people who live in the community or meet specific criteria. Many of these networks rely on a group of volunteers to assist in maintaining and developing the system.

Company or Institutional Access This type of access is provided to an employee or student in an institution. Access is then provided through the organization's computer and connection facilities. A user installs and uses the software provided by the company for dialing into the computer at the company or institution. Once connected to the company's computer, the user now has access to all the capabilities provided by the company including Internet access. An advantage to this type of access is that you are generally making a local phone call with no monthly Internet access fees. Disadvantages are that you must remain an employee or student, and you are subjected to the policies of that organization or institution.

Software

The software you need to access the Internet depends on how you access it and who provides the connection service. What you need are communications protocols that coordinate data transfer to and from your computer and the Internet (like TCP/IP, Serial Line Internet Protocol—SLIP, or Point-to-Point Protocol—PPP) and protocols for the various services you want to access (like e-mail, Web, ftp, etc.). In addition, you may need software that permits you to dial into the university and access their Web resources. This is the software that works behind the scenes and with which you do little once it is installed.

The Internet front-end software is the software with which you interact. You might use a comprehensive program like Netscape or Internet Explorer or one provided by your service provider. Most of the time this software is provided free of charge to you when you subscribe, is available for free downloading, or is available as part of your operating system. Contact your computer center to find out what software is needed to access their services and how you obtain it.

USING WEB BROWSERS

Once you are connected, you will want to start using the Web. A Web browser is the software program you use to access the World Wide Web. Although there are many different browsers available, the two most commonly used are Microsoft Internet Explorer and Netscape Navigator. Both are based on an earlier browser called Mosaic, which was the first browser for accessing this graphical portion of the Internet. Both browsers are available for Windows and Macintosh systems. There are, however, slight differences in the two versions of each browser. Learning the basics of using a browser should not take you long.

While there is much competition between these two browsers, they are for the most part very similar in how you work with them. Both are available for free from each company's Web site (Internet Explorer from http://www.microsoft.com/windows/ie and Netscape Navigator from http://www.netscape.com). The main elements of Web browsers follow the conventions for all windows programs. For example, they both have a title bar, menu bar, toolbar, scroll bars, and status bars. Discussed next are the toolbars for both Internet Explorer and Netscape Navigator.

Since browsers, like most software, are constantly being revised, you might want to check which version of the browser you are using. With each new version, there are more capabilities built into the browser for using the Web. The basic functions, however, remain constant. That is the ability to use the back, forward, stop, search, print, and home buttons.

Orientation to Internet Explorer and Netscape Navigator

Since the toolbars for both are more similar than dissimilar, this discussion will present both.

The Toolbar Figures 9–1 and 9–2 show you the basic layout of the screen for Internet Explorer and Netscape Navigator respectively.

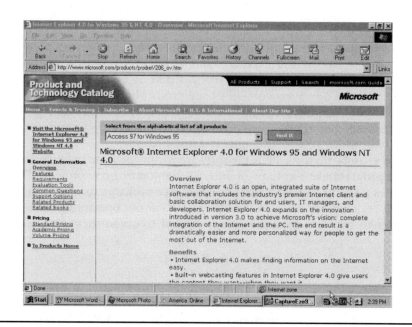

FIGURE 9–1.
Microsoft Internet Explorer Main Screen

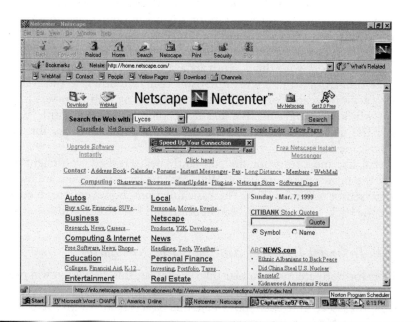

FIGURE 9–2.
Netscape Navigator Main Screen

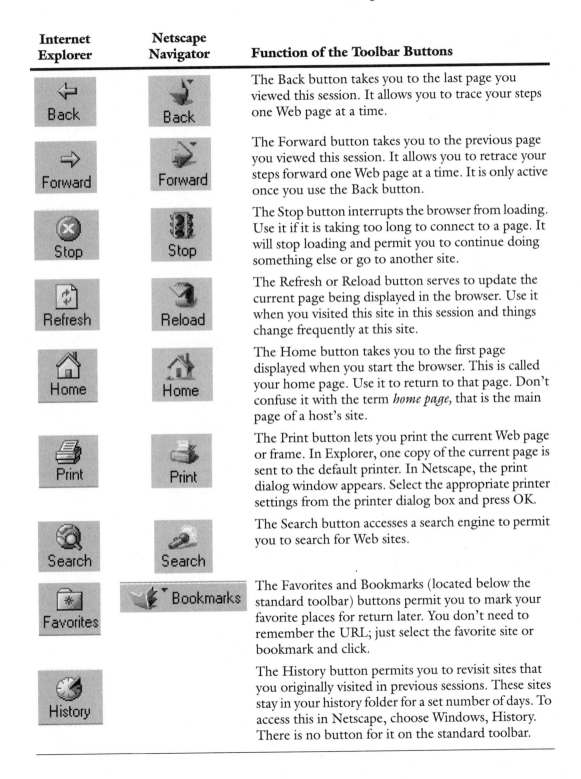

Internet Explorer	Netscape Navigator	Function of the Toolbar Buttons
Back	Back	The Back button takes you to the last page you viewed this session. It allows you to trace your steps one Web page at a time.
Forward	Forward	The Forward button takes you to the previous page you viewed this session. It allows you to retrace your steps forward one Web page at a time. It is only active once you use the Back button.
Stop	Stop	The Stop button interrupts the browser from loading. Use it if it is taking too long to connect to a page. It will stop loading and permit you to continue doing something else or go to another site.
Refresh	Reload	The Refresh or Reload button serves to update the current page being displayed in the browser. Use it when you visited this site in this session and things change frequently at this site.
Home	Home	The Home button takes you to the first page displayed when you start the browser. This is called your home page. Use it to return to that page. Don't confuse it with the term *home page*, that is the main page of a host's site.
Print	Print	The Print button lets you print the current Web page or frame. In Explorer, one copy of the current page is sent to the default printer. In Netscape, the print dialog window appears. Select the appropriate printer settings from the printer dialog box and press OK.
Search	Search	The Search button accesses a search engine to permit you to search for Web sites.
Favorites	Bookmarks	The Favorites and Bookmarks (located below the standard toolbar) buttons permit you to mark your favorite places for return later. You don't need to remember the URL; just select the favorite site or bookmark and click.
History		The History button permits you to revisit sites that you originally visited in previous sessions. These sites stay in your history folder for a set number of days. To access this in Netscape, choose Windows, History. There is no button for it on the standard toolbar.

Starting the Browser Remember from Chapter 4 Software Applications—Common Tasks, there are several ways to start programs. If your institution doesn't have the browser on the desktop, you may need to use the start, programs, browser option. Note that when you start the browser you are sent to a specific home page. This page might be your institution's or the browser's. You have the ability to change this home page by using the set preference feature found in both browsers.

To start the browser, double click the **Browser** icon.

To change the home page in Internet Explorer:

> Select **View, Internet Options**.
>
> If not selected, select text in the **Address** text box in the home page options section of the window.
>
> Type new **URL** and click **OK**.

To change the home page in Netscape Navigator:

> Select **Edit, Preferences**.
>
> Select text in the **Location** text box in the home page section of the window.
>
> Type new **URL** and click **OK**.

Now, when you start the browser it will point to the new home page. Note that this is also the process you use to change how long sites stay in your history folder.

Surfing the Net Surfing the Net refers to clicking hyperlinks to go to another part of this document, to another document, or to another site. To use a hyperlink, click it. You know it is a hyperlink when you place your pointer on top of it and the pointer turns into a hand. Be patient because it sometimes takes the Web pages a while to load. Intensive graphic pages and loading over a modem take longer than those coming in through an Ethernet connection. When traffic is especially heavy on the Internet, it will also slow down your loading time.

If you know the URL for the site you want to visit, type the URL in the locator or address text box located under the standard toolbar. Most current browsers do not require that you type in the http:// part of the address. It inserts that part for you. The computer is very exacting so you must make sure the address is correct.

Go to a site by typing the URL:

> Click the **Text** in the **Locator** or **Address** text box to select the text.
>
> Type the **URL** and press **Enter**.
>
> Click any **Hyperlink** objects or text to surf.

Using History List The history list keeps track of sites visited for the past several days and offers a convenient means of redisplaying pages. Unlike favorites or bookmark lists, which store page locations that you've designated, history items are saved automatically when you display a page. Most browsers store all sites visited in this folder regardless of how you arrived at the site. Some locator or address drop-down lists only store sites where you typed the URL.

To use the history list in Internet Explorer:

Click the **History**  button.

Click the **Day of the Week** you visited the site.

Click the **Site** and/or related **Actual pages** at the site.

To use the history list in Netscape:

Choose **Windows, History**. There is no button for it on the standard toolbar.

Click the **Site**.

Printing a Web Page Note the subtle difference in printing from the two browsers. Internet Explorer sends one copy of the current document to the default printer, but Netscape brings up the print dialog window for you to choose a printer, select pages, and select number of copies. When a Web page prints from the print command, it will print both the graphics and the text.

To print a Web page from Internet Explorer:

Go to the **Web** page you want to print.

Click the **Printer** button.

To print a Web page from Netscape Navigator:

Go to the **Web** page you want to print.

Click the **Printer** button.

Make the appropriate selections in the printer dialog box and press **Enter**.

If working at a site with frames (screen is divided into several sections, each with its own scroll bar), make sure you have the frame you want to print selected before issuing the print command.

Saving a Web Page Sometimes when you are surfing you come across a Web page you want to save because of the content or the tagging. Note that when saving the Web page it saves it as a HTML file with all the code and text, but not the graphics. The graphic objects are separate files, and unless you save them separately, you will not have them. The graphics files are not embedded in the HTML file; the file points to the graphic file.

To save a Web page:

> Select **File, Save as**.
>
> Select the **Location** and **File name**.
>
> Click the **Save** button.

To save a graphic file:

> Right click the **Graphic**.
>
> Select **Save Picture or Image as.**
>
> Select **Location** to download the graphic.
>
> Type a **File name.**
>
> Check the save type as for gif or jpg.
>
> Click the **Save** button.

Creating a Bookmark or Favorite   This is the feature that permits you to save sites you intend on visiting frequently. You use this feature to help you organize this list of Web pages so you can find them later. There are basic functions you can expect from all versions of both browsers with regards to bookmarks and favorites. While the exact procedure will vary, the basic function will exist in all versions of both browsers.

The basic functions are:

- Adding and removing Bookmarks or Favorites from your list.
- Organizing the list of URLs into categories or folders.
- Editing and arranging the bookmarks or favorites.

There are a number of factors complicating the matter of using this feature when using computer lab facilities or campus libraries. You will often find a prescribed set of bookmarks or favorites designated by the library or the lab. There may be limitations to what you may change or add to this set. In addition, you may not have access to the bookmarks and favorites when you use a different computer. For these reasons, it is recommended that you create this folder on your diskette and not on the hard drive. The exact procedure for doing this is described in Exercise 1 and 2 at the end of this chapter.

Function	Netscape Navigator	Internet Explorer
Adding Sites	Go to the **Site**.	Go to the **Site**.
	Click **Bookmarks** on the toolbar OR select **Window, Bookmarks**.	Select **Favorite, Add to Favorites**.
	Click **Add Bookmark**.	Click **Create in** button.
		Select **Folder** and click **OK**.

Function	Netscape Navigator	Internet Explorer
Creating a Folder	Click **Bookmarks** [Bookmarks] on the toolbar or select **Window, Bookmarks**. Click **Edit Bookmark**. Click **Folder** under which you want the new folder added. Right click on **Folder**. Select **New, Folder**. Type **Name Folder** and click **OK**.	Select **Favorites, Organize Favorites**. Right click in **Window**. Select **New, Folder**. Click **New Folder**. Click **Rename** button. Type **Name** and press **Enter**. Click **Close** button.
Organizing Sites & Folders	Select **Bookmark** [Bookmarks], **Edit Bookmarks**. A Bookmark dialog window appears, allowing you to organize your bookmark collection. Note this window functions just like Windows Explorer. Move Bookmark Items Up and Down on the list by dragging and dropping.	Select **Favorites, Organize Favorites**. Select **Folder** or **Site** to move. Click **Move** button. Select **Folder** to move to and click **OK**.
Deleting Sites	Select **Bookmark** [Bookmarks], **Edit Bookmarks**. Right click the **Site** to be removed. Select **Delete Bookmark**. **Close** window.	Select **Favorites, Organize Favorites**. Select **Folder** or **Site** to delete. Click **Delete** button. Click **Yes** to confirm deletion. Click **Close**.

Managing Your Internet Files

When you surf the Internet, the Internet sites you visit send temporary files to your computer. These files are stored in one of two folders located on the hard drive in the Windows folder. They are the **Cookies** folder and the **Temporary Internet Files** folder. These files sent to your computer are for the purpose of speeding the loading of graphics files when you visit the site again and marking what you did at that site. The problem with these files is that they take space on your hard drive and don't seem to be deleted automatically. You therefore need to periodically delete these files. How often you do this depends on how much you surf. Failure to periodically purge these files could lead to a full hard drive.

To delete these files:

Double click **My Computer** and **C hard drive** icons.

Double click the **Windows** folder.

Double click the **Cookies** folder.

Highlight **all the files**.

Press the **Delete** key.

Respond **Yes** to any prompts about deleting these cookie files.

Repeat the process with the **Temporary Internet Files** folder.

This section of the chapter presented some basic functions for working with a browser. Both Netscape Navigator and Internet Explorer were presented to show you how close the browsers are in their functioning. The next section focuses on some basics regarding evaluating quality of design and creating simple Web pages.

CREATING AND EVALUATING WEB PAGES

This section of the chapter covers some basics of Web page creation as well as evaluating the design of a Web page. This is not intended to make you a Web designer, but to give you some pointers with which to start as well as some help on evaluating design. Material on evaluating the quality of the content of a Web site is covered in Chapter 11 Information—Access, Evaluation, and Use. As you begin to visit various Web sites you will begin to appreciate a site that is well designed and develop criteria for what you find most appealing in a site's design.

Creating Web Pages

While the first thing that most Web page creators want to do is start tagging the documents, there is in fact a process for designing Web pages. This process is outlined here and serves as a guide for things to consider when creating Web pages. Paying attention to these items at the start saves you time and energy in the longer term.

- Decide what you want to accomplish with this site. Answer these questions: What is the intent of this site? What do I want to accomplish with this site? What are the purposes and goals of this site? Create a statement that reflects your answers to these questions to serve as a guide during the development and maintenance of the Web site.
- Identify your target audience to help focus your design and content. Many Web sites are created without identifying the who. A design for teenagers may not be appropriate for professional audiences.
- Develop a site map showing the relationship between the parts. What pages will you have? How will they link or relate to others? Keep in mind that users may access these pages in varying ways and may not always start at the beginning.
- Develop criteria for inclusion of content. How will you decide what content to include? What is your criterion for inclusion? Keep in mind the intent of the site and the target audience.

- Decide who will be responsible for maintaining each part of the site. Consider how often the data may need to be updated and then determine a schedule for reviewing and updating the parts.
- Decide on a design that best presents the content. A consistent look to the site helps keep the user oriented as to place. Some things to consider are placing navigational aids consistently in the same place on each page identifying the who, what, when, and where of the content. Make these navigational aids, such as buttons, easy and clear to follow. Set these standards at the start and then use them.

Once these guidelines are addressed there are some specific things to consider regarding design and layout. While these points serve as a guide, good design is a matter of your own personal taste and style, not someone else's. Good design also keeps in mind the intent of the site and the target audience.

- Use common sense. Remember that many people access the Internet through dial-up modems and not the faster Ethernet connections. Graphics take longer to load than text and you will lose your audience if they have to wait too long for the graphics. Use the ten-second rule; that is, your page should load from many different types of connections in ten seconds. Also consider that not everyone will be using the latest technology so may not have the latest version of a browser or the same size monitor you used for design. When in doubt about design, keep it simple.
- Design a template or layout to use with most of the pages. This means to make sure that each page has a descriptive title located in the same place on all pages, buttons and navigational aids to take the user back to the original site home page and to other pages at this site, and identifying information such as who created the page, when it was created or last revised, and how you can contact them if you have questions. Many pages also include information about copyright.
- Use graphics and sound as appropriate. The graphics and sounds should add something to the content, not detract from it. Just because you have the ability to place many graphics on the page, doesn't mean you should. Keep in mind the rules "simple is better" and "white space is good." Consider that many users find graphics and sound distracting. Other users may access your page in settings where sound is distracting to others. Pay attention to copyright requirements especially when using graphics you did not create.
- Keep graphics reasonable in size. Try to maintain a balance between size, resolution, color, and look. That means you should try and keep the size between 25K and 30K with a resolution of 72 dpi. Use the appropriate graphic file format—gif files for images and jpg for photos. Use thumbnail graphics (small postage size pictures) and give the user the option to look at the graphic in a larger version. Keep in mind that what most users see when your page loads is the first four inches of a printed page.
- Select colors carefully. Make sure the colors work together and are easy to read or are pleasing on the eyes. If you don't have color sense, have someone else design the color scheme or use an already developed color scheme. Be especially careful of colors if you want users to print your pages.

Now you are on your way to begin designing your page. This next section deals with a brief introduction to HTML. While there are other tagging or markup languages like Standard Generalized Markup Language (SGML), HTML is by far the most commonly used one.

HTML

Once the documents are designed in terms of layout and content, the documents need to be coded or tagged. The concept of HTML is to provide a mechanism for displaying text and graphics based documents in Web browsers. It describes the contents of a Web page by specifying fonts and font-related attributes as well as location or layout of the text and graphics. HTML is a series of tags embedded in the Web document that tells the browser how to display the page. The tags look like the example here.

```
<HTML>

<HEAD>

<TITLE>Document Title</TITLE>

</HEAD>

<BODY>This is my first attempt at a Web page. </BODY>

</HTML>
```

When a browser locates a Web document by using the URL including a path to the page or by being sent there through a link, it interprets these tags regardless of the platform the user is using. This means that the Web pages are displayed on Windows, Unix, and Macintosh computers. These pages will basically look the same.

There are many tools available for creating HTML documents.

- ASCII Editors like NotePad that comes with Windows. This requires you to type the tags and text directly into the document.
- HTML converter programs like MS Word and WordPerfect. It takes the document you create and converts it to a HTML file adding the tags for you.
- HTML editors like FrontPage and Hotdog. These are software programs with a graphical user interface that helps the developer create HTML files without having to type the tags.

Each of these tools has advantages and disadvantages. For example, using a converter program like Word results in documents appearing differently from what you saw in the word processor. The program has to interpret the formatting and convert it into HTML tags. This is not always done cleanly, so you may still need to play with the tags to have the document display as you designed. Exercises 4 and 5 provide experience with creating a simple Web page.

TRANSFERRING FILES

One of the functions that most Internet users want to be able to accomplish is the ability to transfer files from a server on the Internet to their computer. Before the advent of the Web, using ftp (file transfer protocol) was the only way to transfer files from one computer to another over the Internet. Ftp is the communications protocol and program used to transfer data from one location to another. To do this you had to access ftp, then type commands like fetch, put, etc. to tell the computer what to do. Now with Web browsers, transferring files is as simple as following directions on the screen.

If you want to save the current Web page in HTML format or capture a graphic, follow the directions given earlier in this chapter. The browser is great for transferring these files. If, however, you want to transfer a variety of other types of files like compressed (Zip and TAR), program (exe), and pre-formatted files (pdf), use File Transfer Protocol (ftp). The use of ftp is becoming easier as many Web documents that facilitate file transfer embed the ftp commands in the HTML code. That means, you, the user, click something like a download button and follow the directions on the screen.

To use ftp you need the following:

- A computer, your local one, with ftp, and connected to the Internet.
- A computer, remote server, running ftp, and connected to the Internet.
- The Internet address for the remote server. This is usually ftp.same-second-domain.same-high-level-domain.
- If needed, an account on the remote server. Many ftp sites are run as anonymous, which means you don't need to log in or, if you do, you use something like anonymous for the login and your e-mail or nothing for the password.

Two commonly used terms regarding transferring files are download and upload. Download is moving a file from one computer (generally a server) to another (generally your PC). It is a generic term that doesn't specify how you do it, just that the files were transferred. Uploading is transferring a file from your computer to a server. This is the reverse direction and is used when you want to move your local HTML files, for example, to the Web server for publishing on the Net.

While you can use a communications protocol called telnet to run TCP/IP and remotely log in, our discussion here is implementing ftp through Web browser facilities.

To access ftp through your Web browser:

Start your **Web** browser.

In the location or **Address** text box, type **ftp://ftp.domain.domain**.

Select the **File** to transfer or click the **Download** button.

Click **OK** to save the file to disk.

Select location to place the file and filename, if needed, and click **OK**.

The file is now being transferred.

Here are some points to consider when retrieving files from the Internet.

- Know what you are downloading. Some ftp sites are cryptic and assume you know the file-name and how the site is organized. When at an ftp site, look for a file that describes the site and how it is organized. This is usually an index, read.me, or files.1st type of file. Select it and read how things work at that site.
- Keep security in mind. Downloading files from the Internet can introduce a virus into your system. Most sites take precautions to prevent viruses in their files, so the chances are good that the files will be clean. However, to be on the safe side, it doesn't hurt to check your

downloaded files (especially exe and com files) with an anti-virus program before installing on your computer. Many people believe you have a greater chance of getting a virus from e-mail files than from ftp sites.

■ Know the system requirements for the file. Many sites also assume you know what computer system you are using—Windows 95, 98, or NT—as there are different versions of files for the different systems. Many sites will also tell you how large the file is, how much space is needed on the hard drive to run the program, and how much memory the program requires. Make sure the file is the correct one for your system.

■ Obey copyright laws. There are several different types of files for download. Freeware files are yours to use without cost. There are many free graphics files for use in creating your Web pages. While some are totally free for use, others have some restrictions such as free for use at nonprofit Web sites. If you use the file, some sites require you to acknowledge the developer or site in your Web site. Shareware files are yours to try and if you like the program, you pay a small fee to register the program. Many times the registered version is a later version than the shareware one. The last type of files are program files; these require you to pay for them. Some of these programs let you have a trial version before you pay for it; others require that you buy the program before you can download it. The trial versions usually last 30 days and then become unusable.

Summary

This chapter covered some basics of using the Internet, specifically, some terminology and concepts such as Web, URL, ftp, and HyperText. An introduction to connecting and the related requirements followed. A brief orientation to the two most commonly used browsers was presented showing how similar they are. Since the Web is composed of Web pages, the chapter concluded with a brief discussion of creation of Web pages and evaluation of Web page design.

EXERCISE 1: INTRODUCTION TO MS INTERNET EXPLORER AND BROWSING

Objectives

1. Define selected words related to a Web site.
2. Identify different types of Web addressing.
3. Use Internet Explorer to access the World Wide Web and connect to different sites.
4. Create and edit a **Favorites** Folder.
5. Print a document from the World Wide Web.
6. Transfer both a home page and graphic file from the Web.

Activity

1. Define the following words.

    Home page. What are its two meanings in Web jargon?

    What home page do you open to when you connect to your college lab?

    What is a link or hyperlink?

2. Understand Web page addresses.

    What is the difference between an e-mail address and a Web address or URL?

    Here are some addresses. Decide what type of address each is.

    > 43.134.020.12
    >
    > whitehouse.gov
    >
    > Nancy Brown
    >
    > Nbrown@aarme.com

    What might be the host name for a computer at the US Government's Department of Commerce?

    Pat works in the Nursing Department of the University of Pennsylvania. What might be the full Internet address?

    Want to find out who owns a particular domain name?

    Double click the **Internet Explorer** icon.

    Click the **Address** text box to highlight the text.

    Type http://www.networksolutions.com/ in the address text box as shown in Figure 9–3 and press **Enter**.

    Click **WHOIS Search** text on left side of screen.

    Type **disney.com** in the search text box and press **Enter**.

    Who owns this domain name and what is the primary IP address?

Click the **Back** [Back] button on the standard browser toolbar. Highlight text in search box.

Type **nbc.com** in the query text box and press **Enter**.

Who owns this domain name and what is the primary IP address?

Click the **Back** button on the standard browser toolbar. Highlight text in search box.

Type **nursing.com** in the query text box and press **Enter**.

Who owns this domain name and what is the primary IP address?

Click the **Back** button on the standard browser toolbar. Highlight text in search box.

Type **healthcare.com** in the query text box and press **Enter**.

Who owns this domain name and what is the primary IP address?

3. Use Internet Explorer to connect to sites.

Click the **Text** in the **Address** text box in Internet Explorer so it is highlighted.

Type **http://www.mapquest.com** and press **Enter**.

Click **ONLINE MAPS** and type your **Address, City, State,** and **Zip code** in the correct text boxes.

Click **Get Map** [Get Map] button. How accurate is your map?

Click the **Text** in the address text box so it is highlighted.

Now, type **weather.com** and press **Enter**.

Type **Your Zip code** (your actual zip code not the words) in the zip text box and click **Go**.

What is the forecast for the next five days in your city?

Click the **Back** [Back] button two times to go back to mapquest.

Click the **Printer button** at the right bottom side of screen—Printable Maps.

Click the browser **Printer** [Print] button to print a copy of the map.

4. Create and work with **Favorites**.

Click **Favorite, Organize Favorites** on the menu bar.

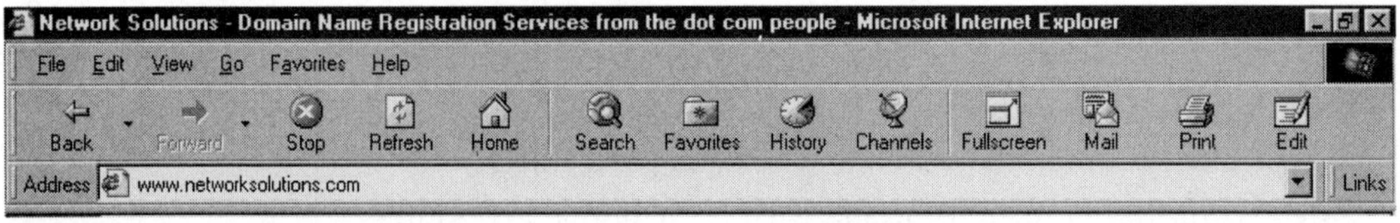

FIGURE 9–3.
Internet Explorer Bars

Right click in the **Favorites** window.

Select **New, Folder**, click **New Folder**, select **Rename** button, and type **Learning Folder**, press **Enter**, and click **Close** button.

Click the **Drop-down Address** [▼] button and click the **weather.com** site.

Select **Favorites, Add favorites**, click **Create in** button, click **Learning Folder**, and click **OK**. The weather site is now added to your favorites folder.

Type **pacprod.com/card.htm** in the address text box and press **Enter**.

Click the **Favorites** folder, **Learning Folder**, and **weather.com**. This takes you to the weather site.

Click **Favorites** folder to remove the folder list from the screen.

Because you may not be able to keep a favorites folder on the hard drive in the lab, you will want to keep your folder on a diskette. You can do this one of two ways—create the favorites folder and at the end of each session copy it to your diskette OR create a word file and paste the URLs of your favorite sites into it.

Click **Favorites** folder to open it. Select **File, Learning Folder**, and **Send to**.

Select the **3½" drive icon**. Folder is now copied to the diskette in the A drive.

To access this folder in the future from your browser, select **File, Open, Browser**. Make sure the list of file types is set to **All Files**[*]. Highlight **Site** or **Folder** and click **Open**.

To access the Word file, start **Word, Open** the Folder, and click **URL**. If you are not in a lab with a direct connection, make sure your browser is running in the background.

5. Save Web pages.

Type www.cdc.gov in Location Text box and press **Enter**.

Click **Health Information, Airbags**. Select **File, Save as** from the menu bar.

Change location to **3½" drive** (click drop-down arrow in Save in Text box area, click **3½" drive**). Click **Save** button.

Open **Word** and the **Airbags** file. What do you notice about this file? Close **Word**.

Now, open **Airbags** file in your Web browser. What is missing?

To save a graphic file:

Type **www.clip-art.com** and click **Medical** button on left side.

Right click the **Ambulance**. Select **Save Picture As** from the shortcut menu.

Select **Location** to download the graphic.

Select **File name** and click the **Save** button.

Close any open windows and exit your browser.

---

[*] and you are looking in the **3½" Floppy drive** storage space.

EXERCISE 2: INTRODUCTION TO NETSCAPE NAVIGATOR AND BROWSING

Objectives

1. Define selected words related to a Web site.
2. Identify different types of Web addressing.
3. Use Internet Explorer to access the World Wide Web and connect to different sites.
4. Create and edit a **Bookmark** folder.
5. Print a document from the World Wide Web.
6. Transfer both a home page and graphic file from the Web.

Activity

1. Define the following words.

   Home page. What are its two meanings in Web jargon?

   What home page do you open to when you connect to your college lab?

   What is a link or hyperlink?

2. Understand Web page addresses.

   What is the difference between an e-mail address and a Web address or URL?

   Here are some addresses. Decide what type of address each is.

   43.134.020.12

   whitehouse.gov

   Nancy Brown

   Nbrown@aarme.com

   What might be the host name for a computer at the US Government's Department of Commerce?

   Pat works in the Nursing Department of the University of Pennsylvania. What might be the full Internet address?

   Want to find out who owns a particular domain name? Double click **Netscape Navigator** icon.

   Click in the **Location** text box to highlight the text.

   Type **http://www.networksolutions.com/** in the **Location** text box as shown in Figure 9–4 and press **Enter**.

   Click **WHOIS Search** text on left side of screen.

   Type **disney.com** in the query text box and press **Enter**.

   Who owns this domain name and what is the primary IP address?

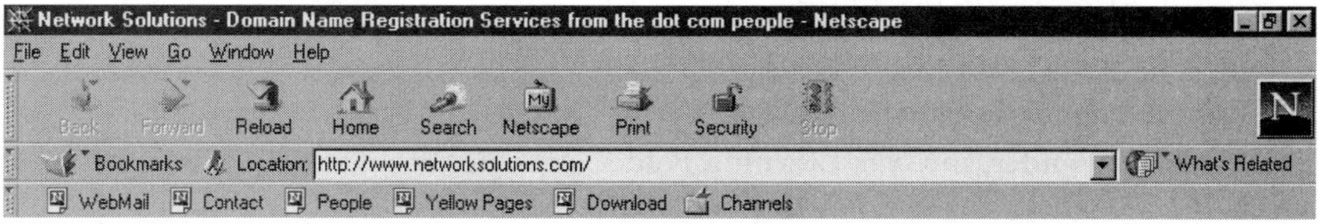

![Netscape Navigator browser window screenshot showing the title bar "Network Solutions - Domain Name Registration Services from the dot com people - Netscape", menu bar with File Edit View Go Window Help, the navigation toolbar with Back, Forward, Reload, Home, Search, Netscape, Print, Security, Stop buttons, the Location bar showing http://www.networksolutions.com/, and the personal toolbar with WebMail, Contact, People, Yellow Pages, Download, Channels.]

FIGURE 9–4.
Netscape Navigator Bars

Click the **Back**  button on the standard browser toolbar. Highlight text in search box.

Type **nbc.com** in the **Query** text box and press **Enter**.

Who owns this domain name and what is the primary IP address?

Click the **Back** button on the standard browser toolbar. Highlight text in search box.

Type **nursing.com** in the query text box and press **Enter**.

Who owns this domain name and what is the primary IP address?

Click the **Back** button on the standard browser toolbar. Highlight text in search box.

Type **healthcare.com** in the **Query** text box and press **Enter**.

Who owns this domain name and what is the primary IP address?

3. Use Netscape Navigator to connect to sites.

    Click the **Text** in the **Location** text box so it is highlighted.

    Type **http://www.mapquest.com** and press **Enter**.

    Click **ONLINE MAPS** and type your **Address, City, State**, and **Zip code** in the correct text boxes.

    Click **Get Map** [Get Map] button. How accurate is your map?

    Click the **Text** in the **Address** text box so it is highlighted.

    Now, type **weather.com** and press **Enter**.

    Type **Your Zip code** (that is your actual zip code) in the **Zip** text box and click **Go**.

    What is the forecast for the next five days in your city?

    Click the **Back**  button two times to go back to mapquest.

    Click the **Printer button** at the right bottom side of screen—Printable Maps.

    Click the browser **Printer** [Print] button to print a copy of the map.

4. Create and work with **Bookmarks**.

Click **Bookmarks**, **Edit bookmarks** on the menu bar.

Right click in the **Bookmark** window.

Select **New Folder**, and type **Learning Folder**, press **Enter**, and click **Close**.

Click the **Drop-down address** [▼] button and click on **weather.com** site.

Select **Bookmarks**, **Edit bookmarks**, click **Learning Folder**, and click **Close** button.

Click **Bookmark** [Bookmarks] button, **Add bookmark**. The weather site is now added to your Bookmark folder—Learning Folders.

Type **pacprod.com/card.htm** in the **Location** text box and press **Enter**.

Click the **Bookmark** [Bookmarks] button, **Add Bookmark**, **Learning Folder**, and **weather.com**. This takes you to the weather site.

Because you may not be able to keep a Bookmark folder on the hard drive in the lab, you will want to keep your folder on a diskette. You can do this by creating a Word file called bookmarks. Create a simple two-column table with one column labeled Description and the other URL. Go to the site, highlight the URL, click copy button, go to your Word document, and pasting the URLs of your favorite site into it. To use the URL, make sure your browser is running in the background and you are connected to the Internet. Click the URL and this takes you to the site.

5. Save Web pages.

Type **www.cdc.gov** in the **Location** text box and press **Enter**.

Click **Health Information, Airbags**.

Select **File, Save as** from the menu bar.

Change location to **3½" drive** (click on drop-down arrow in Save in text box area, click **3½" drive**). Click **Save** button.

Open **Word** and the **Airbags** file. What do you notice about this file? Close **Word**.

Now, open **Airbags** file in your Web browser. What is missing?

To save a graphic file:

Type **www.clip-art.com** and click **Medical** button on left side.

Right click the **Ambulance**. Select **Save Picture as** from the shortcut menu.

Select **Location** to download the graphic. Select **File name** and click the **Save** button.

6. Close any open windows and exit your browser.

EXERCISE 3: DOWNLOADING FILES FROM THE WEB

Objectives

1. Download a variety of file types.
2. Identify the differences between downloading, file save, and **save target as**.

Activity

1. If necessary, start your **Browser**.

2. Obtain a file through your browser from a download Web site.

   In the **Location** or **Address** text box, type **www.download.com** and press **Enter**.

   Click **Utilities** from the directory structure.

   Click **File Compression** and scroll to **WinZip(32 bit) for OS 95/98/NT**.

   Click **WinZip(32 bit)** file. What is the version, date, and size of this file?

   Click the **Download** button. Click **OK** to save this program to disk.

   Note the address in Figure 9–5 towards the top of the window.

   Change the Save in text box to the **3½" disk** drive and click **Save**.

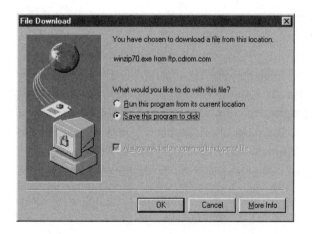

FIGURE 9–5.
File Download Screen

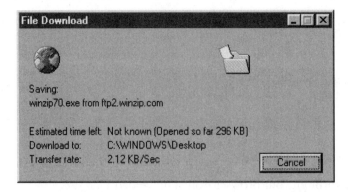

FIGURE 9–6.
File Download Progress Screen

The file is now downloading (see Figure 9–6).

Again notice the address from which it is downloading.

Click **OK** at the prompt telling you the download is complete.

3. Obtain a file through your browser from an ftp site.

In the **Location** or **Address** text box, type **ftp://ftp.pkware.com** and press **Enter**.

What do you need to know to obtain the correct file? How different is this site from the one in number 2?

Click **files.1st**. What is the filename and size of the file that will run in Windows 95/NT?

Click the **Browser back** button.

Click **Pk270wsp.exe**. At this point the process is the same as that in 2 so click **Cancel**.

Now, go to **www.pkware.com**. This is the Web site for the same file.

What is the difference in the user interface?

Click **Pkzip for Windows** on the left side of the Window.

Click **pk270wsp.exe**. At this point the process is the same as that in 2 so click **Cancel**.

Note that the files in 2 and 3 are compressed files. Before you can use them, you need to unzip them. To do this, you double click the file and follow the screen directions.

4. Obtain another file through your browser from an ftp site using right click.

Type **ftp://ftp.irs.ustreas.gov** in the location or address text box.

Double click **Pub** directory, **Irs-pdf** directory.

Right click **f1040ez.pdf** and select **Save target as**.

Select **3½" Drive** for Save in and click **Save** button. The file is now downloading.

Click **OK** to the download complete prompt. Close **Browser**.

Double click the **f1040ez.pdf** file in the **My Computer, 3½"** drive window.

What happened?

Pdf files require the system to have Acrobat Reader installed on the computer to read and display these files. Some files require special programs to read and display them. Most sites that use pdf files have a link to a free copy of the Acrobat Reader software.

EXERCISE 4: CREATING A SIMPLE WEB PAGE WITH HTML

Objectives

1. Design a simple HTML file.
2. Use a text editor to enter HTML tags.
3. Add a graphic and links.

Activity

1. Obtain a quick reference guide for HTML tags. Use methods for searching outlined in Chapter 11 and search for a reference on HTML tagging. Why do you feel this is a good site for beginners? Justify your answer.

   Include URL here:

   Select two of the following sites to provide reference sources about HTML tagging for you when you develop your home page. Either save them to disk or print them for reference when doing your home page design.

   http://www.mcli.dist.maricopa.edu/tut/tags/tag1.html

   http://www.ncsa.uiuc.edu/General/Internet/WWW/

   http://builder.com/Authoring/Basics/ss09.html

2. Find the following images that you need to download to your disk for use on your HTML document.

Graphic:	Filename:	URL:
An icon or button to use on your home page		
A line to separate some of your content		
A background image or color for your home page		
A picture that represents something for your home page		

Additional sites you might consider for animated gifs, icons, and buttons are:

http://www.cybernettix.vuurwerk.nl/

http://www.clip-art.com

http://www.freestuffcenter.com/awesome/

http://www.clipartconnection.com

3. Create HTML pages with an ASCII editor.

Go to **Start, Programs, Accessories,** and click **Notepad.**

Type **<HTML>,** press **Enter,** type **<HEAD>,** and press **Enter.**

Type **<TITLE>YOUR NAME HOMEPAGE</TITLE>** and press **Enter (that means to type your name and not the capitalized words YOUR NAME HOMEPAGE).**

Type **</HEAD>** and press **Enter.**

Type **<BODY>** and press **Enter.**

Type **<H1>Level One Heading</H1>** and press **Enter.**

Type **This will be the first paragraph in my document. <P>** and press **Enter.**

Type **Hey this is too much typing in one day! <P>** and press **Enter.**

Type **Maybe I'll give you a picture to look at......<P>** and press **Enter.**

Type **<IMG SRC="image file name and extension"> <P>** Use one of the images you downloaded from above and type its filename and extension. Make sure it is in the same folder as your html file.

Type **<A HREF="http://www.yahoo.com">Click here for Yahoo! </A>** and press **Enter.**

Type **</BODY>** and press **Enter.**

Type **</HTML>.**

Save the file on your diskette as **myhtml.html.** Make sure you type the extension.

Open Netscape Navigator or Internet Explorer, choose **File, Open file,** select **myhtml.html** and click **OK. Print** it and **attach** it to this exercise.

Click on the **Click Here For Yahoo!** Did your link work? If not, make sure you are connected to the Internet.

That's all there is to it. Most people, who don't tag all the time, refer to references when looking for the appropriate tags or use the source code from other sites when they find something they like. But in order to do that, you have to have some basic understanding of the codes. When creating your page, refer to the quick guides from above.

EXERCISE 5: CREATING A SIMPLE WEB PAGE USING MS WORD

Objectives

1. Design a simple home page using MS Word.
2. Edit the page.
3. Add a graphic and links.

Activity

1. Plan. First, you are to create two pages—one will be the index page or home page and the other one will teach you how to link from the home page. Place your graphic files in a folder titled images on your diskette in the A drive.

2. Create an HTML file.

   Start **Word**.

   Select **File, New**, and click **Web Page** tab.

   Select **Web Page Wizard** icon. (If asked to access a newer version, click **No**.)

   Select **Simple Layout** and click **Next**.

   Select **Community** and click **Finish**.

   Highlight **Insert Heading Here** and type **Creating HTML with Word**.

   Select **Replace the....menu**.

   Type **Creating an HTML file using Word is simple and fun**.

   Select **Type some text.....** and type **Here is a list telling about me**.

   Continue selecting text for the bullets typing one statement beside each bullet:

   - **Who I am....I am a health professions student.**
   - **Picture of me working.**
   - **What I do for fun...read and travel.**

   Press the **Enter** key and type **Where I go to school...name of college**.

   Highlight and delete **Type some text**.

   Highlight **Related Page 1** and type **Me at Work**.

   Highlight **Related Page 2** and type **About Me**.

   Highlight **Related Page 3** and type **Travel**.

   Highlight **Travel**, including the vertical bar at the left, press **CTRL+C**, move the cursor after **Travel**, and press **CRTL+V**.

   Highlight **Travel**, type **College (Your college's name)**.

   Save the document on your diskette as **Index.html**.

3. Edit the document.

   Select the **Heading** and format it as **AmeriGarmndBT**.

   Click the decrease font size [A] button on the formatting toolbar once.

   Click in the **Heading**, click **Right-justified** button on the formatting toolbar.

   Note: Editing the document is just like editing other Word documents.

   Click the **Save** button to update the file.

4. Insert graphic.

   Go to the **Top** of the document (the cursor should be to the left of C in Creating).

   Select **Insert**, **Picture**, **From File**, click **No** if prompted to save, double click **Popular**.

   Select **Amhappy** file.

   Click the **Graphic** and use the **sizing handles** to make it smaller (about $1\frac{1}{2}$"). **Save** the file.

5. Create second HTML file.

   Follow the directions in 2 and 3 to **create a second** file.

   Call the file **Travel** and include the following text:

Heading	**Places I Like**.
Text	**I love to travel with my family throughout the US and abroad**.
Picture	One either **scanned** or from the **Internet** of a place you like.
Delete extra text in place holders.	
Text at bottom	**Home Page, Me at Work, About Me, College**. **Save** the file.

6. Create links to each other.

   Click **Window, Index.html**.

   Select the text **Travel** at the bottom of the page.

   Select **Insert**, **Hyperlink**.

   Click the **Browse** button in Link to File or URL text box area.

   Select the **A drive** and click the **Travel** file. Click **OK**. You've now created a link from the file to the Travel File.

   Select the word **Travel** in what I do for fun and repeat the above process to create a link to the travel file.

   Save the file. Now, click **Window, Travel.html**.

   Repeat the above process to create a link to the **Home page** (Index.html file). **Save** the file.

7. Show the documents.

   Start your **Browser**.

   Select **File, Open,** and click **Browse**.

Select the **Index.html** file on the 3½" drive.

Click the linked text to move between the two documents.

Print each document.

8. Now, continue until all pages were created and appropriate links made.

ASSIGNMENT 1: EVALUATING WEB DESIGN QUALITY

Directions

1. Use methods for searching outlined in Chapter 11 and search for a reference on evaluating quality design for Web pages. Why do you feel this is a good site?
2. Write the URL of the site you visited here:
3. Go to http://www.cyberbee.com/guide2.html. What are the indicators of quality design discussed at this site?
4. Go to http://www.orat.ilstu.edu/classes/inet/documents/criteria.html. What are the indicators for quality design discussed at this site?
5. Go to http://www.glover.com/sucky.html. What are the ten "sucky" design issues that are discussed at this site? Now, click the link to "Sucky to Savvy." Which of his design points do you agree with and which don't you agree with? Why?
6. What do you think constitutes quality in the design? Are there other things you might add to these lists that are not there?
7. Select a Web site to critique using selected design criteria.
8. Type your responses to the above questions using your word processor.

ASSIGNMENT 2: CREATING A PERSONAL HOME PAGE

Directions

1. For this assignment you will create a personal home page. You may use whatever software you prefer to create it from an ASCII editor to HTML converter to HTML editor.

2. The following is expected for this home page:
   - Follows the guidelines given in class and in the references for good design.
   - Includes at least one of each of the following:
     One button
     One graphic or image found on the Web
     Colored background

> One picture (make sure you aren't violating copyright; it is easier if you take a picture you have and scan it)
>
> A link to your biosketch
>
> A link to a Web page at another site
>
> A link to your college or university home page

- Uses only graphics that are appropriate for the content.

3. Part of your grade will be a presentation to your classmates of your home page. Be prepared to show your home page and talk about its development. This means that you need to make sure that all your graphic and HTML files are on your diskette in the proper places.

Chapter 10

Computer-Assisted Communication

OBJECTIVES

1. Identify the components needed to establish computer-assisted communication.
2. Describe computer communication modalities: e-mail, listservs, bulletin boards, chat rooms, Internet conferencing, threaded discussions.
3. Send e-mail messages and attachments.
4. Join a listserv and participate in the discussion.
5. Access newsgroups, bulletin boards, and chat rooms.
6. Identify criteria for selecting the World Wide Web for online learning.

INTRODUCTION

Communication is the process and structure of sending and receiving messages by a variety of means. In computer-assisted communication, the computer enhances the communication process by either structuring the message or providing a channel to send and receive messages. This chapter focuses on using a computer system as a channel for communicating messages over both short and long distances. Messages sent by a computer system take many forms. For example, they may take the form of a short e-mail note, an article published online, a database, a downloaded computer software program, or an online course.

TERMS RELATED TO COMPUTER-ASSISTED COMMUNICATION

The following terms are important to understand when examining different computer-assisted communication modalities. They are introduced here and more specific information about some of them appears later in the chapter.

Asynchronous This term was first used in data transmission, referring to sending and receiving data a byte at a time with a start and stop bit delimiting each byte. Now it is also used to reference a communication exchange when the people involved are communicating at different times. For example, e-mail is asynchronous since you and the person you are communicating with do not need to be on the computer at the same time.

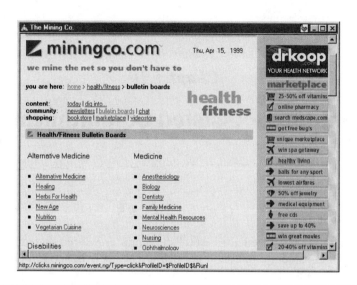

FIGURE 10–1.
Accessing Bulletin Boards about Health

Bulletin Board	Similar to their counterparts hanging on a wall, these are public areas for messages. They are typically organized around specific topics and may be part of an online service and accessed through Internet search engines. Bulletin boards may be open to everyone or may be restricted to members of certain groups and accessed through passwords. See Figure 10–1 for examples of bulletin boards accessible through the health/fitness link from http://home.miningco.com.
Chat	Chat is real-time communication between two or more users via a computer. Most Internet service providers have built-in chat features.
Chat Room	A designated area or "room" where individuals gather simultaneously and can "talk" to one another by typing messages. Everyone who is online usually sees the messages. See Figure 10–2 for an example of a World Wide Web site where you can access chat rooms related to health (http://dir.yahoo.com/health/chat/).
E-mail	Electronic mail is a message composed and sent over a computer network to a person or group of people who have an electronic mail address. E-mail can be sent over a local area network or over the Internet.
Emoticon	Emoticons are a way to show an emotion via text on the computer to help make up for the inability to read body language.

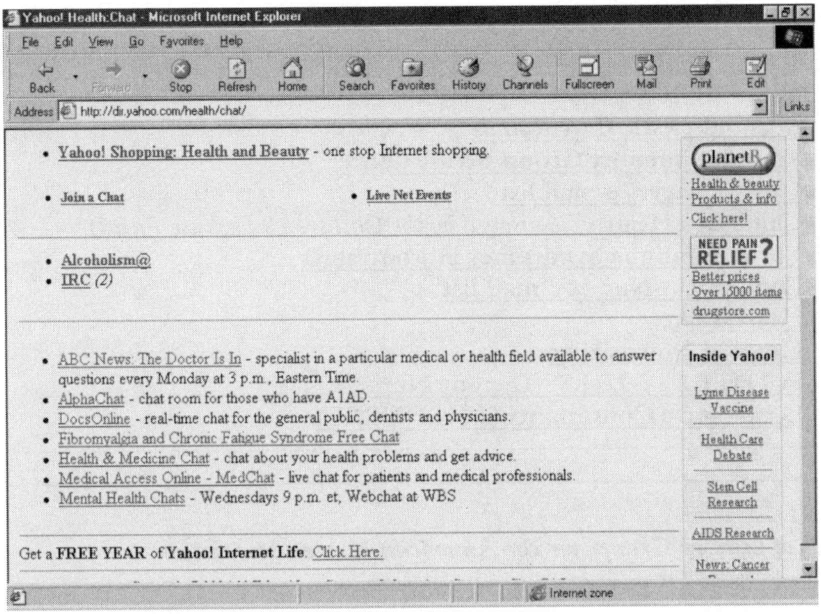

FIGURE 10–2.
Accessing Chat Rooms about Health

Internet Conferencing	This occurs when two or more persons interact over the Internet in real time, receiving more or less immediate replies. This can involve interaction via text, audio, or video.
Listserv	Listserv is the name for a software program that manages automated mailing lists; however it is commonly used to refer to all mailing lists. When you post a message to a listserv, everyone on the mailing list receives the message via e-mail. Table 10–1 shows some listservs of interest to nurses.
Newsgroup	A group of information and articles organized around a particular topic, such as Alzheimers Disease or Child Abuse, is a newsgroup. Newsgroups generally require that you have access to a newsreader, although you can circumvent that by using Dejanews. You can post a message to the newsgroup for all to read and respond.
Online Course	This refers to educational experiences and/or materials on the Internet. The actual amount of "online" experience in a course varies. Course materials may be online and other learning experiences may take place through traditional methods, or all learning experiences

Nursing Listservs	http://www.nursingworld.org/listserv/index.htm#list

Adenoid Cystic Carcinomas
Amputee Support Group Breast Cancer
Case Managers e-mail list
Children's Health *(sponsored by the Children's Defense Fund)*
Chronic Fatigue Syndrome/Fibromyalgia
Connecticut Nurses e-mail list
Heart Talk
Hospital Downsizing
IVTHERAPY-L (I.V. Therapy Nurses)
Legal Nurse Consultants (LNCNURSE)

TABLE 10–1.
Partial List of Listserv Groups for the American Nurses Association

	may be initiated and conducted through Web sites, e-mail, and other online computer experiences.
Synchronous	This term was originally used in data transmission to mean moving streams of data at the same time and rate. When applied to communication among people on the computer it refers to individuals communicating in the same time set. Chat rooms or NetMeetings are examples of synchronous communication since individuals involved are all on the computer at the same time.
Threaded Discussion	This online information exchange is similar to a bulletin board, except that topics within each interest area are identified and organized together so that you can access and read just those discussions rather than all items posted.

COMPONENTS NEEDED FOR COMPUTER-ASSISTED COMMUNICATION

Both the sender of the communication and the receiver of that message must have the appropriate hardware, software, and a connection to the network in order to communicate. The basics of computer-assisted communication require a sender, channel, medium, and receiver. In computer-assisted communication the sender includes not only the person creating the message, but the computer. The communications medium and channel refer to the "how" of the communications—how the message is being transferred from one place to the other. The medium may include such devices as telephone wires, twisted pair, fiber optic cables, or satellites. The computer must be connected to the communications medium by either a modem or network connection (network card in the computer). It is essential that both computers use software that supports the same communications protocol so that they can "talk" to each other. Chapter 9 provides more detail on computer hardware and the basic communications software needed.

Most computer labs and hospitals are networked. The network consists of all the computers and related devices that are connected together for the purpose of sharing devices, programs, and data. Other terms related to these connections include:

Server	The computers in the network that act as a manager for the network. The server runs user and computer software programs, stores data, and controls network traffic.
Local Area Network (LAN)	A network that exists within one or more buildings. Networks vary in size and have a variety of organizational structures. There may be several small LANs connected together within one institution.
Wide Area Network (WAN)	Several LANs that are separated by distance and connected by a backbone are referred to as a WAN.
Backbone	Backbone is a high-speed network connecting together several powerful computers or LANS.
Internet	The Internet is a worldwide system for linking computer networks using TCP/IP communication standards.
TCP/IP standards	This stands for Transmission Control Protocol/Internet Protocol and is the basic communications standard for using the Internet.

ELECTRONIC MAIL

E-mail or electronic mail is a way to send messages to others in electronic form. You write e-mail as you would write a letter with your word processor. However, instead of printing the message and sending it via the postal system, you typically click a "Send" button on your e-mail program and your mail arrives at its destination within a matter of seconds or minutes, depending on where it is going. Just as there are many different word processing, graphics, and spreadsheet programs, there are different mail programs. Often one comes with your computer. Eudora and Pegasus are popular mailers. Mailers are also included with both Netscape and Internet Explorer, and from your Internet Service Provider. Many search sites, as well as other service providers, provide free mail services. All these programs typically involve a point and click approach to accessing and sending mail. Some institutions, however, use a mail system that is dependent on typing commands rather than selecting them from a menu. While this chapter provides general information about using e-mail, it does not provide step-by-step procedures for using a specific program. Check the help information online or the documentation for the system in your institution for assistance using a specific e-mail system.

E-mail messages consist of two parts, the header and the body. The body is the actual message. The header has at least four sections that provide useful information.

Date	This includes the date and time the message was sent.
From	This tells you who sent the message as well as their e-mail address(es).

| To | This indicates who receives the message as well as their e-mail address(es). |
| Subject | This is the topic discussed in the e-mail. |

E-mail users are given a certain amount of space for e-mail messages on the server of their institution or by the Internet Service Provider or e-mail provider. If e-mail messages are not read and deleted, eventually the space allotted will become filled and other messages will be returned to senders. Thus, you should read your mail often and delete messages no longer needed. Most programs also allow users to systematically store messages that they wish to keep in folders. By moving previously read messages to folders, the Inbox of the mail system is kept uncluttered and new messages are more readily visible when the mail program is started.

E-mail Addresses

All e-mail systems provide users with individual addresses. On a local area network an e-mail address operates much like interoffice mail. A user's local e-mail address usually consists of the User's ID only. Mail sent over a WAN is like mail sent via the postal service in that a full Internet address is needed. Web page and e-mail addresses are different, however. In an e-mail address, there is always an @ symbol that separates the User ID from the rest of the address. A URL never has an @ symbol in the address and always starts with http://. Chapter 9 provides more information about URLs.

There are three parts to an Internet e-mail address. For example, your address might be whitman_n@mail.lynchburg.edu.

User ID	The first component is the computer name of the individual on the computer system where he or she receives mail. No one else on that system has the same User ID. The User's ID in the example above is **whitman_n**
OR	
Distribution List ID	One of the e-mail functions that is especially useful when sending e-mail to a group of people is the creation of a distribution list. It is also called an **alias** or **mailing list**. With this function the sender creates and saves a list of names and addresses. The list is assigned a name. Each time the sender addresses an e-mail message using the list name, each person whose e-mail address is on the list receives the message. For example, you might have a list called **classN402** to identify your classmates in a certain nursing class. When you address the message and select the distribution list, all list members' IDs appear.
@	The "at" sign is always between the User's ID and the user's mail system address.
User's domain or mail system address	This is the location address for everyone who uses that local computer mail system. This part of the address functions like your home address. Everyone in your family uses the same apartment or house address. In the example above the location address is **mail.lynchburg.edu**.

E-mail Netiquette

Just as there are rules governing what is acceptable to say and do during social interactions, there are guidelines for acceptable ways of communicating using e-mail. Netiquette is the name given to electronic communication conventions. Some of the main rules of netiquette include the following:

1. Start your message with a greeting, just as you would any communication, and make it specific to the recipient(s): "Hi Kurt," "Mary," or "Greetings Colleagues."
2. Include in your message only what you want others to read. **Never** assume your message is private.
3. Be clear and concise. E-mail messages include only your words. When you communicate with a person face-to-face you use intonation and body language as well as words to send your message. With e-mail, you cannot observe the listener so you do not have immediate feedback or the ability to adjust the message midway. You can include "emoticons" like the smiley :-) to signify something pleasant or happy. Standard emoticons include the following:

   :-) basic smiley

   ;-) winking smiley—means "just kidding"

   :-(sad face

   8-) smiley with sunglasses

   :-o surprised face

   For other emoticons, visit http://www.geocities.com/SouthBeach/Marina/2492/layout.html.
4. Keep it short. Don't quote huge amounts of material or include the entire original message when you reply unless it is pertinent to your reply. When replying, put your reply early in the message body so readers don't have to wade through material to get to your response.
5. Limit formatting. Some programs don't read underlining, bold, etc.
6. Use the underscore symbol before and after words to represent underlining when needed, for example, for a journal title.
   a. Keep line length to 60–70 characters.
   b. Use *asterisks* around a word to make a point.
7. Specify the content of your message in the subject line so readers know what to expect.
8. Never type in all caps. THIS IS CONSIDERED SHOUTING.
9. Make your message a good representation of you. Check your spelling and grammar.
10. Respect copyright. Always give credit to others for their work and follow copyright rules for using material. See Chapter 12 for guidelines related to copyright.
11. Avoid flaming. Flaming is voicing very strong antagonistic opinions or attacking someone.
12. Sign your message. Your signature should include at least your name and e-mail address. It can also include your postal mail address, telephone number, title, and professional affiliation but should be no longer than four lines. You can create a "signature" file ahead of time and use it as a standard on all your mail.
13. Never send chain letters. They are forbidden on the Internet.

E-mail Attachments

A file sent along with an e-mail message is called an attachment. Any type of file can be sent via e-mail—text files, graphics, spreadsheets, and even video. E-mail systems are set up to handle text, not the binary files associated with graphics and color images often included in attachments. Therefore, attachments are encoded by the sender's system to a text file that can be sent via e-mail; on arrival they are decoded by the receiver's system. Attaching files to e-mail messages is no longer difficult; few programs involve having to know the commands for encoding and decoding that were once necessary. MIME (Multipurpose Internet Mail Extensions) is the Internet standard for multimedia mail attachments. MIME is useful for sending files to either Macintosh or Windows computers. However, some older mail programs don't support MIME and may use BinHex or uucode. When sending attachments, find out what the computer you are sending to can decode. Check your documentation for the procedure for configuring your mail system to handle MIME attachments. Also be certain that the recipient of your file has the software to run the file you are sending. For example, if you are sending an Excel document, the recipient will need to have Excel software.

A few commonalties related to sending and receiving attachments are discussed here. Review your documentation or online help to learn more of the specifics for handling attachments on your system.

Inserting Attachments. Most mail packages have a menu command or a tab that starts a separate dialog screen to insert an attachment. Once on the dialog screen you can browse your computer and point and click the file to be added.

Reading Attachments. Most programs use an icon on the e-mail message list screen that indicates an attachment is present. For example, Microsoft Outlook uses a paper clip image to indicate an attachment. In order to open and view it, the receiver must have the same software, or something that will interpret the original software and allow it to be read. Typically, clicking on the attachment indicator either opens the file or opens a dialog box that allows the viewer to save the attachment to a file or to open the attachment. To protect your computer, it is wise not to open attachments without checking them for a virus unless you are certain of the sender. Save the attachment to a file—just be sure to note in what folder the file is being saved, then check it with an antivirus program prior to opening.

LISTSERVS

People with common interests frequently join together to form an organization. The type of interests and the structures of organization have wide variations. The joining together of people with common interests also occurs in the virtual world of the Internet. The term listserv comes from one of the software programs used to support this process. Individuals subscribe to a group with a specific focus and send e-mail, called "posts," to the listserv. The post is automatically sent to all members of the list. An example of listservs of interest to nurses is found in Table 10–1 located earlier in this chapter.

Listserv Program

This software program maintains the mailing list for a group of people with common interests. To join the group, or to subscribe, individuals send an e-mail message to the listserv's e-mail address. Because this message will be read and answered by a computer program the message must follow the specific format required by the listserv software. There are several different listserv software programs. Some examples of common listserv programs include Listproc, List-Serv, and Majordomo.

The List

The membership list includes the group of people who have joined together by subscribing to the same list. The list will have a computer name that reflects the interest of the group. For example, **snurs-l** is the name of a list for undergraduate nursing students. To communicate with other people on the list, you send a message to the list's e-mail address. Your message will then be sent as an individual e-mail message to each person on the list. When the message is distributed to each member on the list, it is referred to as "posted to the group."

Types of Lists

There are two types of lists. On a moderated list, each e-mail message to the list is reviewed and approved by a person before it is posted. On an unmoderated list no one reviews posts before they are sent to members. Most lists are unmediated. The list relies on the integrity of its members to abide by the list rules.

Joining a List

Most lists have directions that can be accessed either through e-mail or on the Web site that introduces the listserv. Be sure to save the directions for later use once you subscribe to a list-serv. Procedures for joining listservs are similar. The following steps represent the typical approach to joining a list.

1. Address the e-mail message to the listserv's e-mail address, not the list's e-mail address. For example, **listserv@abvm.cc.buffalo.edu** is the address of a listserv.
2. Put no other information in the header. Leave the subject line blank.
3. In the body of the message type the following:

   Subscribe <list name> <firstname lastname>

   For example: **Subscribe snurs-l Ramona Nelson**

   Some listserv software programs accept the word **sub** in place of the word **subscribe**, while others require the word **join**. Some listserver software programs require your e-mail address in place of your first and last name.
4. Put no other information in the body of the e-mail message. Do not sign your name, or thank the listserv. Remember you are NOT communicating with a person. You are sending commands to a computer.
5. If you are unsuccessful you will receive an error message from the computer. This message will try to tell you what mistake you made. If you don't understand the message, get help at your local site.
6. If you are successful, you will receive a welcome message from the listserv. It may contain a great deal of information that you do not understand, but save this message!!
7. If you will not read your e-mail for a period of time, send a message to the listserv suspending your mail service. If you want to stop receiving mail from the list you must send an

unsubscribe message to the listserv's address. The specific directions for stopping mail or for unsubscribing are included in the Welcome Message from the list. If you fail to do this and your mailbox becomes full, messages are bounced back to the listserv. This is very poor list etiquette.

Posting an E-mail Message to a List

It is wise to read several postings on a list before posting a message. Each list has it's own culture. It is helpful to know the list and the nature of the list before posting.

1. Address the e-mail message to the list's e-mail address, not the listserv's e-mail address. For example, **snurs-l@abvm.cc.buffalo.edu** is the address of the list. Note the difference in the listserv's address (**listserv@abvm.cc.buffalo.edu**) and the list's address (**snurs-l@abvm.cc.buffalo.edu**). In both cases the domain part of the address is the same, but the User ID part of the address is different. When you post a message to the list, you are communicating with people and not a computer. Note also that many lists require you to type your ID and password before you can post to them.
2. Put the topic of the message in the subject line. This is very helpful to receivers reading their e-mail directory. If your posting is a response to another person's e-mail, use the same words to identify the subject topic as the previous sender used. Many mail programs will insert the subject and address if you use the reply function. If you use the reply function with an e-mail message from a listserv, check to be sure that the mail program inserted the correct list address.
3. When typing your message, use appropriate netiquette.
4. Since some mail programs clip off the header on incoming messages, always sign your message with your name and e-mail address at the end of the message.

NEWSGROUPS

Usenet is an informal group of computer systems that exchange news. While most of the news on Usenet is carried on the Internet, Usenet predates the Internet and includes a number of computer systems that are not on the Internet. The news exchanged is organized into newsgroups. These newsgroups can be conceptualized as a cross between a listserv and a bulletin board. People with a common area of interest subscribe to a listserv. The same is true for a newsgroup. Once you subscribe to a listserv each message that is posted to the list is sent to you individually. This does not happen with a newsgroup. With a newsgroup the messages are posted to a central location in your local system. To read these messages and interact with the group you must use a software program called a newsreader. Today most Web browsers have newsreaders built into them, so more people are involved in newsgroups.

Newsgroups are organized by topics in a hierarchical tree structure. The first part of the topic identification is general. Each successive part becomes more specific. For example, the newsgroup related to nursing has the following name: **sci.med.nursing**. The newsgroup for nurse practitioners is named **alt.npractitioners**. Table 10–2 describes general Usenet names.

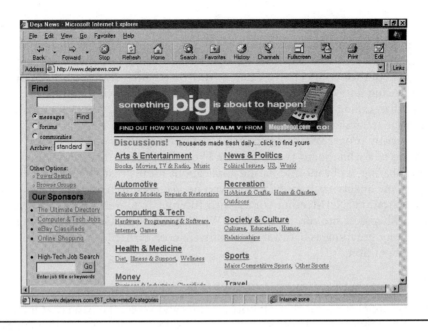

FIGURE 10–3.
Accessing Newsgroups

You may read a newsgroup by going to DejaNews (www.dejanews.com), a service that maintains a list of newsgroups and allows Web access. See Figure 10–3 for the opening screen that assists you to search for the group you want. You may use the name, e.g., sci.med.nursing, or search a specific topic to see what newsgroups are related to your interest. After you find a newsgroup on your topic, you can read the current postings by telling your software to get the articles from this newsgroup. In most applications, you can do this by double clicking the name of the newsgroup from the newsgroup list.

TABLE 10–2.
Usenet Names and Meanings

Examples of General Usenet Names	Meaning
alt	Alternative
comp	Computers
sci	Science
misc	Miscellaneous
soc	Social issues
talk	Debate oriented discussion
news	Usenet news
rec	Recreation

INTERNET CONFERENCING

Internet conferencing involves two or more people interacting with one another over the Internet, who engage in a real-time conversation and receive more or less immediate replies, depending on the speed of their connections. Chat, or text-based interactions, has been the main form of this conferencing until recently. Now audio and video conferencing via the Internet is beginning. Rather than calling a meeting or phoning your colleagues, you use a software program and the appropriate audio and video accessories to speak to and see your colleagues over the Internet. Currently programs like Microsoft's NetMeeting allow audio and/or video conferencing, sharing of a whiteboard (writing space like a blackboard that everyone in the meeting can see), and sharing applications. Sharing applications means that I can open and show you a spreadsheet of my quality assurance data and you do not need to have the spreadsheet software to see this application. NetMeeting comes with Internet Explorer 4.0 or can be downloaded free from the Microsoft site on the Internet. While audio and video conferencing is not yet a common meeting situation, as hardware and software evolve, there is no doubt that Ma Bell will have more competition.

CHAT

Although there are chat rooms that support graphics and voice, the basic chat interface is text. Text chat involves two or more people communicating by typing messages that appear in a text window, visible to the other people in the same chat room. People use chat to communicate about specific topics, to meet new people online, and because it offers more rapid response than e-mail. In fact, chat rooms rank third, behind search engines and e-mail, as the most-used resources on the Internet. Twenty-six percent of the time spent on the Internet is spent in chat rooms (Rupley, 1998). However, like chatting in a crowded room, there are often many simultaneous conversations taking place. In text chat, you will see all the messages that are part of those different conversations in the order they were entered into the system. Thus, following the sequence of a particular line of the conversation may be confusing at first.

Most chat systems allow you to send private messages to individuals in the chat room as well as to participate with the group. Some chat programs, such as ICQ and ichat Pager, allow you to compile a "buddy list" of your friends on the Internet. Using these programs, you can set up your own chat room and chat privately with your friends. The same "instant message" is available to AOL subscribers; their buddies do not need to subscribe to AOL, but can simply download the software. The process for participating in chat rooms is similar in most programs:

- Log in.
- Choose a username, the name that everyone else in the chat room will see. You can use your real name or a nickname for better privacy—it's up to you. As with other user IDs, each name must be unique.
- Read messages in the current chat session. Messages from those participating in the chat session as well as system messages and information about people entering and leaving the room appear in a box on your screen. Each message is preceded by the username of the person submitting the message, so you can tell who said what.
- Type your message into the text entry box and press Enter.

Using one of the many search engines on the Internet you can find a chat room of interest. Most search engines support chat rooms. There are also topic-specific chat rooms located on many other Web sites; for example, the Yahoo Health Chat page shown in Figure 10–2 lists some health-related chat rooms you can join. Chat rooms are usually organized around topics of interest, age, or other categories. Chatiquette is similar to netiquette in terms of the words and behavior acceptable while participating in a chat room. For more information about chatiquette, visit http://search.zdnet.com/cgi-bin/texis/zdhelp/zdhelp/single.html?Ueid=914763.

ONLINE LEARNING

With advances in technology, some educators are beginning to put educational materials online. In some instances entire courses are being taught via the Web with no regularly scheduled classroom sessions and no in-person contact among students or teacher. Web-based systems are asynchronous, thus students are able to use Internet based materials from wherever they are, whenever they want, and as often as they want. Traveling to an educational site is no longer necessary as students access materials from any computer with Internet access. However, there is more to facilitating learning than merely having course materials on the Web. When you find an online course, examine it to determine how well it includes the following:

- A list of goals or outcomes that describes what you can achieve from the course and how this will be useful.
- Clearly outlined expectations for the projects/homework expected and how the grade is achieved.
- A variety of learning experiences guided through online information and resources.
- Modules that organize topics into manageable units for learning.
- Opportunity for interaction between the students and teacher.
- A way to ask questions and receive answers.
- Control, to some extent, of the learning environment to set the pace and progression through course modules.
- Examples to facilitate understanding of material being studied.
- Opportunity to practice using material and to apply material to problems or cases.
- Feedback on practice and your use of the material.
- Tools to help you reflect on what is being learned and to guide you in setting the next steps in the learning process.
- Resources in the form of hyperlinks, tables, charts, summaries, and references.

Students who are looking for an online learning experience should also consider their own motivation as well as the structure of the course. When examining whether or not you might do well with an online course, ask yourself the following questions:

- Am I self-directed so I can identify what I want from the course and use the course materials to do so?
- Am I disciplined so that I will keep up with the work without the structure of a regular class session?
- Can I feel satisfaction from interaction online versus in person?

If you describe yourself as goal-directed, disciplined, and comfortable interacting on the computer, online learning may be of interest to you.

SUMMARY

This chapter introduced terminology and procedures for using common methods of computer communication. Using e-mail, subscribing to listservs and newsgroups, and accessing chat rooms and bulletin boards are all useful methods of exchanging ideas and information about health and health care delivery. Emerging trends are to use the computer for Internet conferencing and educational experiences. Criteria for evaluating online learning were provided as a basis for making personal decisions about this method of learning.

REFERENCES[*]

Baldazo, R. & Mathog, M. (October 16, 1996). *Web phones.* Retrieved April 18, 1999 from the World Wide Web: http://www.cnet.com/Content/Reviews/Compare/Webphone.

Dyer, B. (1998). *Modular design of Web pages.* Retrieved January 28, 1999 from the World Wide Web: http://www.dyroweb.com/wbt/modular.html.

Eudora Tech Support: Help Desk. (1999). Retrieved April 19, 1999 from the World Wide Web: http://www.eudora.com/techsupport/howto/AtchMethods.html.

Hambridge, S. (1995). RFC 1855: *Netiquette guidelines.* Retrieved April 18, 1999 from the World Wide Web: http://www.dtcc.edu/cs/rfc1855.html.

McDaniel, R. (October 21, 1998). *The beginners guide to Internet chat.* CNET (1995–1999). Retrieved April 19, 1999 from the World Wide Web: http://www.cnet.com/Content/Reports/Guides/BegChat/index.html.

McManus, T. (1996). *Delivering instruction on the World Wide Web.* Retrieved January 27, 1999 from the World Wide Web: http://ccwf.cc.utexas.edu/~mcmanus/wbi.html.

Mudge, S. M. (1999). Delivering multimedia teaching modules via the Internet. *IETI 36*(1), 11–16.

Rinaldi, A. (1998). *Electronic communications.* Retrieved April 19, 1999 from the World Wide Web: http://www.logan.net/help/netiquette.html.

Rupley, S. (1998). Ready for visual chat? *PC Magazine* December 29, 1998. Retrieved April 20, 1999 from the World Wide Web: http://www.zdnet.com/zdnn/stories/news/0,4586,2180088,00.html.

Steffanos, G. & Steffanos, M. (May 9, 1998). *Internet conferencing. 1996–98* S K Web Construction. Retrieved April 20, 1999 from the World Wide Web: http://www.skwc.com/95/Windows95Conf.html.

---

[*]When entering an URL, do not type the period that follows it in this list.

EXERCISE 1: USING E-MAIL

Objectives

1. Access an e-mail system.
2. Change your password.
3. Read, save, and delete your mail.

Activity

1. Obtain an account from your computer center.

   An account gives you permission to use the system. This permission comes in the form of a User ID and unique password. If your instructor or school has not provided you with an account, you will need to set up a computer account before doing this exercise. If you have a User ID and password you already have an account, unless the User ID and password do not work with the computer system that your instructor wants you to use.

2. Find the documentation.

   Most institutions have documentation for computer programs available to users. Short handouts are usually available free either in print or at the institution's Web site. More detailed documentation may be sold through the computer center and/or bookstore. Find out where and how you can obtain documentation in your institution. Obtain a copy of the documentation for signing-on to the system and for using e-mail. Once you have an account you may also be able to access online help.

3. Sign on.

   Follow the directions for signing on to the computer system. Generally this means type your **User ID** and press the **Tab** key to go to the next text field. Type your **Password** and press **Enter** or click **OK**.

   Remember the password will not appear on the screen. In most mail programs it appears as ****** in the **Password** text box. If a message appears on the screen saying **invalid password**, **login incorrect**, or something similar, try typing your User ID and password again. Some systems are case sensitive, so you need to note if you should or should not use capitals in either your User ID or password. Note, however, that most systems give you three tries to get in and then your account is locked out and you will need to see the account administrator to have it unlocked.

4. Change your password.

   When you sign on for the first time, some computer systems force you to change your password before proceeding. If your system does not require you to change your password, this should be your first action after signing on. Check your documentation for the specific process for changing a password.

In newer mail programs:

Click the password **Icon**, OR Select an option on a **Menu**, OR Click a **Hypertext** link.

In older or mainframe based systems:

Type a command like **Set password** or **Passwd** and press **Enter**.

When prompted for your current password, type **Your current password** and press **Enter** or click **OK**.

When prompted, type your **New Password** and press **Enter** or click **OK**.

When prompted, type your **New Password a Second** time and then press **Enter** or click **OK**.

When typing passwords throughout this procedure the passwords do not show on the screen. Processing the change is usually instant though on some systems there may be a time lag before the new password takes effect. Check your system documentation.

5. Access and read your mail.

   Start the **Mail** program.

   Click the **Icon** or type the **Command** to open the Inbox containing your mail.

6. Open and read each message.

   Double click or highlight the **Mail message** and press **Enter**.

   If this approach does not work, look at the screen for directions and read the written documentation for your system. After you read each e-mail message, look at how your mail directory changed.

7. Exit the mail program.

   In windows based e-mail programs,

   Click the **Close** button in the upper right corner OR

   Click **File, Exit** from the menu bar.

   In command based programs,

   Type **exit, quit, eoj, logoff,** or **logout** or some such command and press **Enter**.

8. Send a message.

   Find the **E-mail address** of a friend. Asking your friend for his/her address is the easiest way to do this. In college settings there may be a faculty, staff, and student directory online that contains listings of addresses.

   Start the **E-mail** program.

   Type the **E-mail address** of your friend in the To: text box. Note many programs permit you to select the address from your e-mail address book by double clicking it.

   Press the **Tab** key twice or click in the **Subject** text box. You don't need to CC yourself and pressing the tab key twice passes the CC textbox.

   Type in the **Subject** and press **Tab** or click in the **Message** text box.

Type and format **Your message**.

Click the **Send** icon.

The procedure for composing an e-mail message varies greatly from one system to another. The above is the general process for many of today's e-mail programs. If this doesn't work, read your local documentation for the following information:

1. How do you initiate the function to compose a message?
2. How do you enter the address of the person who will receive this message?
3. How do you enter the e-mail message?
4. When the e-mail message is ready, how do you give the send command?

One way to test your understanding of the correct procedure at your location is to practice by sending yourself a message. Once you master the procedure, practice sending messages to a friend.

9. Reply to a message.

   Open a **Mail Message** (Double click it).

   Click the **Reply to Sender** button.

   Note the program inserts the sender's address and subject in those textboxes. The **Subject** text box uses the same subject and adds a RE: to it.

   Compose **Your response** and click the **Send** button.

   In some mail programs you will need to type the **Reply** command. If you have received a message as part of a distribution list, find out how to reply to the author and how to reply to everyone on the list.

10. Save or delete each message.

    Highlight the **Message**.

    Press the **Delete** key or button.

    In some Web-based mail programs you delete messages by clicking in the square box next the message, and then click the delete button.

    Read your local documentation for the save and delete procedures. If you do not delete messages your mailbox will become full and eventually new messages will be bounced back to the sender. Some mail programs leave the undeleted messages in the inbox, while others move them to an older message folder. You will know the message is in your inbox if the message is listed in your message list each time you start the mail program. Most systems permit you to move messages into online folders. Read your documentation for a procedure for saving messages in folders.

11. Exit the e-mail program.

    In Windows e-mail programs:

    Click the **Close** button in the upper right corner or select **File, Exit** from the menu bar.

In command based programs:

> Type the **Command** as indicated in your system documentation (**exit, quit, eoj, logoff, logout**) and press **Enter**.

It is important to exit the e-mail system with the computer still running. If you turn the computer off or just walk away without exiting e-mail, someone else may be able to access your account without signing on. Once you exit the e-mail program, complete the computer sequence for shutting down the computer as specified by your lab, library, or other locale.

EXERCISE 2: PARTICIPATING IN CHAT

Objectives

1. Enter a chat room.
2. Read messages and participate in a chat.

Activity

1. Start your Web browser and go to a Web site.

   Double click the **Browser** icon.

   Type **http://www.excite.com** in the **Location** or **Address** text box and press **Enter**.

   Click **People and Chat**. You will find it towards the bottom of the screen under the Search window.

2. Select and enter a chat room.

   On the People and Chat page that appears next, click **Chat by Interest** at the left of the page.

   Click **Health and Wellness**.

   At the sign on screen, click the option—**Chat as a Guest**.

   On the next page give yourself a user name that will be your ID in the chat room.

   Click **Chat Now**.

3. Participate in a chat.

   Once you enter the chat room you will see the list of people in the chat room along the right of the screen. Your user ID will be listed and it will indicate you are a guest.

   Read the messages.

   When you are ready, type **Your own message** at the bottom of the page and click **Send**.

4. Exit the chat.

   When you finish click **Exit** chat.

   Note some of the other options available to you to locate a person, go to a private room, get help, and send a private message to one of the people in the chat room.

ASSIGNMENT 1: ACCESSING A NEWSGROUP

Directions

1. Access DejaNews (www.dejanews.com) from your Web browser.

   At Dejanews' home page, click **Health**.

   Scroll down and select a topic.

   Click **Discussions** tab.

   Select a **Forum Topic**.

   Read the messages.

2. Print the Web page that contains the post listings.

3. Select a specific topic that has at least eight messages and follow that thread. Select the discussion thread by clicking on the first message; read that post, then click on **next>** to go to the next (or **<prev** if you want to go back to the post you read previously).

4. Use your word processing package to answer the following questions:

   - What discussion topic did you select?
   - What was the general theme of messages to this topic?
   - What were your reactions to reading about this topic?
   - Would you like to participate in a newsgroup? If so what topics might be of interest? If not, what are your reasons?

5. Submit your responses to the above question and your Web page printout.

ASSIGNMENT 2: COMPARE AND CONTRAST LISTSERV AND LITERATURE SEARCH

Directions

1. Subscribe to a health-related listserv. Review your messages each week for the next four weeks. Make an annotated list of the topics discussed during those four weeks. At the end of the three weeks send a post to the listserv. At the end of the four weeks send a message to the listserver to **unsubscribe**. Turn in a copy of messages that you have posted as well as the list of the five top topics discussed.

2. Use an automated literature database to do a literature search. Limit the search to the last two years. Search for articles related to the focus of the listserv. For example, if the listserver relates to home health nursing then use the words **home health nursing** as keywords when doing the literature search.

3. Turn in an annotated list of the five most common topics discussed in the literature. Write a brief paper comparing and contrasting the two lists of topics.

ASSIGNMENT 3: INTERNET RESOURCE DOCUMENT

Directions

1. In this assignment you will create an Internet resources document that can be used by other students. The document should include only those resources that can be accessed from your site. Resources on the Internet change frequently so check each resource before adding it to the document. That means to make sure the address is correct and the site is still available.

2. Work in small groups (three to five people) to create the resource document. Your resource document should include each of the following related to specific topics of interest to your discipline:

   a. A list of chat rooms with information on how to access them

   b. A list of listservs with directions for subscribing

   c. A list of newsgroups with directions for how to access them

3. After each small group completes its document, the class will create a master document identifying all resources found by the class.

ASSIGNMENT 4: EVALUATING ONLINE COURSES

Directions

1. Use a search engine (see Chapter 11) to search for online courses. You might try the terms "distance learning" and "online courses." When you find one that is not password protected and that you can explore, compare it to the criteria for examining online courses at the end of this chapter.

2. Using your word processor, make a flyer listing each criterion. Beside or under each of these, identify how well the course you examined meets these criteria. Give enough information to lure someone to a good course or steer them clear of one you think hasn't yet been well developed. Be sure the course title and Web address is on your flyer. Be creative with your design and include graphics if you wish.

3. Submit your flyer.

Chapter 11

Information—Access, Evaluation, and Use

OBJECTIVES

1. Use a variety of search strategies to access information from library and Internet resources.
2. Use a systematic approach to evaluate the quality of information accessed from a variety of sources.
3. Identify appropriate and inappropriate uses of information.
4. Explain general principles for footnoting and documenting information resources.

INTRODUCTION

Information literacy includes the acquisition of knowledge and skills needed to access information, to evaluate the information accessed, and to make appropriate use of that information. This chapter is organized in terms of these three concepts. First, this chapter focuses on how you can access information. More specifically, in this chapter you will learn how to access information that has been stored in computer systems. The skills that you will learn make it possible for you to access all kinds of information including accurate, inaccurate, and misleading materials.

Inaccurate and misleading materials do not come with a label telling you that there is a problem with the information. In fact many times the author will try to ensure that the information looks like high-quality information. You as a reader must determine the quality of the information.

Even good information can be misused. For example, you may have found an excellent article or Internet site explaining the importance of adequate vitamin intake during pregnancy. You then use this information in developing a teaching booklet for pregnant women. However, if you fail to include information about the problems that can occur with overdosing on certain vitamins during pregnancy, the women who read your booklet may be misinformed.

ACCESS

Accessing information begins by understanding how data is stored in the computer. The data is entered into the computer in a very orderly and systematic arrangement called a database. As you learned in Chapter 8, a database is made up of files that contain records. Each record refers to a specific entity and includes a set number of fields. Data related to the entity are stored in the fields. For example, if the entity is a journal article the fields most likely include the author(s), article title, journal source, and an abstract of the article, along with several other fields. The process of searching for data in a database involves matching the specific information about an entity with the field where the data is stored. For example, if you were looking for a book that was written by the author Joos you would want the computer to look in the author field for the name Joos. Each time Joos is found in the author field it would refer to a book written by Joos. However, if the author field contains only one name, Smith, and the title field included the name Joos, this may be a book about Joos but it is not a book written by Joos.

One key type of database that is presented in this chapter is a bibliographic database. Bibliographic databases include information related to articles, books, and other print materials. In most cases the information identifies the title, author, and abstract along with several other details about the item. Increasingly, bibliographic databases also include the full text. Table 11–1 lists common bibliographic databases used in health care. These are only a few of the many important health-related bibliographic databases. To learn more about other health related bibliographic databases visit http://www.nlm.nih.gov/.

A variety of different database management systems can be used to search a bibliographic database. Many users become confused between the bibliographic database and the bibliographical database management system. PubMed is an example of a bibliographical database management system. PubMed is a World Wide Web retrieval service developed by the National Library of Medicine (NLM). PubMed provides access, free of charge, to MEDLINE. It also contains links to the full-text versions of articles at participating publishers' Web sites. The URL for PubMed is http://www.ncbi.nlm.nih.gov/PubMed/. There are several other bibliographical database management systems that can be used to access MEDLINE. Because different libraries and different Web sites may use different bibliographical database management systems this book does not contain specific commands for using these. Each bibliographical database management system does contain a help section. This is where you find the specific information for searching.

General Principles for Searching

Two factors determine how much time and effort you need to exert when searching for information—your level of expertise with the topic and your knowledge of search strategies. An expert in a specific field can do a very efficient, effective, and focused search. For example, if you are an expert in maternity and are looking for information about a specific complication of pregnancy, you could be expected to find information very quickly. This is because an expert knows the language and how knowledge is organized within the field.

However, if you are not an expert the process of searching for information is in many respects recursive. You usually begin by identifying a topic about which you want more information. For example, you may take a course on managed care and be assigned to report on a controversial issue related to managed care. As you begin the search for information on the topic of managed care, you will find related information that doesn't really apply. At the same time you may find that there is more information about this topic than you are able to use. In the process of selecting materials that will apply and eliminating materials that do not apply, your search will become more focused. This initial exploration can be frustrating, but it is very important. It is during this initial stage that you become familiar with the terminology and the way that the

NAME	DESCRIPTION
AIDSLINE	AIDSLINE (AIDS Information Online) is produced by the U.S. National Library of Medicine. It is a bibliographic database focusing on research, clinical aspects, and health policy issues related to AIDS (Acquired Immune Deficiency Syndrome). This database includes articles from over 3,000 journals as well as government reports, technical reports, meeting abstracts and papers, monographs, special publications, books, and audiovisual materials.
BioethicsLine	BioethicsLine is produced jointly by the Kennedy Institute of Ethics and the U.S. National Library of Medicine. It includes citations related to bioethics. Documents are selected from the disciplines of medicine, nursing, biology, philosophy, religion, law, and the behavioral sciences.
CancerLit	CancerLit is produced by the U.S. National Cancer Institute. CancerLit is a database of bibliographic records pertaining to all aspects of cancer therapy. Approximately 200 core journals contribute a large percentage of the records.
CINAHL	The Cumulative Index to Nursing & Allied Health (CINAHL) is published by Cinahl Information Systems. CINAHL includes literature related to nursing and allied health. Almost all English-language publications from nursing and allied health are indexed along with the publications of the American Nurses Association and the National League for Nursing. Selected journals are also indexed in the areas of consumer health, biomedicine, and health sciences librarianship. In total more than 500 journals are regularly indexed. There is between 60 and 70% overlap between this index and MEDLINE. In other words there are several citations specific to nursing and allied health included here that would not be found in MEDLINE. This resource can be located at http://www.CINAHL.com.
HealthSTAR	HealthSTAR is produced cooperatively by the U.S. National Library of Medicine and the American Hospital Association. The database focuses on health care delivery and contains citations to the published literature on health services, technology, administration, and research. It includes both the clinical and nonclinical aspects of health care delivery.
HSTAT	HSTAT is a free, electronic resource that provides access to full-text documents useful in health care decision making. HSTAT includes clinical practice guidelines, quick-reference guides for clinicians, consumer brochures, and evidence reports sponsored by the Agency for Health Care Policy and Research (AHCPR). It can be accessed at http://text.nlm.nih.gov.
MEDLINE	MEDLINE is produced by the U.S. National Library of Medicine. This database is considered by many as the primary bibliographic database of biomedical literature. MEDLINE includes medical, dental, nursing, allied health, biological and physical sciences, humanities, and information science literature related to medicine and health care. More than 3,900 journals are indexed, plus selected monographs of congresses and symposia. Abstracts are included for about 67% of the records.
Other	Several other useful databases may be found at http://www.nlm.nih.gov.

TABLE 11–1.
Selected Bibliographical Database in Health Care

related information is organized. If your approach is to look for a few related articles or Internet sites and then stop your search there, you are missing a significant part of your education.

Indexing, Standard Languages, and Keywords

A record within a database may include several fields. The database management system that interfaces with the database will offer the user the opportunity to search on these fields. Sometimes the database management program is designed with the expectation that the user understands the concept of searching on specific fields. For example, many library database management systems are designed so that the user can search for a specific author. In these systems the user would enter a command such as au=Whitman or a=Whitman. The search results from these systems would include all books that were authored by Whitman.

On the other hand there are also library database management systems that are designed for users who are less familiar with these concepts. With these systems any term that is entered by the user will be compared to several fields. For example, the user would enter the term Whitman and if this term occurred in the title, author, or even the abstract it would be included in the search results. When the database management system offers the opportunity to search on a specific field, some of the more common fields and commands are included in Table 11–2.

The two fields that are used most frequently during a search are keywords and subject. Both of these fields identify the topic discussed in the reference being accessed. However, keywords and subject terms are developed very differently. Using the same term as a keyword and then as a subject will often produce overlapping but different search results. Keywords are terms selected by the author, publisher, or even the developer of the library database management system to identify the topic of the article. Some library database management systems are designed so that any word that appears in the title and/or abstract will function as a keyword. However, keyword terms are not standardized in any way. For example, an article about cirrhosis may be indexed on the keyword "liver" or "hepatic" or "cirrhosis." The same article in different library database management systems may have different keywords associated with it.

Subject terms, on the other hand, are very standardized. Individuals who are experts in understanding indexing and taxonomy concepts develop these in a systematic process. Standard sets of subject terms are often referred to as a controlled vocabulary. One example of a con-

Abbreviation	Field
Au or A	Author(s)
Ti or T	Title
Yr	Year published
Pb	Publisher
K	Keyword
Su	Subject

TABLE 11–2.
Common Searchable Fields in Bibliographical Databases

trolled vocabulary is MeSH (Medical Subject Headings). MeSH is used in indexing MED-LINE. This means that there are people who read each article and then select the specific indexing terms from the controlled vocabulary. If you use a subject term, you will find all the materials that relate to that term. Because keywords are not standardized, searching on a keyword may lead to incomplete results.

There is a second key point that you need to understand about subject terms. Different databases can be indexed with different subject terms. For example, CINAHL has its own controlled vocabulary that is different from MeSH. This means that the same article may be indexed under different terms in these two bibliographical databases.

Now that you understand how this works, let's take a minute to apply these concepts to a search approach. Start with identifying your topic. Next, select a database that best fits your topic. For example, if you are interested in nursing diagnosis, CINAHL would be a better database than MEDLINE. Next, use the name of your topic as a keyword. Conduct a keyword search. Look over your results and select a reference that is clearly related to your topic. Review the citation to see what subject terms were used to index this reference. There will be several different subject terms. For example, the article may be about types of injuries that occur when children are abused. The subject terms may refer to trauma, children, or abuse. Select the subject term that best fits your area of interest. Now, conduct a search on that subject term. At this point you will have too many or too few references.

Boolean Search Strategies

Boolean search can be used to limit or expand your search. Each time you search on a term your results from that search can be viewed as a database or a collection of articles. There are several approaches that can be used to expand or exclude databases from this database. Chapter 8 introduced these concepts and they are expanded here.

And By searching on two topics using the word **AND** between the two topics you will be able to find materials that are about both topics. For example, if you were searching for information dealing with computers and health care your search might look like this: **Computers AND "health care."** Each of the citations that were listed in your search results would be about both computers and about health care. In many systems using the symbol **+** in front of both terms will function the same as using the term **AND** between the terms. In other words, the term **AND** is used to give you a more focused search. You will note that I put quotes around the phrase **health care**. In most systems using quotes will result in the terms being used as a phrase rather that two separate terms. Two separate terms means the words can appear anywhere in the citation; using quotes means they are next to each other.

Or Sometimes you are looking for information when there are several closely related terms. For example, you may be looking for information on abuse. In this case IPA (refers to intimate partner abuse), family abuse, or family violence may be used to index the materials. If the search uses the term **OR** between each of these terms, the citations in the search result may be indexed on any of these terms. **OR** is used to expand a search.

Truncation Sometimes your topic may have several closely related words. One example is nurse, nursing, and nurses. In this case using truncation may be more efficient than **OR**. With truncation you type the beginning of the term and then use a symbol to indicate that you will except any citation including a term that begins with these letters. The specific symbol will depend on the specific database management system in use. Some common symbols include nurs*, nurs?, and nurs$. Remember that when you use truncation your search results will include every term that begins with the beginning letters. For example, what other terms do you know that begin with the letters nurs in addition to the terms nurse, nurses, and nursing?

Not The term **NOT** is used to eliminate a set of materials. For example, you may be interested in information about assistive health devices but you do not want citations dealing with pacemakers. In this case your search would be **"assistive health devices" NOT pacemakers**.

Near The term **NEAR** is used when the terms should be located within the next few words. For example, you may be looking for information on teaching people about computers. In this case your search might be as follows: **teaching NEAR computers**.

Figure 11–1 is a diagram that demonstrates the concepts of **AND**, **OR**, and **NOT**. There are several other operators that can be used to expand or limit a search. Many times you can find additional information by reading the help section included with the online library at your institution or the Internet search site.

Search Sites and Engines

The Internet contains a vast amount of information. Search sites are places on the Internet where you go to find information. Search engines are software used to find and index information. There are several hundred different search sites and engines on the Internet. Each one has a different interface or appearance, yet they all have several common features. Understanding how to use search sites begins by understanding relevant terms.

Directory A directory is a hierarchical grouping of WWW links by subject and related concepts. These are created by people who searched the Web and then grouped the links by subject. Not all search sites include directories.

Hits Hits are a list of links that are returned as search results when a search engine is used.

Meta-directory A meta-directory is a directory of links to other directories. These are sometimes called a directory of directories or directories of directories.

Meta-search Engines Meta-search engines are not really search engines. They work by taking the user's query and searching the Web with several different search engines at one time. They are gaining in popularity for they permit one stop searching.

Query Query refers to the combination of terms that the user enters into a search engine in order to conduct a search.

Ranking This is a process of indicating how relevant a hit may be. Many times a search engine will organize the search results by their ranking. However, the methods used by search engines to rank pages varies; thus, ranks may not always be useful to you.

Robot Robots are used to create a database of links that are accessed when a user conducts a search. These are special kinds of computer programs that can search the Web, locate links, and then index the links to create the database. Indexing is usually done by using the words in the URL and title of the HTML file and counting the frequency of words used at the Internet site.

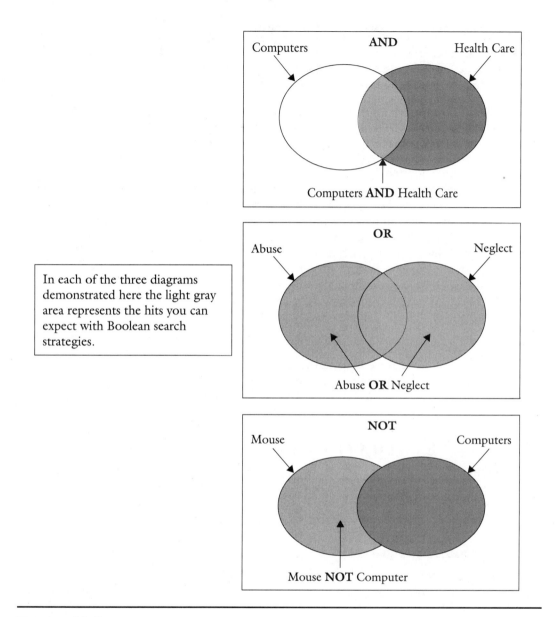

In each of the three diagrams demonstrated here the light gray area represents the hits you can expect with Boolean search strategies.

FIGURE 11–1.
Understanding Boolean Search Strategies

Some robots search the full text while others review a portion of the site. Robots are also called spiders and crawlers.

Search Engine The software that is used to create the database and permit the users to search it. Sometimes this term is used to mean a search site.

Search Site This is a server or a collection of servers dedicated to indexing Internet Web pages, storing the results, and returning lists of links that match particular queries. The indexes are normally generated using spiders. Sometimes search site and search engine are used to mean the same concept, but they are two different terms.

Stop Word A stop word is a word that is ignored in a query because the word is so commonly used that it makes no contribution to relevancy. Examples are words like *and, get, the*, as well as *you*.

Using a search engine begins by accessing the search engine site on the Internet. Search engine sites can be located by clicking on the icon search in both Netscape and Internet Explorer. This will return a list of search sites. Select any of the search sites. On the home page of the search site there will be a window or box where you can enter your query. Before you try your query it is often helpful to access the help section. Sometimes this section is referred to as search tips. Because each of the search engines is different you will find variations on each search engine. Think of this like a car. Each model is different but there are many common functions. The process for searching is very similar to the process you used when doing library searches.

In many cases your first searches will result in a large list of irrelevant hits. One of the reasons for this is that many search engines automatically assume OR is intended between any of the words in the query. Thus, if you are looking for things about University of Virginia, on many search engines you will get things that include "university" and "Virginia." Only some of these will contain both terms and relate to your desired subject. The Power Searches, Search Tips, or Help included with the search engine can assist you to narrow your search. Boolean search strategies will also help you focus your search. Many search engines use a + in front of the term for AND. A – in front of the term for NOT. A blank space between terms can be considered as either an AND or an OR, depending on the search engine.

EVALUATION OF INFORMATION

While finding information that is specific to your topic can be a challenge, finding quality information can be more of a challenge. When you use information, it is your responsibility to be sure you use high quality information. There are several attributes of quality information and they provide a basis for developing criteria to evaluate information.

Information Attributes

Information attributes apply to all information including health-related information. This section reviews these attributes and demonstrates how they can be used to develop criteria for evaluating the quality of information.

1. Timely: Information that is timely is true at this point in time. In other words, it is current. For example, in 1992, the Agency for Health Care Policy and Research (AHCPR) released clinical practice guidelines on urinary incontinence. You may be able to find a copy of them in your library. In 1996 these guidelines were updated to reflect new findings. The updated version can be accessed at http://text.nlm.nih.gov/ftrs/pick?dbName=cuic&ftrsk=44042&cp=1+t=9301591&collect=ahcpr along with other current guidelines. When you access information on the Internet or in a library always check the date of the information at the site of the information. A word of caution applies when checking the date. Many search engines on the Internet will return results that include a date. Here is one of the citations the author found on Alta Vista using the search term "health guidelines":

14. Public Health Guidelines for Enhancing Diabetes Control

Perspectives in Disease Prevention and Health Promotion Public Health

Guidelines for Enhancing Diabetes Control Through Maternal- and Child-Health URL: aepo-xdv-www.epo.cdc.gov/wonder/prevguid...66/p0000166.htm

Last modified 5-Jun-98—page size 2K—in English [Translate]

However, here is the title on the first page of the document:

Perspectives in Disease Prevention and Health Promotion

Public Health Guidelines for Enhancing Diabetes Control

Through Maternal- and Child-Health Programs

MMWR 35(13);201-8,213

Publication date: 04/04/1986

As you can see the document is no longer timely. Reliable sources will usually include the date the material was last updated on the document or on the Web page.

2. Accurate: Information is accurate when it does not contain errors. Using Alta Vista as a search engine and "causes of aids" as the search term, this author found the following citation:

2. AIDS & HIV

WHY HIV DOES NOT CAUSE AIDS AND AIDS IS NOT CONTAGIOUS. (The following paper is reproduced and posted by permission of the author, Micael Martinez) As you . . .

URL: well-being.com/aids&hiv.htm

Last modified 27-Jul-96—page size 393K—in English [Translate]

You may want to look at this site and determine if you find the paper accurate. If you decide the paper is inaccurate, think about why you reached that conclusion. One clue is that accurate information can be consistently found at several different reliable sources. Would the information you found at this site be supported by information published by the CDC?

3. Verifiable: Verifiable information can be checked at more than one source. There is consensus among experts and consistency on how the data is reported. Verifiable information is usually supported by quantifiable data. An example of verifiable information is the impending nursing shortage. In this case you might check government statistics, predictions from your professional organization, and health foundations such as the Pew Foundation.

4. Accessible: Accessible refers to how easy it is to obtain the information. For a number of years MEDLINE was not generally available to the public. In the first six months that access to MEDLINE was offered free on the Internet, one third of all searches were conducted by the general public as opposed to professional health care providers. MEDLINE had become accessible to a widely diversified audience.

Information is accessible if you enter a search term for information and that information is in your search results. Three factors have a major influence. First, the terms or language used to store the information. If this is a bibliographical database—what words are in the title or in the abstract? How was the document indexed? If the information is located on the Internet, access depends on what words are used on the Web page and the approach used by the Internet search engine to indexing. For example, does the Internet search engine search the whole document or only the first paragraph?

A second factor that determines access is the number of references that refer to the original document. In a bibliographical database references are in the footnotes. Sometimes it is possible to click the footnote and be linked directly to the article. On the Internet access is also determined by links. If there are several Web pages that link to a document you are more likely to find them either by browsing or by using a search engine.

The third factor that will determine accessibility is your ability to focus a search. Initial searches often find too much or too little information. One of the most effective approaches is to find one document that includes information you find useful and then use information about this document to find additional material.

Review the document to determine the key or subject words that would locate this document. Note the database where the document was stored. For example, was it on a site maintained by the Center for Communicable Diseases (http://www.cdc.gov) or a major medical center? Is the document in CINAHL but not in MEDLINE? Use this information and the search strategies that you reviewed to search for related documents.

5. Freedom from bias: Biased information has been altered or modified in order to influence the reader. Sometimes the bias is blatant and easy to identify. Do an Internet search using the term abortion. As you know this is an area where there are strong opposing opinions. Look at several sites to determine if information is accurate and free from bias. Bias is easier to identify when you disagree with the opinion being expressed or when the information is clearly inaccurate. Sometimes the information is accurate and the bias is subtle. For example, drug information provided by a drug company most likely includes information about side effects. The information, however, may be in small print near the end of the document. The indications for using the drug may be in larger print and at the beginning of the document. Each time the drug is referred to in the document the trade name is used as opposed to the generic name. These approaches influence you to consider the indications for the drug before its side effects and to think of the trade name before you would remember the generic name.

6. Comprehensive: Comprehensive information is complete. Because there is always more that can be said about any topic, it can be difficult to determine if the information is comprehensive. Information is not comprehensive if missing details mislead the reader. For example, there may be two hospitals in your local community where coronary artery bypass surgery is done. One hospital may have a higher post-op death rate than the other has. This information could lead you to conclude that one hospital provides better care than the other does. However, if the first hospital was a community hospital that took only low risk patients and the second hospital was a major medical center for high-risk patients, the different death rates may be explained.

7. Precise: Information is comprehensive if all the details are provided. However, the information lacks precision if the details are not specific. For example, a map on the Internet may include the specific street where a clinic is located. However, the map may fail to provide the street number for the clinic. Precision occurs when the details provided meet the specific information needs of the reader.

8. Appropriate: Appropriate refers to how well the information answers the user's questions. Is the information on target? For example, you may be looking for information on preparing clinic nurses for a new information system. You may be able to find a great deal of information about the new system but nothing that helps you to prepare the new users. The information that is found is precise, timely, accurate, and meets all the other criteria of quality information. It just does not focus on the specific information needed.

9. Clarity: Information lacks clarity if there can be one or more meanings applied to the same information. For example, "There are several sites on the Internet that provide health information. Some sites provide quality information while others do not. This is one of these sites." The reader is left to infer if this is a site that provides good or poor quality information.

Criteria for Evaluating the Quality of Online Information

Knowing information attributes can help evaluate online information. Using those attributes, you can evaluate the source of the information, its accuracy and currency, and how easy it was to access and use the information online.

1. Source: When accessing and using information try to start with a reliable source. Reliable sources are usually verifiable and accurate. The source of the information on the Internet refers to both author information and where the information is located on the Internet. Many times these two concepts of source can overlap. You may find information about the role of weight in diabetes on an Internet site maintained by the American Diabetic Association or you might find the information on the personal site of individuals well known for their research on diabetes and weight. Many times personal sites use a ~ in the URL to direct you to a personal directory. When evaluating the author as a source, it is helpful to identify the author's name, title or position, degrees or education, and professional affiliation. Remember that this information may be included as part of the information on the Web pages and yet not be accurate. The author could state that s/he is the chairperson of the department of a major university and in reality be a ten-year-old child learning to design a Web page. It is up to you as the user of the information to validate the source.

The URL is your major clue for the location of the information. Let's look at the following URL: http://www2.widener.edu/Wolfgram-Memorial-Library/webeval.htm.

http: indicates this is a site located on the World Wide Web

www2 is the specific name of the server where the information is located

Widener is the name of the institution where the server is located

edu indicates that this is an educational site

Wolfgram-Memorial-Library is the directory on the server where the document is located.

webeval.htm is the actual document. The name of the document indicates it deals with evaluation of Web based materials.

Reliable Web sites often provide information on both the author and the Internet location. The following is taken from the URL that was just examined.

An article explaining how to use these materials appears on pages 49 through 55 in the November/December 1996 issue of "Computers in Libraries" magazine.

Copyright Jan Alexander & Marsha Tate, 1996–1999

Date Mounted on Server: 8 August 1996

Last Revised: 12 May 1999

If you have any comments or suggestions please contact:

Jan Alexander (Janet.E.Alexander@widener.edu) or

Marsha Ann Tate (Marsha.A.Tate@widener.edu)

Wolfgram Memorial Library, Widener University

One University Place

Chester, PA 19013

URL for this page: http://www2.widener.edu/Wolfgram-Memorial-Library/webeval.htm

Many thanks to Maria Varki, Head of the Reference Department, for encouraging us in this project, and to Mike Powell, Reference Librarian, for his invaluable technical assistance.

Return to The Teaching Pyramid

Return to Library Main Menu

Return to Widener Main Menu

2. Current: Current information is information that has been updated as new information has evolved. The Web page itself should indicate the last time the information was updated. This is not the same as the last time the page was modified. If a spelling error is corrected the page is modified; however the information has not been updated.

Another clue that the information is current is the reliability of the links. There are two ways to evaluate the links. First, do they function? Links on the Internet change constantly. If a site is not being well maintained, the links will become outdated and no longer function. Second, does this site link to current information? On a well-maintained site, links that no longer connect to quality information are removed.

3. Easy to navigate: Quality information is usually organized in a logical format. Logical technical approaches are then used to guide the user through the information. This may be as simple as a table of contents that provides an overview of the information in the document or as complex as the use of multiple frames. Sometimes a site map is used to provide an overview of the information at the site. The use of color and graphics can help or hinder the navigation of a site. A site may be comprehensive, but if the site is not well organized and the navigational aids do not function well, the user may never find the quality information located on the site.

Since a search engine may start the user anywhere in the site, effective navigational aids are important. The example used here, http://www2.widener.edu/Wolfgram-Memorial-Library/webeval.htm, is located in the middle of a site dealing with Web resources. Note the navigational aides throughout the page and how they quickly give you an overview of how the information is organized.

4. Objective information: Objective information is free of bias. But the Internet is also an excellent place for the expression of opinions as well as advertisement of ideas, products, and positions. Biases on the Internet are acceptable if they are clearly stated. Http://www.democrats.org/index.html is the URL for the Democratic Party. Http://www.rnc.org/ is the URL for the Republican Party. One could expect different viewpoints from these two sites. Alta Vista includes a directory titled **Abortion Debate**. This directory includes sub-directories titled **Pro-Choice** and **Pro-Life**. Many sites include an area titled "about." The "about" section should indicate who has sponsored the site and if the sponsor holds certain opinions. Here is an example taken from the following site:

http://www.cais.com/agm/main/about.htm

About This Site

The purpose of this Web site is to provide information to the pro-choice community, to others with an interest in abortion and abortion-related issues, or to women seeking an abortion. Most of what you'll find is original information, not just a collection of links (except the "Information About Abortion" section).

I do not pretend to be unbiased—this is a pro-choice Web site, after all. I do, however, present accurate, objective information. When I engage in "editorializing," I'll let you know. If any visitor to this site is aware of any inaccuracies, please let me know.

I say "I" rather than "we" because this site is not the product of any organization. Although various individuals or groups have contributed information, this is primarily the effort of one person, done in what passes for my spare time.

I do not engage in philosophical debate over abortion, and present no arguments—philosophical, moral, religious, scientific, or otherwise—concerning the legality of abortion. I have no interest in convincing anyone that my views on abortion are correct. I just provide information. Make up your own minds.

5. Error free: Several of the criteria already listed will help you determine if an online resource is error free. There are additional clues that are also helpful. First, watch for errors in spelling and grammar. If a site is sloppy with these kinds of details, they may also be sloppy with the accuracy of the information they are providing. Second, be cautious if you find information on only one site and no other information verifying it at other sites. For example, you may find an Internet site telling you about the malaria epidemic in Alaska. Malaria is caused by a parasite that is transmitted from person to person by the bite of an infected Anopheles mosquito. These mosquitoes are present in almost all countries in the tropics and subtropics. Given these facts about the cause of malaria, do you think that it is likely there could be an epidemic in Alaska?

Health Care Information on the Internet

What's the problem?

> Not all health information is created equal, and not everything out there is correct. When knowledgeable people have "surfed" the Web, they have found dangerously misleading or incomplete health information that looks quite legitimate on the surface. The medium itself contributes to the problem. Anyone can make anything look slick and professional on the Web. Just because you're reading something on a computer screen doesn't mean it's any more credible than something you heard at a party or on a talk show. While most health information on the Internet was put there to help people, not all of it will necessarily be good for you. [Source http://www.scipich.org/IHC/problems.htm]

Additional Criteria for Health Information

The criteria that were already discussed deal with any information on the Internet. They apply to health care information, but are not specific to health care information. There are however additional criteria that apply when the information is health related.

1. Intended audience is clear: Does the site clearly state who the intended audience is, including the skills and knowledge needed to interpret the information provided by the site? This information is often included in an area titled "mission" or "about us."

2. Confidentiality of personal information: Many health care sites collect personal health care data. For example, there are many sites with self-assessment areas. A quality site will clearly state what data is collected and how the data is used. Remember that anyone can publish anything on the WWW including a statement of privacy that is incomplete or inaccurate. Be sure you know the site and the sponsors of that site before you provide personal information to an Internet site.

3. Source of the content–references: An Internet site that provides health information needs to be able to document the source of that information. As a user of that information you need to evaluate the source of the information and if the sources listed are in fact real. The reference list itself can include references that do not exist.

4. Reading/comprehension level: There are several tools that can be used to evaluate reading level of materials posted on the Internet. The word processing package presented in this book includes one such tool. Comprehension is a more difficult question. Comprehension deals with the health care background of readers and their ability to understand the information being presented. Since the Internet can be accessed by anyone, it is important for the site to help the reader with this question. It is helpful if the intended audience is well identified.

Sites with Health Care Information Criteria

The quality of health care information on the Internet is of concern to many health care providers. A number of sites located on the Internet provide guides for evaluating health care information.

Rollins School of Public Health at Emory University has developed a form that can be used to evaluate health-related sites on the Internet. The form is designed for health educators and clinicians to evaluate the appropriateness of Web sites for health education for their clientele. This form is located at: http://www.sph.emory.edu/WELLNESS/instrument.html

Health On the Net Foundation (HON) is a not-for-profit organization located in Geneva, Switzerland. Among its many activities HON has developed a Code of Conduct for providers of health care information. The code isn't intended to rate the quality or the information provided by a Web site. It defines a set of rules designed to make sure the reader always knows the source and the purpose of the data being read. This organization can be located at: http://www.hon.ch/home.html. You will note that the Emory University form included a reference to this code on the evaluation form.

Mitretek Systems is a nonprofit organization. It established the Health Information Technology Institute to take "the lead in the application of innovative technology solutions to ensure quality health care." One area of focus is the quality of health care information on the Internet. A paper, "Criteria for Assessing the Quality of Health Information on the Internet," is located on their site at http://hitiWeb.mitretek.org/

In 1996 the Office of Disease Prevention and Health Promotion of the U.S. Department of Health and Human Services (DHHS) convened a Science Panel on Interactive Communication and Health (SciPICH). Interactive health communication (IHC) defined as the interaction of an individual—consumer, patient, caregiver, or professional—with an electronic device or communication technology to access or transmit health information or to receive guidance on a health-related issue. Their Web site includes a template for evaluation of these health education tools as well as a comprehensive list of references. The Web site is maintained by DHHS as a free informational service to the public and is located at http://www.scipich.org/.

USING INFORMATION

The final step in information literacy is the effective use of information. This is a very broad topic. The statement—"You can say anything with statistics"—is a comment on the use of information. In this book the discussion is limited to documenting information from the Internet.

Footnotes and Documentation

All information accessed on the Internet should be documented just as you would document information from other sources. However, on the Internet there are some additional issues. First, it is easy to forget that the copyright laws also protect information posted on the Internet. This can even apply to e-mail messages posted to a listserv. Second, just as it is easy to post information on the Internet, it is also easy to remove that information. Therefore, the citation for information obtained from the Internet should include some additional data such as the date the information was developed, if this information is provided by the Internet site, and the date the information was accessed. There are several Internet sites that give directions for formatting an Internet citation.

Internet Sites for Citing Internet Information

The American Psychological Association (APA) is one of the most common formats used in health care. The APA maintains a Web site and includes information on how to use the APA format to cite Internet resources. This is located at http://www.apa.org/journals/webref.html.

In addition to the APA, there are other accepted citation formats. Several of these are demonstrated on a site maintained by the General Library at the University of Texas at Austin. This site is located at http://www.lib.utexas.edu/Pubs/guides/general/citing.html. This library gives you permission to use these resources. You may want to look at this permission at the bottom of their home page located at http://www.lib.utexas.edu/.

Like the University of Texas at Austin, many libraries include this type of information on their Web sites. Often they will include a list of links to resources for citing Internet resources. Two sites that demonstrate this approach include http://www.nova.edu/library/citation.html and http://www.lafayette.edu/library/cite.html. This second site includes a list on components that should be included in any Internet citation.

SUMMARY

This chapter focused on information literacy. This included strategies to find information, evaluate the quality of information, and cite information from the Internet. Quality health care requires good information. As a health care provider it is your responsibility to search out the latest high-quality information and make appropriate use of that information in providing health care.

EXERCISE 1: USING A SEARCH SITE

Objectives

1. Use the help section of an Internet search site.
2. Conduct an Internet search using Boolean search strategies.
3. Identify a directory, search tool, meta-directory, and meta-search engine.

Activity

1. Access a search site.

   Type the following URL in your browser **Location** or **Address** text box: **http://www.yahoo.com**. You are now on the home page of Yahoo.

   On this page locate the following four areas. The **Help Icon, Advance Search**, the area where you **enter your query** and the **list of subjects** within the directory.

2. Use a directory.

   Click the subject area that deals with **Health**. The next page will be a subdirectory.

   Click one of the **Topics** from the subdirectory. Look near the top of the page to see if there is a path statement that will tell you how deep you are in the directory. The path may look something like this: **Home > Health > Women's Health >**.

3. Use a home navigational aid.

   Click the **Home** link to return to the Yahoo home page.

Click the **Help** section. Does all the help relate to searching Yahoo?

Did you learn anything new on this page?

4. Use advanced search.

Click the **Back** button on your browser to return to the Yahoo home page.

Click **Advance Search**.

Look around in this section. Move your mouse around and see if you find some links that you did not realize were there.

Click the **Back** button to return again to the Yahoo home page.

5. Find and orient to new search engines.

Use Yahoo to find at least **two** other **Search** engines on the Internet.

Use the same approach demonstrated with Yahoo to orient yourself to the search engines.

6. Conduct a search.

Go to the **Search engine** you prefer.

Design a query to search for **Search Engine Tutorials**.

7. Compare online tutors.

Select a **Tutorial** from the hits on your search and one of the following tutorials.

Complete the two tutorials.

Which of the two did you find most informative? Why?

http://www.ultranet.com/~egrlib/tutor.htm

http://www.Webpro.co.za/services/search.htm

http://www.eons.com/research/tutorials.htm

http://www.mannlib.cornell.edu/reference/workshops/WebSearching/

http://www.notess.com/search/

http://www.monash.com/spidap.html

As you are looking for a site with tutorials for search engines be sure to at least take a quick look at this site: http://www.lib.berkeley.edu/TeachingLib/Guides/Internet/FindInfo.html

8. Meta-search engine classifications.

Metat-search engines can be classified in many ways. Some examples include classification by topic searched (medicine, law, art), by how sites are found and indexed (robots and people), and by how many search engines are being used to conduct the search at one time. There are sites on the WWW where lists of links to several search engines are presented. These sites classify the search engines in a variety of ways.

Locate at least **five** sites that include 15 or more search engines.

Locate sites where the search engines are grouped under certain headings.

Create a table that includes a column for 1) the site, 2) the classification, and 3) an example of a search site in that classification.

Search engines may be classified in more than one way and your groupings or classifications may overlap. Here are some sites to get you started. Do not include these sites in the five sites that you located for this exercise.

http://www.lib.berkeley.edu/TeachingLib/Guides/Internet/ToolsTables.html

http://www.internetminer.com/mse.htm

http://informatics.library.ucsf.edu/Search.htm

http://www.amdahl.com/internet/meta-index.html

http://www.rcq.usherb.ca/ihea/ihea.htm

EXERCISE 2: EVALUATING INFORMATION ON THE INTERNET

Objectives

1. Develop a tool that can be used to evaluate information on the quality of information on the Internet.
2. Evaluate the effectiveness of the tool for a user who has limited knowledge of the topic presented at an Internet site.

Activity

1. Evaluate information sites.

   Review three sites from the following:

   http://www2.widener.edu/Wolfgram-Memorial-Library/pyramid.htm

   http://www.albany.edu/library/internet/evaluate.html

   http://www.ciolek.com/WWWVL-InfoQuality.html

   http://www.ala.org/parentspage/greatsites/criteria.html

   http://members.aol.com/xxmindyxx/evaluate/question.html

   http://www.library.ucla.edu/libraries/college/instruct/Web/critical.htm

   http://sosig.ac.uk/desire/internet-detective.html

2. Develop evaluation Web content tool.

   Using information from the selected sites as well as the text, design a tool for evaluating Web pages.

   Select two health related Internet sites with information for the general public. One site should have high quality information. The other site should have inaccurate information.

   Ask a high school student or college freshman who would be expected to have a limited health care background to review the sites using your form.

3. Answer the following questions.

   a. Did the student collect information for all sections of your form?

   b. When information was missing, did s/he note this? For example, if the date the page was last updated was missing, did they note this?

   c. Did s/he validate the data or information that they collected? For example, if the author of the information at the Internet site indicated that s/he was a college professor, did the student check the directory of the college to see if s/he was listed?

   d. Was the student able to differentiate the quality of the information at the two sites?

   e. If the student was correct, what factors influenced the student in making this decision? In other words, how was s/he able to recognize the quality of the information?

   f. If s/he was incorrect, what factors mislead the student? Remember the student may be correct about one page and not the other.

   g. From this experience, how would you revise your form? What would you stress if you were teaching patients to evaluate information on the Web?

ASSIGNMENT 1: EVALUATING HEALTH CARE INFORMATION ON THE INTERNET

Directions

1. Begin this assignment by designing two forms for evaluating health related information at an Internet site. Design one form that can be used by a health care provider. The second form should be designed for use by the general public. The forms should be no longer than two pages and should include directions for use.

2. Pilot both forms with at least five users. Exercise 2 should be helpful to you in planning your pilot.

3. Write a paper about this project including the following information. Explain the rationale for the design and content of each form. Describe how you selected your users and what happened when you piloted the forms with the users. Outline your findings or the results of your pilot. Redesign the forms based on your pilot and include the revised forms in your paper. Don't forget to cite references using the appropriate format.

4. After the paper is completed, design a poster presentation based on the paper. You may find PowerPoint helpful for this part of the assignment. Present the poster presentation to your classmates.

5. Turn in both the paper and the poster presentation.

Chapter 12

Legal and Ethics Issues Related to Electronic Data

OBJECTIVES

1. Describe legal/ethical concerns related to computer use by health care professionals.
2. Identify appropriate activities to support legal and ethical use of computers for health care delivery.
3. Identify methods for protecting a computer connected to the Internet.
4. Identify implications of copyright law related to using materials found on the Internet.

INTRODUCTION

Computer systems are more widespread than ever in health care agencies today. They are used for patient care, health insurance surveys and audits, research, financial records, and inventory management. Putting large amounts of data on computers has been a concern for many years. Within health care agencies, computer systems can be used as specialized systems for medical information, patient documentation, patient education, or communication. In addition, health care is provided via computers, and professionals in one state provide care to individual patients in another state. This leads to legal implications regarding professional licenses. Accessing information via the Internet, sharing computer disks, and using materials found at various Internet sites also raise ethical and legal concerns. This chapter will focus on legal and ethical concerns related to using computer systems for storing and sharing patient data, providing patient care across legal jurisdictions, the implications of copyright law, and the safety and security of using the computer.

USING COMPUTER SYSTEMS FOR STORING DATA

All large organizations today use computer systems to store data. This is true of most hospitals as well as many other health care agencies. While computer systems are used for purposes other than management of personal data, such as financial records and inventory management, the legal/ethical implications related to storing personal data is of primary concern. There are three major concerns related to storing personal data, be it individual personalized information or patient records, in computers:

1. providing for privacy and confidentiality of data
2. maintaining a safe and secure system
3. recognizing and prosecuting criminal abuse of computer data and equipment.

PRIVACY AND CONFIDENTIALITY

To protect privacy and confidentiality, issues relevant to data storage and use must be addressed. Problems of ensuring privacy and confidentiality of data include data storage issues and data use issues.

Data Storage Issues	Incomplete or inaccurate storage of data
	Unnecessary storage of data
Data Use Issues	Access of data for unauthorized use
	Intentional or accidental manipulation of data

Personal Privacy and Confidentiality

There is a great deal of concern about what is kept in the various databases of different companies and the government. For example, information about you and your driving record is stored by the Department of Motor Vehicles where you are licensed; social security benefits information is stored by the government; and many mail order companies have information such as your phone number and address. Knowing what data is stored about you is important to protect your privacy. Currently at issue is the right of the government to store personal DNA information in its databanks in order to help link criminals to specific crimes. Most of us realize when we complete forms, such as warrantee or registration forms asking for our name, address, and other information, that this data may be sold to other companies. Now, similar questions are being asked in order to receive Internet services. Individuals who use the Internet for sensitive transactions, such as checking bank balances or using a credit card to purchase goods, are concerned about the privacy and security of this data. In fact, simply using the Internet generates information about the individuals—where they go on the Net, who they interact with via chat rooms and listservs, and what products they buy. Some of the newest tracking systems can build a detailed database of personal information (CDT's Guide to Online Privacy, 1998). Questions arise about what happens to that information, whether or not it will be "sold" to other companies, and how else it might be used.

Patient Privacy and Confidentiality

Though we often think medical information is private, people both inside and outside of the health care industry share medical information. Besides physicians and other health care providers, your information may be shared with insurance companies and government agencies like Medicare or Medicaid. Access to your records is obtained when you agree to let others see them, usually by signing consent forms or blanket waivers when you receive health care. With the increasing use of technology, medical information is stored in a variety of computer databases both in local institutions and in other places serving a number of health care institutions. With the passing of PL 104-191, the Health Insurance Portability and Accountability Act of 1996, Congress made provisions for a standard unique health identifier for each individual, employer, health plan, and health care provider in the health care system, making it even easier to access individual data. While the law also includes penalties for infringement of the integrity and confidentiality of data, privacy advocates continue to be concerned about secondary uses of medical information, employer access, and unauthorized access (Privacy Rights Clearing House, March 1993/Revised January 1999, p. 2).

SAFETY AND SECURITY

Protecting the safety and security of patient data involves identifying the threats to computer systems and initiating procedures to protect the integrity of the data and system. Threats occur primarily in two areas, accidental destruction of data and intentional breaks into the system. Accidental destruction of data involves natural disasters such as damage by water, fire, or chemicals; electrical power outages; disk failures; and exposure to magnetic fields. Breaks into the system involve unintended as well as unauthorized use of equipment, computer time, or data and the intentional destruction of equipment or data. In 1996, the National Research Council identified five threat levels for information stored in health care computers:

"Threat 1: Insiders who make "innocent" mistakes and cause accidental disclosures of confidential information. This could be as simple as a lab sending a fax to a wrong phone number, or a nurse pulling up one patient's medical records instead of another.

Threat 2: Insiders who abuse their record access privileges. Browsing seems to be a problem with many electronic record systems. The Internal Revenue Service, for example, has had persistent problems with curious employees looking through the tax records to which they have access. It's unreasonable to think that hospitals will somehow avoid this affliction.

Threat 3: Insiders who knowingly access information for spite or for profit. During the 1992 Democratic primaries, a pathologist at Beth Israel was contacted by a member of the press who wanted access to Paul Tsongas' medical records. The reporter offered good money, and a less ethical pathologist could easily have retrieved the file—probably without having that information traced back to him.

Threat 4: An unauthorized physical intruder who gains access to information. Many hospitals rely on physical security to protect information stored inside a computer: the terminals are put in a special room or behind a desk to which only authorized personnel are supposed to have access. Unfortunately, hospitals are not as secure as hospital administrators would like to believe. If that journalist had simply put on a white lab coat and gotten a fake badge, the person might have been able to retrieve Tsongas' medical records unassisted.

Threat 5: Vengeful employees and outsiders, such as vindictive patients or intruders, who mount attacks to access unauthorized information, damage systems, and disrupt operations. A doctor who practices at an HMO recently told me of a problem that her group has been having: An employee—they think they know who—has been accessing the HMO's scheduling computer and deleting patient appointments. The scheduling desk then thinks the appointment slot is free, and two or three patients show up at the same time" (http://www.2048.com/06med.htm).

COMPUTER CRIME

New laws are being enacted to define computer crime since the Internet, with its global connectivity, allows more and more access to computers from external sites. However, it is still difficult to detect and prosecute some computer crime. Although the terms listed below are more readily identified with computer crime in areas other than health care, all types of crime could occur within a health care computer system.

Terms Related to Computer Crime

Hacker	This originally referred to a compulsive computer programmer; it now has a more negative meaning and is often confused with "cracker."
Cracker	This is a hacker who illegally breaks into computer systems and creates mischief.
Data Diddling	This involves modifying valid data in a computer file.
Encryption	This is a method of coding sensitive data to protect it when sent over the Internet.
Firewall	Term used for preventing spread of external problems into a local system or confining problems occurring within a local system, such as a virus, and preventing their transmission to other external computer systems.
Salami Method	This method of data stealing involves taking little bits at a time.
Software Piracy	This is unauthorized copying of copyrighted software.
Trapdoors	These are methods installed by programmers that allow unauthorized access into programs.
Trojan Horse	This involves placing instructions in a program that add additional, illegitimate functions; for example, the program prints out information every time information on a certain diagnosis is entered.
Time Bomb	This involves instructions in a program that perform certain functions on a specific date or time such as printing a message or destroying data.
Virus	This involves a program that once introduced into a system replicates itself and causes a variety of mischievous outcomes. Viruses are introduced from infected diskettes, e-mail attachments, and downloaded files.
Worm	This is a destructive program that can fill various memory locations of a computer system with information, clogging the system so that other operations are compromised.

Prosecution of Computer Crime

Prosecution of computer crime is difficult for several reasons. When data is stolen, it is not always seen as valuable, thus those responsible may not be prosecuted. In addition, some crimes detected are not reported. Though methods for tracking entry into computer systems are becoming increasingly sophisticated, discovery of computer crime may be difficult. Laws are catching up, but still lag behind computer technology and associated crimes. In some situations, there are questions about who "owns" data. Many of the early laws that were developed protect individuals from having data about them stored in a computer without their knowledge.

Currently, laws are being proposed to alter the copyright law and protect intellectual property on the Internet. Corporations are beginning to search out and prosecute those who circulate copyrighted material on the Internet (Nodel, 1999). The concept of "fair use" is also being debated. The Copyright Act of 1976 permits the use of limited portions of copyrighted materials for educational purposes in nonprofit educational institutions. In the past, those guidelines related only to text and not to other media. Current guidelines suggest that "up to three minutes of a motion media work, up to 1000 words of a text work, or up to 30 seconds of the music and lyrics from a musical work can be used—as long as none of these quantities constitutes more than ten percent of the original" (Milone, 1997). According to the Berne convention of the copyright law, "almost everything created privately and originally after April 1, 1989 is copyrighted and protected whether it has a notice or not" (Templeton, 1999).

Main Laws Related to Computers

Freedom of Information Act of 1970 This law allows citizens to have access to data gathered by federal agencies.

Federal Privacy Act of 1974 This law stipulates that there can be no secret *personal* files; individuals must be allowed to know what is stored in files about them and how it is used. This applies to government agencies and contractors dealing with government agencies but not the private sector.

Electronic Communications Privacy Act of 1986 This law specifies that it is a crime to own any electronic, mechanical, or other device primarily useful for the purpose of the surreptitious interception of wire, oral, or electronic communication.

Computer Fraud and Abuse Act of 1984, amended in 1986 This law specifies that it is a crime to access a federal computer without authorization and to alter, destroy, or damage information or prevent authorized access...if such conduct causes the loss of $1000 or more during any one-year period.

U.S. Copyright Law, 1976 This law stipulates that it is a federal offense to reproduce copyrighted materials, including computer software, without authorization.

U.S. Copyright Law, 1995 Amendment This amendment protects the transmission of digital performance over the Internet, making it a crime to transmit something for which you do not have proper authorization.

U.S. Copyright Law, No Electronic Theft Act, 1997 This addition to the copyright act creates criminal penalties for copyright infringement even if the offender does not benefit financially.

Digital Millennium Copyright Act of 1998 This legislation places the United States in conformance with international treaties that prevail in other countries around the world. The new act provides changes in three areas: protection of copyrighted digital works, extension of copyright protection by 20 years, and addition of criminal penalties and fines for attempting to circumvent the copyright. It provides for copy protection for the creative organization and structure of a database, but not the underlying general facts, requires that "Webcasters" pay licensing fees to record companies, and limits ISP's copyright infringement liability for simply transmitting information over the Internet.

Since copyright and privacy on the Internet are such important concerns, there are many Internet sites that provide useful information about "cyberlaw." Among these are the Cyberspace Law Center (http://cyber.findlaw.com/clc/) and CyberSpace Law Lessons for Non-Lawyers (http://www.ssrn.com/update/lsn/cyberspace/csl_lessons.html). Both of these sites have more information about privacy, copyright, and other laws related to electronic data. The Cyberspace Law Center also has a search engine so that specific areas of interest may be examined.

PROTECTION OF COMPUTER DATA AND SYSTEMS

The privacy and confidentiality of data as well as the safety and security of the entire system can be protected by procedures initiated by the health care agency. Steps taken by individual health care providers are also important to maintaining data security. Agency responsibilities include protecting data from unauthorized use, destruction or disclosure, and controlling data input and output. Individuals are also accountable for managing data responsibly.

To protect data from unauthorized use, destruction, or disclosure, agencies should:

1. Restrict access to data; develop password systems and/or call back procedures.
2. Develop coding procedures for sensitive data.
3. Use transaction records to follow access and periodically audit them.
4. Develop systems to identify users by electronic signatures, fingerprints, or retina prints.
5. Locate CPUs in private areas that are patrolled.
6. Protect systems from natural disasters; locate them in areas safe from water and other potential physical damage.
7. Develop backups and redundant systems so that data are not lost accidentally.
8. Develop and enforce policies for breaches of security.
9. Store only needed data.
10. Dispose of unneeded printouts by shredding.

To manage data responsibly, individuals should:

1. Input data accurately.
2. Collect no data that are not used.
3. Keep data out of view of others.
4. Discuss no private information.
5. Keep secure own password/means of access to data.
6. Report breaches of security.
7. Keep harmful materials such as food, drink, and smoke away from computers.

PROTECTING YOUR PC

While most health care agencies store information on large computers, there are agencies that use microcomputers. Even in institutions with larger computers, individual health care providers use PCs. Now that the Internet is used to access information, including health information, it is important to know how to safeguard information on the PC.

While some of the same guidelines related to safety and security of the larger computer are important for the PC, there are additional guidelines to protect the PC system and its data. Often individuals are concerned about the privacy of information on their computers and about what information may be accessed on their PC when using the Internet. Project OPEN is an online public education network created to help address some of the issues arising with the rapid development of computer technology (http://www.isa.net/project-open/layout.html). The following is a summary of action steps to protect the data on your PC.

1. Use existing safety and security devices.
   - If others have access to the computer, lock your computer and lock the door of the room where it is located.
   - Be creative with passwords; avoid the obvious ones, like initials or special dates, and don't tape them on the wall or under your keyboard! A combination of numbers and letters is often useful. Change passwords frequently.
   - Use an approved surge protector.
   - Use whatever methods your e-mail system provides to protect your mail from snooping, tampering, and forgery.

2. Protect your system from viruses.
   - Install software or download files safely.
     — Load only sealed software from a reputable vendor.
     — Download data only from reputable systems that are regularly checked for viruses.
   - Use a recent release of antivirus software for all questionable files.
     — Set your system to automatically scan files.
     — Develop a habit of testing suspect files, downloaded files from unknown sites, and diskettes given to you by others before opening the files.
     — Scan all e-mail attachments before opening. Do NOT set your mailer to automatically open attachments.
     — Copy files from other disks only when you know the disks have been tested.
   - Regularly perform system backups.
     — If data is lost due to a virus, it is useful to have full backups.

3. Protect sensitive data.
   - Store sensitive data on floppies or Zip discs rather than a hard disk or network, and lock them up.
   - Name sensitive files cryptically.
   - Use the password system for your software if it has one.
   - Hide important files by using utilities and other devices.
   - Dispose of paper output carefully.
   - Know what you have on disk.
   - Eliminate old or unnecessary backup files.

4. Use the Internet and online resources responsibly.
   - Examine the implications related to where your e-mail address may be listed and the use of other information you provide to your online service provider and other Internet resources you use.
   - Never give out personal information on a chat.

- Check NO. Many online companies give you the option to have your e-mail address used for sending future information. Be sure to check NO if you do not want that service and want to ensure your e-mail address is not passed on to others.
- Configure your browser to the appropriate security level. At the time of this writing, you can do this with Internet Explorer and Netscape Navigator.
- Use the secure server when you are given that option. Companies often provide you with the option to use a secure server that provides additional protection when you are sending private information such as a credit card number via the Internet.
- Look for the padlock icon. When using Internet sites to send data, the padlock icon, usually in the lower part of your screen, signifies your data is encrypted and you are on a secure site.
- Know the policies related to using e-mail. If you transfer messages from your service provider to your own computer, you will have more privacy protection than if you leave them on the provider's server.
- Recognize that to make some Web sites work, you will need a "cookie" on your computer. A cookie is a small file sent to your hard drive when you interact with certain World Wide Web sites. It contains information about what you did on that Web site and, in some instances, communicates personal preferences when on the site. Cookies do not "scan your hard drive" and are read only by the site or site group that originally sent the file.

PROVIDING PATIENT CARE VIA COMPUTER

Telemedicine is used in a variety of places across the country. In these situations, patients can live in one state and be served by health care providers whose "office" is located in another state. For example, a nurse may provide health education, via the computer, to a client in another state, or a physician may examine a patient in another state using computerized diagnostic aids. This raises legal issues. Currently, in order to protect the public, state law defines the legal authority and accountability of health professionals practicing within the state. States' laws vary. When the patient is in one state and the health provider in another, which state's law governs? Until such time as there is national licensure, some think it seems logical that the law protecting the patient/client would be the law for the state in which that individual resides. However, there has also been recent discussion about labeling the provider practice base as the location of care. In this situation, the state law governing the provider would be that of the state in which the practice is located. When health professionals provide care that crosses state boundaries, they need to have licenses as well as knowledge about the laws of each state in which they practice. Which state's law will govern health care providers whose practice crosses state lines has not yet been fully determined.

SUMMARY

Storing data and exchanging data via the computer has caused many ethical and legal concerns. This chapter focused on issues related to confidentiality and privacy of data, as well as ownership of data and the associated copyright laws that apply to computer data. Securing computers and data is a challenge for large computer networks and important for individuals using PCs and sending personal data over the Internet. The arrival of telemedicine has created legal challenges for health care professionals. At this time, it is not certain how practices crossing state lines will ultimately be governed.

REFERENCES[*]

American Hospital Association. (1999). Statement by the A.H.A. to the subcommittee on government management, information and technology government reform and oversight committee re: medical records privacy, H. R. 52. Retrieved April 14, 1999 from the World Wide Web: http://www.aha.org/ar/gr_conf.html.

Beck, D. A. (1996–98). *Fair use in copyright.* Bitlaw: A resource on Technology Law. Retrieved March 30, 1999 from the World Wide : http://www.bitlaw.com/copyright/fair_use.html.

CDT's guide to online privacy. (1998). Retrieved April 18, 1999 from the World Wide Web: http://www.cdt.org/privacy/guide/start/index.html.

Cyberspace Law Center Home Page (1994–99). Retrieved April 15, 1999 from the World Wide Web: http://cyber.findlaw.com/clc/.

Garfinkel, S. L. (1996). *Security and community in the next century, Chapter 6: The Body's own privacy.* Retrieved April 21, 1999 from the World Wide Web: http://www.2048.com/06med.htm.

Lessig, L., Post, D., & Volokh, E. (1999). *CyberSpace law lessons for non-lawyers.* Retrieved February 25, 1999 from the World Wide Web: http://www.ssrn.com/update/lsn/cyber-space/csl_lessons.html.

Milone, M. N. (1997). Fair use guidelines for educational multimedia. *Technology and Learning 17*(5), 50. Retrieved February 9, 1999 from the World Wide Web: http://Web3.infotrac-custom.com/infotrac_custom/session/605/172/476.

Nodel, B. (July 23, 1999). *Online thieves collide with the law.* Retrieved February 22, 1999 from the World Wide Web: http://www.msnbc.com/news/178744.asp.

Privacy Rights Clearing House. (March 1993 / Revised January 1999). *Fact Sheet # 8: How private is my medical information?* Retrieved April 15, 1999 from the World Wide Web: http://www.privacyrights.org/FS/fs8-med.htm.

Templeton, B. (1999). *10 big myths about copyright explained.* Retrieved March 30, 1999 from the World Wide Web: http://www.templetons.com/brad/copymyths.htm.

Title 17—Copyrights Chapter 1—Subject Matter and Scope of Copyright. Retrieved April 4, 1999 from the World Wide Web: http://www4.law.cornell.edu/uscode/17/101.html.

---

[*]When entering an URL, do not type the period that follows it in this list.

EXERCISE 1: LEGAL AND ETHICAL ISSUES

Objectives

1. Apply information about the ethical and legal use of computers to commonly encountered situations.
2. Clarify personal attitude about the legal/ethical use of computer hardware and software.

Activity

Beside each situation below, place a check by the term that best reflects your opinion. Be prepared to discuss your responses.

1. Kevin gives his password to Beth, another student not enrolled in a computer class for which a lab fee is charged. The password allows access to the school computer. The unauthorized student uses three hours of computer time in a timesharing environment.

   Kevin, enrolled in class:

   ETHICAL____   UNETHICAL____   COMPUTER CRIME____

   Beth, not enrolled in class:

   ETHICAL____   UNETHICAL____   COMPUTER CRIME____

2. A physical therapist gives her/his password to a friend who is a graduate student in PT so that s/he may review a patient record and extract the data needed for a clinical paper.

   Physical therapist:

   ETHICAL____   UNETHICAL____   COMPUTER CRIME____

   Graduate student:

   ETHICAL____   UNETHICAL____   COMPUTER CRIME____

3. A copy of a commercial word-processing package used in a school computer course is given to a friend who is not taking the course.

   ETHICAL____   UNETHICAL____   COMPUTER CRIME____

4. Using a terminal, a health care worker breaks a security code and reviews confidential patient data. No use is made of the information. "I was just curious," is the response when caught.

   ETHICAL____   UNETHICAL____   COMPUTER CRIME____

5. Brian is creating a Web page and finds a terrific background on another page. He copies the background to use on his page.

   ETHICAL____   UNETHICAL____   COMPUTER CRIME____

6. Several health care providers are collaborating on an important research study. The Hospital Board of Review has been slow to give permission for data collection via computerized patient records. The research team members, experienced with computer systems, decide to go ahead and begin data collection while waiting to hear from the Review Board.

   ETHICAL____   UNETHICAL____   COMPUTER CRIME____

7. Terry lurks on a listserv that provides a thought provoking discussion about AIDS. The student takes some of the ideas from the listserv and incorporates them into a paper he is writing, but does not credit the source of the ideas.

   ETHICAL____   UNETHICAL____   COMPUTER CRIME____

8. Judy downloads a file that is labeled shareware, useable for 45 days and if further use is desired, payment is requested. Judy really likes the program and continues to use it well after the trial period without sending any payment.

   ETHICAL____   UNETHICAL____   COMPUTER CRIME____

EXERCISE 2: USE OF COMPUTERS IN HEALTH CARE

Objectives

1. Analyze common concerns related to the ethical use of computers in health care systems.
2. Articulate a position about the ethical use of computers.

Activity

1. You have been asked to be a part of a committee considering using computers to connect the main clinic and several satellite clinics, one of which is in the neighboring state. The committee has several tasks:

   a. Convince those who have recently joined the committee that computers will not be prone to unwanted access.

   b. Develop procedures for safeguarding the patient data that will be entered into the computer system.

   c. Ensure legal protection for the health professionals using the computers.

2. Using your word-processing system, prepare a two- to three-page paper that summarizes the points you would stress as the committee works on its tasks. Include your reference list. Submit your paper.

EXERCISE 3: COPYRIGHT AND PRIVACY ISSUES

Objectives

1. Describe copyright and fair use.
2. Identify methods for adhering to copyright law when writing a research paper.
3. Identify some potential security problems when surfing.

Activity

1. Copyright.

   Access the following Web site and visit some of the articles listed that relate to copyright. http://www.tenet.edu/library/citation.html.

   Answer the following questions.

   What is copyright?

   What is fair use?

   What is public domain?

   What are the guidelines for including information in a research paper in order to be in compliance with the copyright law?

   How do you cite a WWW site in a reference list?

   How do you cite an e-mail message?

   Submit your answers to the above questions using your word processor.

2. Privacy.

   Go to www.delphi.com/navnet/privacy.html. Read and interact with this site.

   Answer the following questions.

   What information do you give away while surfing?

   What are cookies and should you disable them?

   What information is already on the Web about you?

   How secure is using e-mail?

ASSIGNMENT 1: USING INTERNET MATERIALS

Directions

1. You are a part of a student group that has been assigned the task of developing some guidelines for using materials on the Internet in such a way as to prevent copyright infringements.

2. Go to some the following addresses, or find your own sites, to help you develop your guidelines:

   http://www.templetons.com/brad/copymyths.htm

   http://www.bitlaw.com/copyright/fair_use.html

   http://palimpsest.stanford.edu/mirrors/faq/copyright/faq/part2

   http://www.ssrn.com/update/lsn/cyberspace/csl_lessons.html

3. Use your word processor and create a flyer that lists those guidelines using a variety of fonts, bold, italics, underlining, and other formatting features in an eye-catching format. Be creative.

4. Submit your flyer.

ASSIGNMENT 2: COMPUTER USE GUIDELINES

Directions

1. Identify the ethical/legal issues you must consider in the situation described below. Type these in outline format using your word processor.

   Situation:

   You are expecting an influx of personnel who will use the laptops now available in your health care agency. You want to encourage use, but protect the misuse of this equipment.

   There is a variety of software available on CD-ROMs as well as on the hard drives of the computers. You expect the personnel will use this equipment to prepare patient summaries, develop quality assurance reports, document supply inventories, and record patient visits.

5. Use your word-processing program to prepare a separate list of guidelines that you can give to the new users. Your guidelines should help increase awareness of using the microcomputer in ways that will protect patient privacy/confidentiality and promote the safety and security of the computer data and equipment.

6. Submit your list of safety and security issues and your guidelines.

ASSIGNMENT 3: ISSUE CRITIQUE

Directions

1. Select one of the following statements to critique:

    a. "There is nothing wrong with breaking security if you accomplish something useful and leave things the way you find them."

    b. "The health care agency owns the data in its computer and is therefore free to do whatever it chooses with that data."

    c. "In the long run, when simple rules are followed, computer records are more secure than hard copy records."

2. Using your word processor, prepare a one- to two-page paper identifying points that support or refute the statement you select. End the paper by stating your position and your reasons for that position.

3. Submit your paper.

ASSIGNMENT 4: COMPUTER ETHICS

Directions

1. Your health agency wants to post some rules on using computers ethically. Use the readings from this chapter and any other sources you wish to create the "Ten Commandments of Computer Ethics."

2. Use your word processor and create an attractive flyer listing your Ten Commandments. Use color and graphics as you wish to make your flyer visually appealing and attractive.

3. Submit your flyer.

Chapter 13

Health Care Informatics and Information Systems

OBJECTIVES

1. Define health care informatics using the concepts of data, information, knowledge, and wisdom.
2. Describe automated health care delivery systems.
3. Identify selected types and levels of computer related personnel.
4. Differentiate between computer literacy, computer assisted instruction, and health care informatics.

INTRODUCTION

This book is a microcomputer literacy book designed for health care students and providers with limited computer experience. Health care providers learn to use microcomputers because these machines are useful tools for dealing with health care information. This chapter introduces the health care provider to the discipline of health care informatics and to several types of automated systems commonly used in health care.

DEFINING HEALTH CARE INFORMATICS AND RELATED TERMS

Health care informatics is concerned with the application of information and computer science concepts and theories to the delivery of health care. Information science focuses on the study of information generation, transmission, and use. The study of information sciences is usually considered to have originated with Shannon and Weaver's theory of information (1949). Their work focused on the communication of information. Their communication model demonstrates the transmission of a message from a sender to a receiver and is the standard used in teaching communication concepts to health care providers.

Since that time the study of information theory has been approached from several different conceptual frameworks. William R. Hersh (1995) in his book *Information Retrieval: A Health Care Perspective* provides a summary of information models. The information model used to explain health care informatics was developed by Blum (1986). Blum, in giving a historical overview of computers in health care, found it convenient to group medical applications according to the objects they processed. He identified three groups of applications. These were data processing applications, information processing applications, and knowledge processing applications.

Using Blum's model, Graves and Corcoran (1989) in their classic article, "The Study of Nursing Informatics," identified the phenomenon of study of nursing informatics as nursing data, information, and knowledge. Nelson and Joos extended this continuum to include wisdom (Nelson & Joos, 1989). Therefore, an understanding of health care informatics first requires an understanding of the terms: data, information, knowledge, and wisdom.

Data

Data are raw facts. They exist without meaning or interpretation. The individual elements on a history and physical or a nursing assessment are data elements. For example, the observation that a patient's hair is red, that his weight is 150 lbs, or that his blood sugar is 200 are raw facts that can be interpreted in many different ways. In themselves, each of these data pieces is meaningless. The red hair may be the result of illness, a hair color product, or just the natural color. The weight may be too high, too low, or the ideal weight for this individual. Depending on the circumstances, this blood sugar could be normal, indicate the patient is improving, or indicate the patient is becoming sicker. The process of populating the fields in a database involves entering these types of data elements into the database.

Information

Information is a collection of data that has been processed to produce meaning. Some techniques that are used to process data include classifying, sorting, organizing, summarizing, graphing, and calculating. A number of tools are used to process data including paper and pencil, short-term memory, and computers. Processing prepares data so that they can be interpreted. The actual interpretation of the data is a cognitive process whereby data are given meaning and become information. Several factors including education, attitudes, emotions, and goals influence this process. As a result each individual gives a unique interpretation to the same collection of data. These interpretations can be similar, or they can be surprisingly different, but they are never the same.

For example, a newly diagnosed type II diabetic has a blood sugar of 350. The client, the physician, and the nurse each provide a different interpretation of this datum. In other words, this datum is meaningful but the meaning is different for each individual involved.

An **information system** is a system that processes data, organizing those data into meaningful units of information. This definition of an information system does not require that the system be automated. However, in health care informatics, where information science is combined with computer science, the focus is on automated information systems that are used in health care. There are many different types of automated health care information systems. Several are described later in this chapter.

It is important to remember, however, that information gained from these systems may be interpreted and used differently by different health care providers. For example, a chart that tracks the increased independence of a client after cerebral vascular accident presents vital nursing information. This same chart when interpreted by the physical therapist provides key rehabilitation information. While members of both of these disciplines use this information to make important decisions about the patient's plan of care, the chart has a different significance or meaning for the nurse and for the physical therapist. This is why the development of an effective interdisciplinary documentation system requires the involvement of each type of health care professional who will be using the system.

It is also important to realize that the same data can produce different types of information. A hospital information system processes order entry data to produce billing information. These same data may be processed by a clinical information system to develop a clinical pathway. Each of these information systems is using the same data but in each case the information produced is quite different.

Knowledge

While information is built from data, knowledge is built from information. **Knowledge** is a collection of interrelated pieces of information. Interrelated information about a specific topic is usually referred to as a **knowledge base**. For example, the statement "this student has a good knowledge base in anatomy" would not sound correct if the word "base" was removed from the statement.

The information in a knowledge base is organized or structured so that interrelationships can be identified. Look at the table of contents in any textbook and you will see an outline of a knowledge base. A well-presented lecture will explain how various facts or pieces of information interrelate. By understanding the information and the interrelationships the learner can understand the concepts and theories that are inherent in the specific knowledge base being explained.

Once the learner develops a knowledge base, the learner uses this knowledge to interpret new data or even reinterpret old data producing new information. The content in a knowledge base plays a major role in determining how data and information are used in the process of decision making. For example, a diabetic client with an extensive knowledge base about diabetics could be expected to make different decisions than a person with a limited knowledge base.

A professional with an extensive knowledge base is usually referred to as a specialist or expert. Note in this discussion that we believe a knowledge base is more than just a large collection of information. It is the interrelationships between the pieces of information that produce the knowledge base. An expert has built up mental processes that provide quick access to a wide array of interrelationships. As a result the expert has access to a new level of knowledge. An expert looks at a patient and sees the patient and his or her problems as a whole gestalt. A novice looks at the same patient and sees only pieces of the information. A novice does not have the quick mental access to all of the interrelationships that the expert has and cannot always see the whole picture of what is happening with a patient. An expert can look at a client and understand immediately just how sick or anxious that client is. A novice on the other hand may see the same patient, collect the same data and not reach the same conclusion. This is one of the reasons that the teaching-learning process in a clinical setting can be such a challenge. The teacher with an expert background will process the same data and information differently than the student will.

A knowledge base can be stored and shared using a variety of media including oral communication, textbooks, and online databases. As a person gains information it is added to an internal knowledge base. It is this internal knowledge base one uses to interpret information and to make decisions.

Automated **decision support systems** are systems that process information, identifying and demonstrating pertinent interrelationships. These systems may be as simple as the bar chart in Figure 13–1, which identifies overtime hours in a health care institution, or as complex as a fully automated staffing system. Complexity in this example refers to how much of the knowledge base is stored in the automated system. It is the individual's knowledge base that is used to interpret the bar chart. Different nurse managers looking at this same bar chart can and do reach different conclusions about staffing on these units.

While decision support systems can help in the decision-making process, they do not make decisions. For example, an automated scheduling system can be used to generate a work schedule for staff in a clinical setting. The automated system will usually contain an extensive online knowledge base. The system will "know" several facts about the staff as well as the institution's staffing rules. However, the scheduling system will not decide who will work when. The professional in charge is responsible for approving the schedule. Decision support systems are an aid to the decision maker. They provide the decision maker with a more complete picture of the interrelations between the information being considered. It is the decision maker who interprets the information and decides what action to take.

Wisdom

In health care, ethical decision making that ensures cost effective quality care requires more than an empirical knowledge base. Knowing when and how to use this knowledge is referred to as **wisdom**. Knowledge makes it possible for a caregiver to explain the stages of death and dying. Wisdom makes it possible for the caregiver to use theories related to death and dying to help a terminal patient express anger and frustration. The development of wisdom requires not

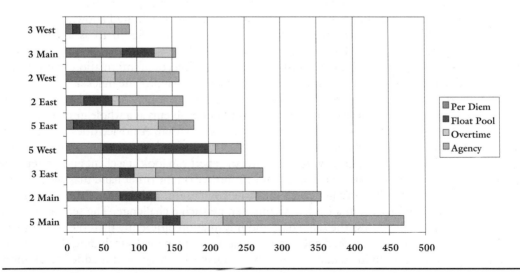

FIGURE 13–1.
Hours of Overtime or Supplemental Staff Used by Clinical Units

only empirical knowledge but also ethical, personal, and aesthetic knowledge. Currently there is no way to fully automate wisdom but certain aspects of this concept are being built into automated systems. **Expert systems** are knowledge-based systems with built in procedures for determining when and how to use that knowledge. Currently, expert systems in health care are being used to advise human decision makers.

AUTOMATED INFORMATION SYSTEMS IN HEALTH CARE

Computer technology has been infused into almost every aspect of health care delivery. This ranges from a stand-alone system used to make appointments in a private office, to fully integrated computer-based patient records maintained by a large integrated health delivery system. The goal of this chapter is to introduce the reader to the concept of automated health care information systems by providing a brief description of the more common systems. A variety of vendors sell health care information systems and many of these have similar functions. These systems are first defined in terms of their purpose or functions. This is followed by a discussion of levels of integration. Finally, the systems are discussed in terms of nursing roles.

Automated Health Care Delivery Systems Classified by Function

Clinical Clinical information systems include a large group of automated systems that process patient data to support patient care. Examples of functions in clinical information systems include collecting patient assessment and health status data, developing care plans, managing the order entry process, keeping medication administration records, developing work lists, and producing reports such as patient problem lists. Two types that are of special importance are point-of-care and departmental systems.

- *Point-of-care systems* are clinical information systems that are used at the point where care is delivered. This location may be on a clinical unit, a patient's home, a primary care office, or any other place where health care is delivered. Point-of-care systems range in size from small hand-held devices to full-sized workstations. The primary uses for point-of-care systems include development of plans of care, documentation of patient data, and access to clinical information. Their primary benefits include decreasing the time used to document care while increasing the quality of the documentation, and increasing access to client data.
- *Departmental systems* are systems that support the daily work or operations of a clinical department. The most common automated clinical departments include laboratory, radiology, cardiology, and pharmacy. Clinical departmental systems accept patient orders; schedule patients, equipment, and rooms; print labels and work lists; as well as maintain inventories. In addition to clinical departments there are nonclinical departments with automated systems. The most common automated nonclinical departments are medical records and material management. The primary benefit of these types of systems is the improved efficiency of the department.

Hospital information systems Hospital information systems (HIS) were originally developed for hospitals. Today, however, they may be located in nursing homes, rehabilitation centers, or any other health care institution. Outside of hospitals they are sometimes called health care information systems. There are three primary functions for hospital information systems.

First, they manage the admission, discharge, and transfer process. Second, they communicate information between the clinical units and the various hospital departments. This includes sending patient orders to hospital departments and reporting results back to the clinical units. In addition, they are also used to request supplies and equipment for the clinical units. These systems almost always interface with the financial systems that are used to track the charges and billing process for the institution. Finally, they are used to print work lists. For example, the HIS may be used to print a list of patients' diet orders. The list is then used to distribute meal trays.

Clinical data repository In health care these systems grew out of the concept of a computer-based patient record. Many of the systems used in health care are collecting patient related data. The clinical data repository can be conceptualized as a warehouse or large database when all data elements from all the different systems could be stored. This makes it possible to integrate the data and obtain a different level of information. For example, by integrating the clinical data with the financial data it would be possible to begin evaluating the cost of each problem on the patient problem list. For these systems to be truly effective a data dictionary that defines each element is required. The National Library of Medicine has been working on this issue for several years. The project is titled the Unified Medical Language Project. More information can be accessed at http://www.nlm.nih.gov.

Financial systems Financial systems include a combination of information systems that are used to manage and report the financial aspects of the institution. These include systems that track income such as billing and contract monitoring, systems used to develop and monitor capital and operating budgets, and systems that track costs to the institution such as payroll and cost accounting. These systems can overlap or interface with the personnel systems. For example, time and attendance systems track who has worked as well as the time that they worked and then it feeds this information to the payroll system.

Personnel systems Personnel systems include a combination of systems used to track the characteristics of employees and/or the use of these employees within the institution.

- *Personnel records systems* maintain individual employee records. For example, health care institutions must know the home address, salary scale, job title and description, professional license number and renewal date, along with a number of other details about each employee. Automated systems make it much easier to maintain accurate data and to search for information about individual employees as well as groups of employees.
- *Scheduling systems* are used to schedule the actual dates and times that an employee will be working or not working. These systems can keep a historical record of vacation, holiday, and sick time used. This is different than the staffing system that is discussed next.

Administrative systems These systems automate the management of data used in the daily operations of the institution as well as data used for strategic and long range planning.

- *Classification systems* use patient data to classify patients by the amount and type of care required. For example, a patient with new second and third degree burns over 60 percent of the body may require six hours of professional nursing time every eight-hour shift. A second patient who is fifth-day post-op from open-heart surgery may require two hours of professional nursing time. The data from classification systems can be used to decide the amount and type of staff assigned to a clinical unit. When classification data are used to make this determination, the classification system is also a staffing system.

■ *Quality assurance systems* attempt to measure and report on cost effective quality care resulting in a high level of patient satisfaction. Some examples of data that are processed in quality assurance systems include patient outcomes or variance reports, performance indicators for providers, infection reports, incident reports, patient satisfaction results, and costing data. These data can be reported for individuals or in aggregate format.

Setting specific systems These systems include any of the functions already discussed; however, the functions are customized for the specific setting. This includes all functions related to clinical, financial, and personnel information management. Some examples of setting specific systems include home health systems, physician office systems, outpatient or ambulatory care clinics, nurse center clinics, and emergency room systems.

Levels of Data Sharing

Stand-alone systems are systems that do not share data or information with any other computer system. A PC based scheduling system located in one department would be a stand-alone system. If the schedule for an employee is changed on this system, that change will not occur in any other institutional system. The personnel and payroll systems would still show the original schedule. Stand-alone systems infiltrate the institution with data redundancy and database discrepancies.

Interfaced systems are systems that maintain their own database while sharing data across a network. For example, a laboratory system may be interfaced with a HIS. The patient orders from the HIS are passed directly to the laboratory system and the lab results are passed directly back to the HIS. When several department systems are interfaced the results have been referred to as spaghetti. Since most of these interfaced systems are from different vendors, and computer systems are constantly being upgraded, maintaining the interface code becomes a constant battle. Patient data can get lost in this complexity.

Integrated systems are systems that share a common database. The clinical data repository system discussed earlier is such a system. All the data related to a client, employee, or financial system are stored in one repository. While this is a simple concept, the process of building a repository is very complex. Most health care institutions operate with a combination of stand-alone, interfaced, and integrated systems. Data are shared at four different levels.

Level one data sharing involves integration of a specific institution service or function. For example, an executive information system will pull census, personnel, and financial data to give an overall picture of the institution's operational status. A product line system will integrate patient data from several different systems to track how patients in that product line move through the organization.

Level two involves sharing data for an individual health care institution. Sometimes this term refers to all patient data. Other times it refers to all institutional data including financial, personnel, and tangible resources.

Level three involves the sharing of data across all institutions owned by the organization. This type of system is referred to as an enterprise-wide system. This level of sharing has become increasingly important with the development of integrated health care delivery systems.

Level four involves sharing data outside of the institutions owned by the enterprise. This is a regional or community health information network (CHIN).

In its early stages, health care computing was built on stand-alone systems. Today the systems are becoming increasingly integrated. This sharing of data across disciplines within health care is one of the factors increasing the integration of services. As this trend continues, health care information systems are becoming more generic. For example, these systems are becoming patient-focused systems rather than medical or nursing systems. While this trend is improving the comprehensiveness of the data, one approach to managing patient data will not meet the information needs for all disciplines. How to develop an integrated, patient-focused health care information system that meets the information needs of different disciplines is an important applied research question in health care computing.

Nursing Information Systems

Nursing information systems convert patient and institutional data to nursing information. The profession of nursing is traditionally discussed in terms of four domains of practice: clinical practice, education, research, and administration. Nursing information systems can also be discussed using these domains.

Clinical nursing information systems provide automated support to the nursing process. These systems are used to collect and record patient data for assessment or monitoring purposes; develop plans of care; print reminders and work lists; document care; and identify goal achievement. With the advent of health care reform and the development of clinical pathways, these systems are rapidly becoming multidisciplinary clinical information systems as described under point-of-care systems.

Nursing information systems that support the administrative role usually deal with the day-to-day operation of the clinical or nursing service department. These include systems such as classification systems, quality assurance systems, and staffing systems. With improved levels of data sharing, administrative systems are beginning to import their data from the clinical information systems. For example, a nurse documents a patient's post-op status and these data are used by the classification system to identify the amount of nursing care needed for this patient's care. Information from these types of administrative systems becomes data for an executive information system. Executive information systems are then used to manage the institution, as well as a basis for strategic and/or long-range planning.

Information systems that support nursing education are used for teaching as well as managing the educational process. Those used for teaching are usually referred to as computer assisted instruction (CAI). Information systems used for management of the teaching process are referred to as computer managed instruction (CMI). CMI includes scheduling, grading, and maintaining student records. Nursing education information systems were initially used in formal educational programs. Today, they are an integral part of staff development and are becoming common in patient education.

The process of nursing research is supported by a variety of different generic computing programs. Every software program in this book can be used in the research process. The development of automated health care information systems has had a major impact on what is possible within the field of nursing research. It is now possible to collect data from an automated database in seconds that would have required months of searching if the same data were stored in paper records. It is also important to note that while software programs can be helpful tools when doing nursing research, the use of such tools does not mean that one is doing informatics research. Health care informatics is a field of study in and of itself with a number of important research questions.

HEALTH CARE COMPUTING PERSONNEL

There are several levels and types of personnel who work in health care computing. Some personnel have their primary background in computer and information science, while others have their primary background in health care. A few are prepared in health care informatics. The educational preparation of people in health care computing varies from on-the-job training to post doctoral preparation.

The Chief Information Officer or Director of Information Services

The chief information officer is administratively responsible for the operation of the information service department. Depending on the organization, this individual may be part of the executive team responsible for strategic and long range institutional planning, as well as the day-to-day operation of the department.

Systems Analysts

Systems analysts are personnel who work with users to define their information needs and design systems to meet those needs. Their education is usually in information or computer science with knowledge of health care acquired from on-the-job experience.

Programmers

Programmers are personnel who design, code, and test new software programs as well as maintain and enhance current applications. These individuals usually receive their educational preparation in computer science or as on-the-job training.

Computer Operators

There are several types of computer operators. The title computer operator usually refers to an individual who actually runs a mainframe or minicomputer. These individuals usually have minimal interaction with health care providers. Microcomputer operators on the other hand work closely with users. They troubleshoot, upgrade, and repair computers as well as install software. Network managers provide this same type of service for local area networks.

Nursing Informatics Specialists

Nursing informatics specialists integrate "nursing science, computer science, and information science in identifying, collecting, processing, and managing data and information to support nursing practice, administration, education, research, and the expansion of nursing knowledge." They support the practice of all nursing specialties, in all sites of care, whether at the basic or advanced practice level (ANA, 1994, p. 3).

Summary

Literacy is the ability to read, write, and use numbers skillfully enough to meet the demands of society. Computer literacy is the ability to use a computer skillfully enough to meet the demands of society. Like literacy, the scope and depth of computer literacy needed by any one person can vary extensively. One person can be very literate with word processing but unable to use any other program. Another person may have a general knowledge of several different programs. In today's automated world all people need to have at least a basic understanding of computers. Health care professionals, like all other educated people, need a basic level of computer literacy.

It is quite possible for a person to learn on a computer and yet be computer illiterate. Computer assisted instruction (CAI) presents educational experiences using a computer. A learner does not need to be computer literate in order to use CAI. While both computer literacy and CAI are important to health care providers, they are not specific to health care. For example, the principles of instructional design apply whether a CAI is health related or not.

Information literacy refers to the ability to access, evaluate, and use information. With the advent of computers, information literacy requires the ability to access databases, especially literature databases and the largest database of all—the Internet. Once information has been accessed, it requires the ability to evaluate the information. Inaccurate and incomplete information must be recognized. This is especially difficult if the reader has a limited knowledge base related to the information being accessed. Finally, information literacy requires the ability to use the information.

Health care informatics is specific to health care. Health care informatics uses tools from information science, computer science, cognitive science, systems theory, and a variety of other fields to convert data to information and then information to knowledge. Then, this knowledge is used to improve patient care.

References

American Nurses Association. (1994). *The scope of practice for nursing informatics.* Washington, DC: American Nurses Publishing.

Blum, B. I. (1986). *Clinical information systems.* New York: Springer-Verlag.

Graves, J., & Corcoran, S. (1989). The study of nursing informatics. *Image: Journal of Nursing Scholarship, 21*(4), 227–231.

Hersh, W. R. (1996). *Information retrieval: A health care perspective.* New York: Springer-Verlag.

Nelson, R., & Joos, I. (1989). On language in nursing: From data to wisdom. *PLN Visions,* Fall, 1989, p. 6.

Shannon, C. E., & Weaver, W. (1949). *The mathematical theory of communication.* Urbana, IL: University of Illinois Press.

EXERCISE 1: LITERACY, CAI, AND HEALTH CARE INFORMATICS

Objective

1. Differentiate between computer literacy, information literacy, computer-assisted instruction, and health care informatics.
2. Identify software programs, both generic and those related to health care.
3. Describe uses of each software group.

Exercise

1. Make a list of all software programs available to you as a student in your current curriculum. Include the programs and databases in your library for accessing reference materials. This is the master list for this exercise.

2. Identify the programs on this list that are not specific to health care. For example, a word-processing program can be used in any field, not just health care. Classify the identified programs by their primary purpose. For example, MS Word would be classified as a word-processing program. Write a brief statement explaining how each group of software would be useful for a health care student or employee.

3. Make a list of the databases in your library and briefly explain what literature is referenced in these databases. Give a brief description of the background or knowledge base the reader should have to evaluate the quality of information included in the references in each database.

4. Identify CAI programs on the master list that can be used to teach health care content. Select five of these programs and describe the level of computer literacy necessary to use each program.

5. Identify one program that can be used to explain the concepts inherent in health care informatics. Explain how you would use this program to explain health care informatics concepts.

EXERCISE 2: DATA, INFORMATION, KNOWLEDGE, AND WISDOM

Objective

1. Develop a personal definition of health care data, information, knowledge, and wisdom.

Exercise

Work in small groups (three to five people) to develop an answer for each of the following questions.

1. When patients complete a health assessment form have they provided you with data or information? Explain your answer.

2. Does knowing a patient's diagnosis provide you with information or knowledge? Does your answer differ if you are referring to a medical or a nursing diagnosis?

3. What is your definition of health care knowledge? How does medical knowledge differ from nursing knowledge? How are they the same?

4. Can wisdom be taught? Explain your answer.

ASSIGNMENT 1: HEALTH CARE INFORMATICS—JOB DESCRIPTIONS

Directions

1. The health care setting where you are employed has decided to install a computer-based patient record. Because computer and health care informatics content was included in your basic education program, you have been added to the implementation team with the title Informatics Specialist. Your first assignment is to write your job description. You have been referred to the following references.

   American Nurses Association. (1994). *The scope of practice for nursing informatics.* Washington, DC: American Nurses Publishing.

   American Nurses Association. (1995). *Standards of practice for nursing informatics.* Washington, DC: American Nurses Publishing.

2. Type the job description using a word-processing program. Include a brief description of the job, a list of required and preferred qualifications, and a list of the job responsibilities.

ASSIGNMENT 2: HEALTH CARE INFORMATICS EDUCATION

Directions

1. Develop an outline identifying the basic health care informatics content that you believe should be included in your basic education. You will find the reference list included in this book helpful for this part of the assignment.

2. Review your educational program and identify what content from your outline is and is not included in your program.

3. When content is not included, identify where it should be added to your program.

4. Based on your analysis in steps 1 and 2, write a two-page position paper on health care informatics as part of health care education. Use your word-processing program to prepare your paper.

ASSIGNMENT 3: HEALTH CARE INFORMATICS

Directions

The table presented below includes several types of automated systems commonly used in health care today. Using references from your library and the Internet, identify common functions that would be associated with each type of system. The first one has been completed as an example of the level of detail needed with this assignment.

Type of System	Primary Functions
Laboratory	1. Data management for administrative functions. For example, create work lists of what lab work needs done, identify when and on whom the lab work must be done, inventory of supplies used, or turnaround time. 2. Generate labels for automated or manual identification and tracking of specimens, from order generation to specimen collection, to completion of lab test. 3. Provide results reporting, either on paper or by computer. 4. Issue alerts on abnormal results, repeat orders etc.

Type of System	Primary Functions
Home Health Care	
Medical Records	
Nursing	
Patient Classification	
Patient Monitoring	
Pharmacy	
Radiology	
Staff Scheduling	
Facilities Management	
Financial	
Human Resource Management	
Materials Management	
Managed Care System	
Quality Improvement	
Other	

Bibliography

Abdelhak, M., Grostick, S., Hanken, M. A., & Jacobs, E. (1996). *Health information: Management of a strategic resource.* Philadelphia: W. B. Saunders.

Austin, C. J. & Boxerman, S. B. (1997). *Information systems for health services administration.* (5th ed). Ann Arbor, MI: Health Administration Press.

Bailey, S. P. (1997). *Problems & cases in health information management.* Lenox, MA: Lenox Publishing Company.

Bakker, S. (Ed.). (1997). *Health information management: What strategies?* Norwell, MA: Kluwer Academic Publishers.

Ball, M. J., Collen, M. F., & Hannah, K. (1996). *Aspects of the computer-based patient record.* New York: Springer-Verlag.

Ball, M. J., Hannah, K. J., Newbold, S. K., & Douglas, J. V. (Eds.). (1995). *Nursing informatics: Where caring and technology meet.* (2nd ed.). New York: Springer-Verlag.

Ball, M. J., Simborg, D. W., Albright, J., & Douglas, J. V. (1995). (Eds.). *Healthcare information management systems: A practical guide.* (2nd ed.). New York: Springer-Verlag.

Ball, M. J., Douglas, J. V., & Garets, D. E. (1999). *Strategies & technologies for health care information: Theory into practice.* New York: Springer-Verlag.

Berner, E. S., Hannah, K. J., & Ball, M. J. (Ed.). (1998). *Clinical decision support systems: Theory & practice.* New York: Springer-Verlag.

Brennan, P. F., Schneider, S. J., & Tornquist, E. M. (1997). *Information networks for community health.* New York: Springer-Verlag.

Camarda, B. (1997). *Using Microsoft Word 97* (Best seller ed.). Indianapolis, IN: Que Corporation.

Davis, M. W. (1998). *Computerizing healthcare information: Developing electronic patient information systems.* New York: McGraw-Hill.

De Dombal, F. T. (1996). *Medical informatics: The essentials.* Woburn, MA: Butter-Heinemann.

Degoulet, P. & Fieschi, M. (1997). *Introduction to clinical informatics.* New York: Springer-Verlag.

DeLuca, J. M. & Cagan, R. E. (1996). *The CEO's guide to health care information systems.* Chicago: American Hospital Publishing.

Drazen, E. L., Metzger, J. B., Ritter, J. L., & Schneider, M. K. (1995). *Patient care information systems.* New York: Springer-Verlag.

Duncan, K. A. (1998). *Community health information systems: Lessons for the future.* Ann Arbor, MI: Health Administration Press.

Edwards, M. J. (1997). *The Internet for nurses & allied health professionals.* (2nd ed.). New York: Springer-Verlag.

Evans, S. (1996). *The PACE Systems: An expert consulting system for nursing.* New York: Springer-Verlag.

Friedman, C. P. & Wyatt, J. (1996). *Evaluation methods in informatics.* New York: Springer-Verlag.

Gibson, C. C. (Ed.). (1998). *Distance learning in higher education.* Madison, WI: Atwood Publishing.

Goodman, K. W. (Ed.). (1997). *Ethics, computing, & medicine & the transformation of health care.* New York: Cambridge University Press.

Halberg, B. (1997). *Using Microsoft Excel 97* (Best seller ed.). Indianapolis, IN: Que Corporation.

Hannah, K. J., Ball, M. J., & Douglas, J. V. (1999). *Performance improvement through information management: Health care's bridge to success.* New York: Springer-Verlag.

Hannah, K. J., Ball, M. J., & Edwards, M. J. A. (1998). *Introduction to nursing informatics.* (2nd ed.) New York: Springer-Verlag.

Hebda, T. L., Mascara, C., & Czar, P. (1998). *Handbook of nursing informatics for nurses & health care professionals.* Reading, MA: Addison Wesley Longman.

Hersh, W. R. (1995). *Information retrieval: A health care perspective.* New York: Springer-Verlag.

Hovenga, E. (1999). *Health informatics.* New York: W. B. Saunders.

JCAHO. (1995). *1996: Accreditation manual for hospitals.* Oakbrook Terrace, IL: JCAHO.

Jennings, R. (1997). *Using Access 97* (2nd ed.). Indianapolis, IN: Que Corporation.

Johns, M. (1997). *Information management for health.* Albany, NY: Delmar.

Jordan, T. (1999). *Understanding medical information.* Stamford, CT: Appleton & Lange.

Kahn, B. H. (Ed.). (1997). *Web-based instruction.* Englewood Cliffs, NJ: Educational Technology.

Lee, N. & Millman, A. (Eds.). (1996). *ABC of medical computing.* London: BMJ Publishing.

Lorenzi, N. M. & Riley, R. T. (1996). *Organizational aspects of health informatics: Managing technical change.* New York: Springer-Verlag.

Lorenzi, N. M., Riley, R. T., Ball, M. J., & Douglas, J. V. (Eds.). (1995). *Transforming health through information: Case studies.* New York: Springer-Verlag.

Mattingly, R. (1996). *Management of health information.* Albany, NY: Delmar.

Maull, K. I. & Augenstein, J. S. (1997). *Trauma informatics.* New York: Springer-Verlag.

McGlynn, E., Damberg, C., & Kerr, E. (1998). *Health information systems: Design issues and analytic applications.* Santa Monica, CA: Rand Corporation.

McWay, D. C. (1996). *Legal aspects of health information management.* Albany, NY: Delmar.

Mills, M. E., Romano, C. A., & Heller, B. (1996). *Information management in nursing and health care.* Springhouse, PA: Springhouse Corporation.

Moorhead, S. & Delaney, C. W. (1998). *Information systems: Innovations for nursing: New visions and ventures.* Thousand Oaks, CA: Sage Publications.

Mueller, S. & Zacker, C. (1998). *Upgrading and repairing PCs.* (10th ed.). Carmel, IN: Que Corporation.

Nicoll, L. (1998) *Computers in nursing: Nurses' guide to the Internet.* Philadelphia: Lippincott-Raven.

Saba, V. & McCormick, K. (1996). *Essentials of computers for nurses.* (2nd ed.). New York: McGraw Hill.

Saba, V. K., Pocklington, D. B., Miller, K. P., & Orthner, H. F. (Eds.). (1997). *Nursing & computers: An anthology, 1987–1996.* New York: Springer-Verlag.

Sackman, H. (1997). *Biomedical information technology: Global social responsibilities for the democratic information age.* San Diego, CA: Academic Press.

Selden, C. R., Humphreys, B. L., Friede, A., & Geisslerova, Z. (1996). *Public health informatics: Current bibliographies in medicine.* Upland, PA: DIANE Publishing Company.

Stasser, S. R. (1998). Information system: *Index of new information for health sciences.* Washington, DC: Publishers Association of Washington, DC.

Tan, J. K. H. (1995). *Health management information systems: Theories, methods, and applications.* Gaithersburg, MD: Aspen.

Thede, L. Q. (1998). *Computers in nursing: Concepts & issues.* Philadelphia: Lippincott-Raven.

Warner, H. R., Sorenson, D. K., & Bouhaddou, O. (1997). *Knowledge engineering in health informatics.* New York: Springer-Verlag.

Weed, L. (1995). *Knowledge coupling: New premises and new tools for medical care and education.* New York: Springer-Verlag.

Zimmerman, M., Duggan, B. M., Penner, M., Parker, C. D., & Keep, N. B. (Eds.). (1996). *Emergency department clinical information systems: A guide for selection & implementation.* Park Ridge, IL: Emergency Nurses Association.

Index